THE REAL WAR
ON CRIME

THE REAL WAR
ON CRIME

THE REPORT OF THE
NATIONAL CRIMINAL
JUSTICE COMMISSION

Steven R. Donziger, Editor

HarperPerennial

A Division of HarperCollins*Publishers*

HarperCollins books may be purchased for educational, business, or sales promotional use. For information please write: Special Markets Department, HarperCollins Publishers, Inc., 10 East 53rd Street, New York, NY 10022.

FIRST EDITION

Designed by Jessica Shatan

Library of Congress Cataloging-in-Publication Data

The real war on crime : the report of the National Criminal Justice
    Commission / Steven R. Donziger
        p.   cm.
    Includes index.
    ISBN 0-06-095165-6
    1. Criminal justice, Administration of — United States. 2. Crime — United States.
3. Crime — Government policy — United States. 4. Crime prevention — United States.
I. Donziger, Steven R.
HV9950.R43   1995
364.973—dc20   95–48975

---

00 ❖/RRD 10

CONTENTS

Chapter One: Crime and Policy   1

Crime Rates: The Numbers Do Not Tell the Full Story • The Key to the Problem: Understanding the Difference Between Crime and Violence • Bait and Switch • "Three Strikes and You're Out" • Truth in Sentencing • Mandatory Minimum Sentences • The Relationship Between Poverty, Family Breakdown, and Criminal Justice • Conclusion

Chapter Two: Prisons   31

The Numbers • Rates of Imprisonment and Crime • The Effects of Incarceration • Rates of Incarceration: The Effect on the Family • The Costs • Sentencing • What Polling Data Reveal About Crime Policy • Conclusion

Probation and Parole • Parole: The Transition from Incarceration to Freedom • Conclusion

Chapter Nine: Pathway to a Safer Society—2020 Vision   195

Recommendation 1 • Recommendation 2 • Recommendation 3 • Recommendation 4 • Recommendation 5 • Recommendation 6 • Recommendation 7 • Recommendation 8 • Recommendation 9 • Recommendation 10 • Recommendation 11

NATIONAL CRIMINAL JUSTICE COMMISSION STAFF

The National Criminal Justice Commission is a project of the National Center on Institutions and Alternatives (NCIA). Founded in 1977, NCIA is a research and practice organization in the field of criminal justice.

Director: Steven R. Donziger

Associate Directors: Eric R. Lotke, Herbert J. Hoelter

Director of Research: Tara-Jen Ambrosio

Chief Statistician and Technical Consultant: Mary Cate Rush

Research Staff: Rachel Singer, Rosalee Kwak, Niall Brennan, Carlos Pimentel

Administrative Support: Alice Boring, John Irvin, Rebecca Ryan

PREFACE

This report is the culmination of a two-year effort by a group of thirty-four citizens to examine criminal justice policy in the United States and to make recommendations as to how that policy can make our country safer. This group came together for a simple reason: the prison system in the United States had expanded by three times since 1980 at a cost of tens of billions of dollars, yet we still felt as frightened as ever of being victimized by crime.

We knew that no business or government agency would triple in size without a strategic plan to manage its growth. Yet we quickly realized that the criminal justice system had no such plan and was being held accountable to virtually nobody—certainly not to us, the taxpayers. The last national report on crime was published in 1969 by the Eisenhower Commission. One year before that, the Kerner Commission published its landmark study on the causes of the urban riots. Two years before that, the President's Crime Commission (with our own Jim Vorenberg serving as executive director) issued specific recommendations to reform the criminal justice system. A quarter century had passed since the last of these reports. Yet during this lengthy period, no president had appointed a group of experts to analyze crime policy or to find solutions that might assuage public fear.

When our Commission set out, members tried to sort through all the facts and figures to determine what impact the criminal justice system had on the lives of ordinary Americans. What the Commission found surprised some and shocked others: rates of crime have remained stable even while the prison population exploded; we have the highest rate of imprisonment in the world; juvenile violence is perhaps our most pressing problem, but only 3,000 of about two million juvenile arrests each year are for homicide; and one out of three young African-American men are under the supervision of the criminal justice system, compared to one out of four only five years ago.

The Commission learned that the battle to stop crime had inverted many of our national priorities. We found that some prisons had new gyms and libraries while many public schools were in a state of disrepair, with overcrowded classrooms and poor equipment; that some prison guards make more than university professors; that we have the highest rate of child poverty in the industrialized world; that in some states we spend about $100,000 to build a new prison cell and another $22,000 each year to operate it; that spending on crime fighting has risen three times faster than defense spending; and that private businesses reap enormous profits from the fear of crime and the expansion of the criminal justice system.

The Real War on Crime is an effort to explain how criminal justice policy affects our safety and our pocketbooks. The report offers a diagnosis of the criminal justice system and proposes solutions to its problems. We believe we have identified the main trouble spots in the criminal justice system so people have the information needed to ask the right questions about the direction of crime policy in America. Until these questions can be answered, we believe that all states—absent some demonstrated urgent need—should impose a three-year moratorium on new prison construction. We provide a host of additional recommendations in the final chapter that are intended to fundamentally improve the way we approach crime control in America. We know some will take issue with our opinions and conclusions. We welcome the debate.

*   *   *

This report simply would not have been possible without the diligence and patience of an extraordinary group of Commission members. I feel privileged to have worked with each of them. Commission members were selected in an effort to guarantee the report would benefit from the broad perspectives of a diverse group of experts and national leaders. We wanted access to the latest research in the criminal justice field but also to the fresh thinking of creative people in other fields. We had prosecutors and police chiefs, defense attorneys and academics, doctors and educators, businesspersons and athletes. All Commission members volunteered their time to attend the meetings, work through the issues, and forge a consensus about what was wrong with the criminal justice system and what could be done to fix it. Commission members gave direction to the content of the report and edited the written drafts that were produced by the staff. While all agree with the overall thrust of *The Real War on Crime*, not all Commission members agree with all parts of the report or its conclusions and recommendations. There was robust disagreement on some issues and we tried as much as possible to reflect that in the report. Commission members and staff also benefited from a very talented group of advisers who lent their expertise on the specific issues with which we grappled. Inclusion on the panel of advisers in no way implies an endorsement of the contents of the report.

The founders of the National Center on Institutions and Alternatives (NCIA), Jerome G. Miller and Herbert J. Hoelter, garnered the financial support to make the Commission happen. Their groundbreaking work for the past two decades in the criminal justice field provided the inspiration to launch the Commission and the insight to sustain it. We extend our warm appreciation to the board members of the L & S Milken Foundation. Their support was invaluable. Eric Lotke drafted large sections of the report, provided vital creative input, and was helpful in distilling the differing wishes of the Commission members into words that all could agree upon. Mary Cate Rush and Tara-Jen Ambrosio helped to organize the research, compile the data, run the Commission meetings, edit the report, and keep our spirits high. Michael Tonry and Katheryn

Russell were instrumental in providing direction during the early stages of the research effort. We are indebted to Rafael Segalyn for guiding us through the publishing world.

Eric Steel, our editor at HarperCollins, made magnificent suggestions throughout the writing process. Others at HarperCollins—particularly Aileen Boyle and Sarah Polen—were always generous with their time and energy. We were fortunate to benefit from the creativity and seasoned judgment of our publicist, Cathy Saypol. Many others, too numerous to mention, assisted with their advice and expertise. They include James Austin, William Chambliss, Gail C. Christopher, Tracy Huling, Barry Krisberg, Mark Mauer, Dan Macallair, Candace McCoy, Karen McLaughlin, Knut Rostad, Rachel Singer, Keith Stroup, Harold Wooten, and Franklin Zimring. We also were helped at various times by members of the very capable staff at NCIA— Alice Boring, Robert Brown, John Irvin, Rebecca Ryan, Hans Selvog, Joel Sickler, and Beatrice Thompson. The Fortune Society in New York City provided office space and encouragement. Mom, Dad, Susan, David, and Sylvie provided moral support. I also would like to thank my special friends and advisers—Jonathon Abady, Jason Adkins, Sharon Styles-Anderson, Cristobal Bonifaz, John Bonifaz, Millard Farmer, Grant Fine, Janet Hoeffel, Judith King, Tony Matthews, Joseph Nursey, Patty Pearcey, Brian Platock, Todd Roobin, Joanne Sunshower, KimEllen Tunkle, and especially my soul mate, Martha McCully.

STEVEN R. DONZIGER
Director, National Criminal Justice Commission
January 1996

FOREWORD

For the first time in more than two decades, a national group of citizens and experts came together to assess the state of America's criminal justice system. The goals of the National Criminal Justice Commission were to provide a comprehensive assessment of crime policy in America, to offer solutions to reduce violence, to recommend policies to make our communities safer, and to determine if the "war on crime" has been effective. After two years of study and consultation with experts in a wide range of fields, the National Criminal Justice Commission has produced *The Real War on Crime*. This report is testimony to the concern all Americans have about crime and violence in our society and our commitment to finding solutions. It represents the views not only of professionals directly involved in the criminal justice system, but also those of citizens who labor daily to make our communities safer places to live.

This project was born from the frustration of seeing little or no change in the capacity of the criminal justice system to affect the rate of crime and violence in our communities. For two decades, the criminal justice system has grown exponentially while our communities are closing libraries, freezing teacher salaries, limiting medical benefits for our senior citizens, slashing student loan programs, and de-funding Head Start and other early intervention programs. We believed this massive sea change in spending and public policy deserved review and analysis. We solicited and received contributions from private foundations to organize the Commission and prepare this report. This funding was combined with the financial support of the private, nonprofit National Center on Institutions and Alternatives, and in early 1994 the National Criminal Justice Commission held its first meeting.

The National Criminal Justice Commission was comprised of a diverse cross-section of American citizens, criminal justice experts, community leaders, national and international scholars, and authors. Our membership included former prosecutors, the director of a national crime commission in the 1960s, an Olympic gold medalist, an editor of a leading magazine of hip-hop culture, an urban real estate developer, and the director of one of the largest food banks in the country. Members also included a police chief, a social historian, and criminal justice experts from Canada, the United Kingdom, and Norway. A complete listing of the Commissioners and biographical information is in Appendix C. This group was organized to dedicate its wisdom and experience to studying the practices and policies of our crime policy. Never before has the challenge been greater.

The Commission was purposely developed to reflect a variety of opinions and a diversity of experiences. Crime and criminal justice have become political symbols. As a result, we felt that our report must be kept as independent as possible. No government money was used and the Commission worked hard to get beyond the political rhetoric and to capture the underlying reality of criminal justice policy.

One of the positive aspects of the growth of the criminal justice system over the past two decades is that information systems and reporting technology have substantially improved. For example, we now can verify that in 1993 there were over 45 million criminal records in the United States. Data from prison wardens inform us unequivocally that over 60 percent of their population has substance abuse problems. We have tried as much as possible to benefit from the proliferation of criminal justice data.

The net result is that we were able to put together the various pieces of the criminal justice puzzle in a way that we hope allows the reader to understand how crime policy works, why it works the way it does, and what our options are for the future.

The responsibility of each Commissioner was to participate in this process, to formulate issues and questions, and to help present to the American public a responsible, informed, and sound analysis of the implications of current policy. Additionally, each Commissioner was challenged to develop ideas for how policies could be improved, how America could become a safer society, and how the American public could contribute to that effort. At Commission meetings, presentations were made by leading experts and advisers from across the country, and Commission members had the opportunity to question, challenge, and request additional information. Commission members reviewed findings, edited the report, and provided guidance and direction for additional information. Absent the inspiration, commitment, perseverance, and patience of the Commissioners, this report would not have happened.

The Commission's fundamental conclusion is that the criminal justice system is in crisis. Citizens in record numbers report that they feel unsafe on their streets and in their homes. As Americans have become more concerned about crime, the criminal justice system has become less effective at reducing it. The prison population has *tripled* since 1980 and expenditures on law enforcement have quadrupled. Yet crime rates are essentially unchanged and fear is higher than ever.

The Commission also found that criminal justice policy is often in conflict with itself. The criminal justice system spends billions of dollars annually on prisons and then underfunds drug treatment, educational programs, and violence prevention programs because there is not enough money. It ignores considerable academic and field research urging it to update antiquated practices and policies. Critically, it fails to meet the needs of the millions of Americans who fall victim to crime each year—victims who might not be victims at all if the criminal justice system were doing its job reasonably well.

Moreover, these practices and policies have helped to divide our country by race. The rate of incarceration for African-Americans is six times the rate for whites—a fact that has as much to do with discrimination as it does with rates of crime. In many major cities one-third or more of the young African-American men are under criminal justice supervision on any given day. The 1968 Kerner Commission observed that "Our nation is moving toward two societies, one black, one white—separate and unequal." Now, over twenty-five years later, our nation is on the same wayward path, and crime policy and the criminal justice system are leading the march.

The costs of our experiment in the massive use of imprisonment are staggering. Taxpayers spent over $100 billion in 1994 to finance the criminal justice system. Our quality of life, including the education of our children and the vitality of our communities, is dependent on how much we spend to finance imprisonment for ever-larger portions of our population. The prison industry absorbs money that would go to health care, job programs, education, and community development. In 1991, for the first time ever, American cities spent more money on law enforcement than education. Despite these expenditures, most people do not feel safe. *The Real War on Crime* tries to understand why we get so little for spending so much.

Criminal justice is a quality of life issue that affects our sense of safety, our willingness to talk to strangers, and the appearance of our neighborhoods. For the quality of life of Americans to improve, the criminal justice system needs to work more effectively to control crime after it occurs and prevent crime before it occurs. *The Real War on Crime* provides a set of recommendations to fundamentally reform the system and to begin to cure its deep afflictions. We have searched the nation and the world for crime and violence prevention programs that are proven effective and can be adopted in communities throughout the United States.

We believe that if our recommendations are adopted, our society will be safer and all Americans will benefit.

HERBERT J. HOELTER
Director, National Center on Institutions and Alternatives
Alexandria, Virginia
January 1996

NATIONAL CRIMINAL JUSTICE COMMISSION MEMBERS

MICHAEL ARMSTRONG, ESQUIRE
Kirkpatrick & Lockhart
New York, New York

PROFESSOR DERRICK BELL
New York University School of
Law
New York, New York

JAMES BERNARD
New York, New York

REED BRODY
International Human Rights
Specialist
New York, New York

SARAH BUEL, ESQUIRE
Assistant District Attorney,
Norfolk County District
Attorney's Office
Dedham, Massachusetts

CONSTANCE R. CAPLAN
The Time Group, Caplan Family
Trust
Baltimore, Maryland

PROFESSOR NILS CHRISTIE
The Faculty of Law, University of
Oslo
Oslo, Norway

LYNN CURTIS, EXECUTIVE
DIRECTOR
The Eisenhower Foundation
Washington, D.C.

KATHLEEN DICHIARA, EXECUTIVE DIRECTOR
Community FoodBank of New Jersey
Hillside, New Jersey

EDDIE ELLIS, EDUCATION COORDINATOR
Neighborhood Defender Services of Harlem
New York, New York

ELAINE JONES, DIRECTOR-COUNSEL
NAACP Legal Defense Fund
Washington, D.C.

BONG HWAN KIM, EXECUTIVE DIRECTOR
Korean Youth & Community Center
Los Angeles, California

PROFESSOR CORAMAE RICHEY MANN
Indiana University
Bloomington, Indiana

PROFESSOR KIMBERLY L. MARTUS
Justice Center, University of Alaska
Anchorage, Alaska

JEROME G. MILLER
President, National Center on Institutions and Alternatives
Alexandria, Virginia

PROFESSOR NORVAL MORRIS
University of Chicago, The Law School
Chicago, Illinois

EDWIN C. MOSES
Olympic Champion
Atlanta, Georgia

PROFESSOR CHARLES OGLETREE JR.
Harvard Law School
Cambridge, Massachusetts

DR. CHUKWUDI ONWUACHI-SAUNDERS
Centers for Disease Control and Prevention
Philadelphia, Pennsylvania

JOANNE PAGE, DIRECTOR
The Fortune Society
New York, New York

CHIEF NICHOLAS PASTORE
New Haven Police Department
New Haven, Connecticut

CAPTAIN WILLIAM PINKNEY
Motivational Speaker
Chicago, Illinois

PROFESSOR DAVID ROTHMAN
Center for the Study of Society & Medicine, Columbia University
New York, New York

ADVISERS AND CONSULTANTS

JONATHAN S. ABADY, ESQUIRE
Beldock Levine & Hoffman
New York, New York

JASON B. ADKINS, ESQUIRE
Cambridge, Massachusetts

ERIK ANDERSEN
Former Warden, Ringe Prison
Denmark

JAMES AUSTIN
National Council on Crime &
    Delinquency
San Francisco, California

JOHN C. BONIFAZ, ESQUIRE
Boston, Massachusetts

PROFESSOR LYNN S. BRANHAM
Thomas M. Cooley Law School
Lansing, Michigan

PROFESSOR WILLIAM CHAMBLISS
George Washington University
Washington, D.C.

PROFESSOR MEDA CHESNEY-LIND
University of Hawaii
Honolulu, Hawaii

GAIL C. CHRISTOPHER
Gail C. Christopher Enterprises
Washington, D.C.

PROFESSOR ELLIOT CURRIE
University of California at
    Berkeley
Berkeley, California

DR. MICHAEL C. ELSNER
Riverdale, Maryland

PROFESSOR MICHAEL
   GOTTFREDSON
School of Public Administration &
   Policy
University of Arizona
Tucson, Arizona

PROFESSOR MARK HAGER
Washington College of Law
The American University
Washington, D.C.

RONALD HAMPTON, EXECUTIVE
   DIRECTOR
National Black Police Association
Washington, D.C.

TRACY HULING
Freehold, New York

PROFESSOR ROBERT JOHNSON,
   CHAIR
Department of Justice, Law &
   Society
The American University
Washington, D.C.

NOLAN E. JONES, DIRECTOR
Justice & Public Safety
National Governors Association
Washington, D.C.

FRED E. JORDAN, JR.
Juvenile Probation Officer
South Carolina

BARRY KRISBERG, PRESIDENT
National Council on Crime &
   Delinquency
San Francisco, California

MARC MAUER, ASSISTANT
   DIRECTOR
The Sentencing Project
Washington, D.C.

DAN MACALLAIR, ASSOCIATE
   DIRECTOR
Center on Juvenile and Criminal
   Justice
San Francisco, California

DR. CANDACE MCCOY
Rutgers University
Newark, New Jersey

PROFESSOR JOHN MCKNIGHT
Center for Urban Affairs & Policy
   Research
Evanston, Illinois

KAREN MCLAUGHLIN
Education Development Center
Newton, Massachusetts

PROFESSOR TRACY MEARES
University of Chicago
Chicago, Illinois

DONALD MURRAY
Associate Legislative Director
National Association of Counties
Washington, D.C.

KAREN E. NEEDELS
Mathematic a Policy Research, Inc.
Princeton, New Jersey

JOSEPH M. NURSEY, ESQUIRE
Atlanta, Georgia

PATTI PEARCEY
B.C. Coalition for Safer
   Communities
Vancouver, British Columbia

DEAN JAMIN RASKIN
The Washington College of Law,
   American University
Washington, D.C.

KNUT ROSTAD
Carter Goble Associates
Washington, D.C.

PROFESSOR KATHERYN RUSSELL
University of Maryland at College
   Park
College Park, Maryland

PROFESSOR HERMAN SCHWARTZ
The American University
Washington, D.C.

PROFESSOR LARRY SHERMAN
Crime Control Institute
Washington, D.C.

MICHAEL E. SMITH, PRESIDENT
Vera Institute on Justice
New York, New York

NELSON C. STANDIFER,
   COMMISSIONER
Midnight Basketball League, Inc.
Hyattsville, Maryland

PROFESSOR RANDOLPH N. STONE
University of Chicago, The Law
   School
Chicago, Illinois

R. KEITH STROUP, ESQUIRE
Citizens for a Safe America
Alexandria, Virginia

PROFESSOR CHARLES W. THOMAS
Private Corrections Project
Gainesville, Florida

PROFESSOR MICHAEL TONRY
University of Minnesota Law
   School
Minneapolis, Minnesota

BARRY WEISBERG
Civic Consultants
Chicago, Illinois

HAROLD WOOTEN
Administrative Office of the U.S.
  Courts
Washington, D.C.

PROFESSOR FRANKLIN E. ZIMRING
Boalt Hall School of Law,
  University of California
Berkeley, California

THE REAL WAR
ON CRIME

ONE

CRIME AND POLICY

We are a nation both afraid of and obsessed with crime. Each day, newspapers tell another story of innocence shattered: the Oklahoma City bombing, the drowning of two young boys in a South Carolina lake by their mother, the brutal stabbings of Nicole Brown Simpson and Ronald Goldman. In the evenings, our televisions are saturated with real-crime dramas such as *America's Most Wanted* and *Unsolved Mysteries*. Since the 1960s, hundreds of different crime bills have been passed by Congress and state legislatures. We have fought a war on drugs. Annual expenditures on police have increased from $5 billion to $27 billion over the past two decades. We have built more prisons to lock up more people than almost every country in the world. We are the only country in the West to employ capital punishment and to use the death penalty against teenagers. Yet Americans in record numbers still report that they feel unsafe in their streets and in their homes.

We have leveled our supposedly strongest weapons at crime, to the tune of about $100 billion tax dollars per year, but we have not accomplished much. Crime rates have not gotten worse—as many would have you believe—but neither have they gotten much better.

Yet still there is the feeling that the criminal justice system is not doing enough. Many suggest that we need more police, more prisons, harsher sentencing, even a return to the chain gangs. While we continue to take tougher and tougher stances, the underlying problem remains: our criminal justice system is failing to control crime in a way that makes Americans feel safe.

A hoax is afoot. Politicians at every level—federal, state, and local—have measured our obsession, capitalized on our fears, campaigned on "get tough" platforms, and won. Since the Willie Horton advertisement dashed the hopes of Michael Dukakis in the 1988 presidential race, almost every serious candidate has tried to appear tough on crime. But appearances are often deceiving.

We will first review the basic facts about crime in America. It is important to approach the facts with caution because you will see that they rarely tell the whole story. The Commission found that some baseline data about crime are simply untrue or are more complicated than they appear, even though they provide the foundation on which much of our crime policy is constructed.

Crime Rates: The Numbers Do Not Tell the Full Story

There is a widespread perception in this country that crime rates are rising. In most categories, crime rates over the last two decades have remained remarkably stable. What has changed is the nature of criminal violence. Partly because of the prevalence of firearms, one category of the population—young males in the inner city—is at an extremely high risk of being killed. This danger sometimes spills over to the suburbs and rural areas, creating fear throughout the country. As this report will demonstrate, violence in the inner city is one of the most pressing issues facing our criminal justice system. But it is not the only issue. There are many other criminal justice issues that receive less media attention, but also have devastating implications for public safety. This report examines many of them—the difference between fear of crime and crime itself, violence, prisons, juvenile crime, domestic violence, policing, and the racial implications of crime policy.

Before delving into these issues, we must keep in mind several basic facts:

•Crime rates are higher today than they were in the 1950s. This is largely because crime increased significantly in the 1960s. But since the early 1970s, crime rates have remained remarkably stable even though they sometimes go up or down from year to year.

•The murder rate in this country dropped 9 percent from 1980 to 1992 and now is almost exactly the same as it was in the 1970s.

•The serious violent crime rate for the United States stands 16 percent below its peak level of the mid-1970s.

•Serious crimes reported to police dropped in 1992, 1993, and 1994.

These statistics tell us only that certain categories of crime have remained remarkably stable over the last two decades. They should not be taken to mean that crime is not a major problem. Crime (particularly homicide) is widespread in this country, and among young people violent crime is expected to increase further in the next few years.

Two Measures of Crime

We have found that there is a huge difference between the public *perception* and the *reality* of crime in the United States—a difference whose causes we explore in detail in Chapter 3 on fear, politics, and the prison-industrial complex. For now, it is important to remember that most people perceive crime to be rising when in reality it has remained remarkably stable for many years.[1]

One major source of confusion about crime rates in the United States is that there are two major methods by which crime is measured, the Uniform Crime Reports (UCR) and the National Crime Victimization Survey (NCVS). It may be startling that these two systems of measurement produce such different numbers. The UCR is tabulated by the FBI, based on arrest information submitted annually by each of the 17,000 different police departments in the United States. Because it is the only survey to provide a state-by-state breakdown of crime rates, the UCR is the measure of crime most cited by the media (who see it as a good local story) and politicians (who talk about it with their constituencies).

However, most criminologists consider UCR figures inaccurate because they tend to exaggerate increases in crime—a fact that is at least partly responsible for the misperception that crime is rising.[2] The UCR overestimates increases in crime for several reasons. First, computers have led to marked improvements in police reporting of crime. Thus, "increases" in crime reported by police are often the result of improved recordkeeping rather than actual increases in criminal activity. For example, in 1973 citizens reported 861,000 aggravated assaults to police, but the police recorded only 421,000.[3] By 1988, citizens reported 940,000 aggravated assaults to the police, and the police recorded 910,000. The number of aggravated assaults did not go up much between 1973 and 1988, but the recording improved dramatically. The same pattern occurred for robbery and rape.

The UCR also is flawed because of the way many police departments tabulate their statistics. If two persons are arrested for a single assault, police usually count the two arrests rather than the one assault. Thus, one crime suddenly turns into two and the total number of crimes becomes inflated. This practice creates the most severe distortions in juvenile crime because juveniles are often arrested in groups.

Moreover, budgetary decisions based on police reports create incentives for police departments to skew their figures upward. The 1994 Federal Crime Control Act, for example, allocates more funds to states with higher levels of crime as recorded by the police. Given these problems, it is not surprising that the UCR reports an increase in violent crime in the last twenty years.

Despite its flaws, the UCR does provide an accurate measure of the homicide rate. This is because murders are rare and serious events that citizens tend to report quickly and accurately to the police, who record them with precision. The UCR indicates that the incidence of murder per capita is lower today than it was in the 1930s, when the rate of incar-

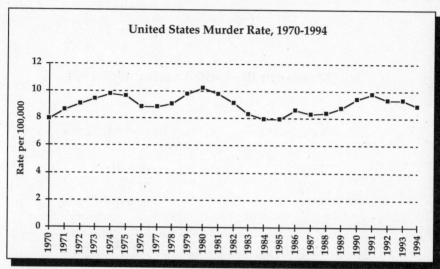

United States Murder Rate, 1970-1994

Source: **U.S. Department of Justice, Federal Bureau of Investigation. Data provided by the Criminal Justice Information Services Division (preliminary data for 1994).**

ceration then was about one-fifth what it is today. The current homicide rate of 9.3 per 100,000 population is nearly identical to the rate of 9.4 per 100,000 recorded in 1973. The total number of murders in Boston, for example, was 135 in 1973. In 1993, it was 98.[4] Our national murder rate is not increasing nearly as fast as many might claim.

We believe—as do most criminologists—that the figures produced by the National Crime Victimization Survey are more accurate. To conduct the survey, staff at the Census Bureau telephone a representative sampling of households around the country to determine how many people were victimized by one of seven crimes in the preceding year. The seven crimes are rape, robbery, assault, personal theft, household theft, burglary, and motor vehicle theft. The NCVS generally is considered more reliable because it uses scientific polling techniques similar to those that determine the Nielson ratings in television. It does not measure murder because the victim cannot be interviewed. The NCVS does not break down crime data for each state, thus making it less interesting to members of the news media who want to find a local angle on crime trends.

Murder in the United States, 1973-1994

Year	Number of Murders
1973	19,640
1974	20,710
1975	20,510
1976	18,780
1977	19,120
1978	19,560
1979	21,460
1980	23,040
1981	22,520
1982	21,010
1983	19,310
1984	18,690
1985	18,980
1986	20,610
1987	20,100
1988	20,680
1989	21,500
1990	23,440
1991	24,700
1992	23,760
1993	24,530
1994	23,249

Source: **U.S. Department of Justice, Federal Bureau of Investigation. Data provided by the Criminal Justice Information Services Division.**

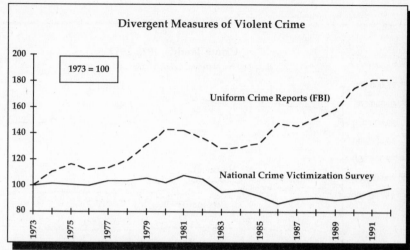

Divergent Measures of Violent Crime

1973 = 100

Uniform Crime Reports (FBI)

National Crime Victimization Survey

Note: Figures were scaled to 100 in 1973 and have been adjusted to take into account population increases.

Source: U.S. Department of Justice, Bureau of Justice Statistics (1994), *Sourcebook of Criminal Justice Statistics—1993*, pp. 247, 352.

The Threat of Violent Crime

It is important to distinguish between crime generally and violent crime specifically. Violent crimes are committed against *people*— murders, rapes, robberies, kidnappings, and assaults. Nonviolent crimes are usually committed against *property*—burglaries, auto thefts, embezzlement, check forgery, fraud, and trespassing. (Burglary, defined as breaking into a dwelling, presents a definitional problem. Though burglary is formally a crime against property, it carries the lurking possibility of violent confrontation and the psychological sense of intrusion associated with violent crime. It is therefore more serious than most nonviolent crimes.) Offenses involving the sale or possession of drugs are also nonviolent, but obviously a violent act associated with the sale or possession of drugs (such as a shooting to protect a drug market) would be a violent crime.

Much violence in our society is not a violation of the criminal law. For example, if someone kills another in self-defense, that person committed an act of violence but not a crime. There is also violence in the media and on television that shapes public perceptions and,

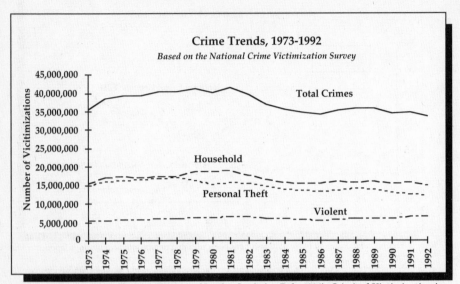

Crime Trends, 1973-1992

Based on the National Crime Victimization Survey

Source: U.S. Department of Justice, Bureau of Justice Statistics (July 1994), *Criminal Victimization in the United States: 1973–92 Trends,* p.9.

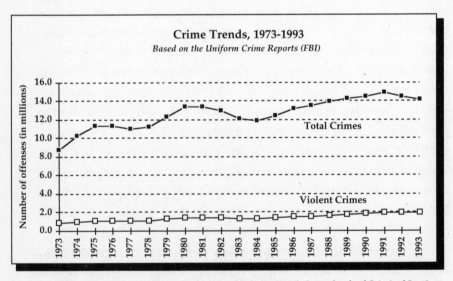

Crime Trends, 1973-1993

Based on the Uniform Crime Reports (FBI)

Sources: U.S. Department of Justice, Bureau of Justice Statistics (1994), *Sourcebook of Criminal Justice Statistics—1993,* p. 352; U.S. Department of Justice, Federal Bureau of Investigation (1994), *Crime in the United States—1993,* pp. 5, 10.

according to some experts, actually influences people to commit violent acts. But violence in the media is not a crime. A violent crime is an act of violence that violates a criminal law passed by the Congress or a state legislature.

The vast majority of crime in America is *not* violent. One in ten arrests in the United States is for a violent crime. Only 3 in 100 arrests in the United States are for a violent crime resulting in injury. The distinction between violent and nonviolent crime is critical and will be used throughout this report in understanding why the criminal justice system is not more effective at making Americans safe. When people think of locking up criminals, they usually have an image in mind of a violent offender—a murderer or a rapist. But we will show that the vast majority of people filling our expensive new prisons are nonviolent property and drug offenders.

Violent crime is a major problem in localized areas of the inner city. In those places, firearms violence—especially against young people—has increased dramatically. During the 1980s, teenage boys in all racial and ethnic groups became more likely to die from a bullet than from all natural causes combined. During the time period from 1985 to 1991, annual rates of homicide for males aged 15 to 19 years increased 154 percent.[5] For African-American male youths, the homicide rate is eight times that of white male youths. If you live in the inner city and are young—particularly young and African-American—your chance of being the victim of a violent crime is incredibly high. And if you are not living in the inner city, the localized violence of some communities reverberates nationally, making everybody *feel* less safe even though most people are *more* safe than they were in the 1970s.

The media has focused much of its crime reporting on the tragic phenomenon of youth homicide. As a result, a myth has been created and projected that all Americans have a "realistic" chance of being murdered by a stranger. While it is always good to take precautions to lower the risk of crime, in reality almost all Americans have an extremely remote chance of being killed or victimized by a stranger. Most violent crime is committed by friends and family. The most common homicide is not random but a person shooting someone he or she knows, often in the home. A 1994 government study of 8,000 homicides in urban areas found that eight out of ten murder victims were killed by a family member or someone they knew.[6] Women are far more likely to be assaulted by their husbands or boyfriends than by a stranger in an alley. Children are more likely to be molested by family or friends than by strangers.

While a few neighborhoods are extraordinarily dangerous, most are relatively safe. Males are more at risk of criminal victimization than females (because males commit much more crime than women, they tend to associate more with criminals and therefore run a higher risk of being victimized by them). Young people—particularly adolescents—are much more at risk than elderly people. The risk of being a victim of a serious violent crime is nearly four times higher for a person 16 to 19 years old than it is for a person aged 35 to 49.[7] The chances of a white woman 65 or older becoming a victim of a serious violent crime (e.g., murder, rape, robbery, or assault) are *one-sixtieth* the odds of an African-American male teenager.[8]

U.S. Crime Rates Compared to Other Countries

Although it is often assumed that the United States has a high rate of incarceration because of a high crime rate, in reality the overall rate of crime in this country is not extraordinary. The one exception is murder. Largely because of the prevalence of firearms, we have about 22,000 homicides per year, about 10 times the per capita murder rate of most European countries. Many comparable countries such as Australia and Canada actually have higher rates of victimization than the United States for some crimes. For the crime of assault with force, 2.2 percent of Americans are victimized each year, compared to 2.3 percent of Canadians and 2.8 percent of Australians. For robbery, 1.7 percent of Americans are victimized annually; in Spain, the number is 2.9 percent. For car theft, the U.S. rate is 2.3 percent; Australia is at 2.7 percent and England is at 2.8 percent.[9] Thus, it is not our higher violent crime rates that lead to our high incarceration rates—the 22,000 homicides per year cannot account for the 1.5 million people behind bars. Rather, American rates of incarceration are higher because of our exceedingly harsh treatment of people convicted of lesser crimes.

The Key to the Problem: Understanding the Difference Between Crime and Violence

We all want to protect ourselves from violent offenders, either by taking the steps necessary to prevent violent crimes or by sending to prison those who commit them. But how do we begin to control violent crime? We must start by understanding the difference between *crime* and *violence*.

We cannot begin to control violent crime until we recognize that *the primary reason most Americans live in fear is not crime but violence*. The United States does not have more crime than other industrialized countries. Rather, it has a *different character of crime*. Criminologists in the Netherlands and the United Kingdom recently compared crime across industrialized countries.[10] With the exception of homicide, the United States had the highest crime rate in only one of the fourteen offenses measured—attempted burglary. Because of the prevalence of firearms on our streets, however, America leads the world in *the proportion of violent crime resulting in injury*. If a person is assaulted with a gun rather than fists, the chances are much higher that injury or death will result. This is why the United States is far and away the world leader in the number of murders.

It is not the amount of *crime* but rather the amount of *violence* that adds to our fear. It is the failure to recognize the distinction between crime and violence that diverts attention from finding more effective methods to make our country safer. In order to understand this important distinction, it is necessary to look at crime statistics a little more closely.

Violent Crime Is a Fraction of Overall Crime

We have shown that violent street crime is but a small portion of overall crime. But even within this "violent" category the actual physical violence is often overstated. The vast majority of violent crimes are assaults where one person hits or slaps another or makes a verbal threat. Only about 8 percent of the victims of violent crime nationally went to a hospital emergency room.[11] Most were released immediately or the same day. Of all the victims of violent crime

Except for Murder, Victimization Rates in the U.S. Are Not Higher . . .

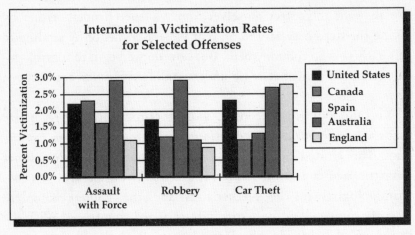

. . . But Fear Is

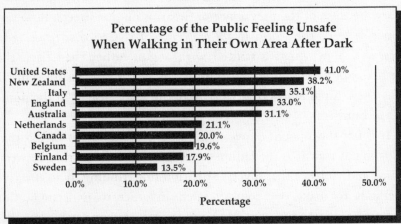

Source: **Van Dijk, Jan J. M. (November 1992),** *Criminal Victimisation in the Industrialized World,* **pp. 10, 24, 33, 57, The Netherlands: Ministry of Justice.**

nationally, slightly over 1 percent required a hospital stay of one day or more.[12] (See chart on page 15.)

Crime Policy in the United States

Unlike many European countries, there is no cabinet official in charge of national crime policy in the United States. Each of the fifty state legislatures determines its own crime policy separately. Some

Definitions of Selected Crimes

Violent Offenses		Nonviolent Offenses	
Homicide	The killing of a person whether intended or not. Includes murder and manslaughter.	Burglary	The unlawful entry of a building in order to commit a crime.
Murder	The intentional killing of a person.	Larceny or Theft	The unlawful taking of property *without* use or threat of physical harm.
Manslaughter	The unintentional killing of a person.	Drug Trafficking	Possession of a controlled substance with intent to sell.
Forcible Rape	Compulsory sexual intercourse by use or threat of physical force.	Drug Possession	Possession of a controlled substance *without* intent to sell.
Robbery	Theft by use or threat of physical force.	Public Order	A variety of offenses such as disorderly conduct, public drunkeness, and loitering.
Aggravated Assault	A physical attack intended to inflict *serious* bodily harm. Physical injury not necessary.	Traffic Offenses	A variety of offenses ranging from driving while intoxicated to driving with a revoked license.
Simple Assault	A physical attack intended to inflict *any* bodily harm. Physical injury not necessary.		

Note: These definitions are amalgamations of the laws in many jurisdictions.

states refuse to send a person to jail for having a small amount of marijuana, while others impose strict sentences. Some states choose to have the death penalty, while others shun it. Some states have mandatory minimum sentences for drug crimes, while others allow judges unfettered discretion to impose sentences. Though policies vary, most states in recent years have adopted tougher measures— longer sentences and more restrictive bail policies, both of which have led to higher rates of incarceration across the country.

Although it is difficult for these reasons to define the exact parameters of a national crime policy, a national "get tough" trend has been evident over the last fifteen years. Since 1968, six major anti-crime bills have passed Congress and been signed into law by presidents. In one way or another, all of these bills have been used by elected officials to convince the public that Washington was getting "tough" on crime by increasing sentences for certain types of offenses. Many of the bills were used to influence crime policy by withholding money from the states unless they adopted certain "get tough" policies favored by the federal government. For example, under the 1994 federal crime bill, a state can receive part of the $9.7

How Crime Breaks Down in America

Arrests for Violent Offenses	13.6%	Arrests for Nonviolent Offenses	86.4%
Murder	0.2%	Public Order	13.5%
Manslaughter	0.1%	Theft Offenses	13.0%
Forcible Rape	0.3%	Driving Under the Influence	10.9%
Robbery	1.0%	Drug Offenses	8.0%
Aggravated Assault	4.0%	White Collar	3.8%
Other Assaults	8.2%	Liquor Laws	3.7%
		Burglary	2.9%
		All Other	30.8%

Note: Totals may not add to 100% due to rounding.
Source: U.S. Department of Justice, Federal Bureau of Investigation
(December 1994), *Crime in the United States–1993, p. 217.*

billion set aside for new prison construction only if it requires inmates to serve at least 85 percent of their sentences before parole (in effect doubling sentences for many classes of offenders). The frequency with which Congress passed anti-crime legislation increased in the 1980s, when prisons were expanding most rapidly.

At the time it was signed into law, the 1968 Crime Control and Safe Streets Act was the most extensive anti-crime legislation in history. It provided for emergency wiretapping, tightened controls over interstate firearms transfers, and allocated hundreds of millions of dollars to localities to upgrade their law enforcement capability. The 1984 anti-crime legislation increased penalties for drug offenses, established mandatory sentences for certain firearms offenses, and reformed bail laws to allow for increased pretrial detention of dangerous offenders. In 1986, Congress passed another bill that established stiff mandatory sentences for possession of crack cocaine. The bill made such sentences 100 times greater than those for powder

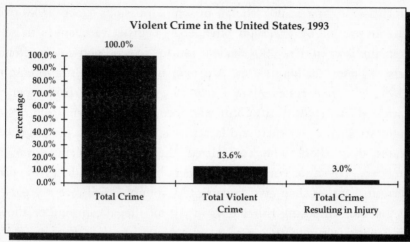

Violent Crime in the United States, 1993

Sources: U.S. Department of Justice, Federal Bureau of Investigation (December 1994), *Crime in the United States–1993* , pp. 5, 10; U.S. Department of Justice, Bureau of Justice Statistics (March 1994), *Criminal Victimization in the United States, 1992*, p. 88.

cocaine, even though, as we will explain in Chapter 4, there was little or no difference between crack and powder except the race of the people using them. A 1988 bill increased funding by billions of dollars for federal drug control efforts. The federal crime bill of 1994—the most expensive in history—added the death penalty to dozens of federal offenses, allocated $23 billion for law enforcement (this includes the $9.7 billion for prisons), and directed another $6.1 billion for crime prevention programs. Although the full impact of the 1994 crime bill has yet to be felt, it will almost certainly contribute to higher rates of incarceration in the federal prison system.

Nonviolent Offenders Fueled the Prison Expansion

Since 1980, the United States has undertaken one of the largest and most rapid expansions of a prison population in the history of the Western world. Between 1980 and 1994, the prison population tripled from 500,000 to 1.5 million. The number of people under some form of correctional supervision (in prison or jail, on probation, or on parole) surpassed 5 million people at the end of 1994, or 2.7 percent of the adult population.

Most of the increase in the prison population during this time was *not* accounted for by violent offenders. Fully 84 percent of the increase in state and federal prison admissions since 1980 was accounted for by *nonviolent* offenders.[13] Legislative changes in sentencing laws in the 1980s made it routine to send nonviolent offenders to prison for long terms. A person arrested for a drug offense in 1992 was five times more likely to go to prison than a person arrested in 1980.[14] In California, people who committed lesser offenses such as car theft and larceny went to prison at much greater rates than those who committed the serious violent crime of robbery.[15] Even for petty offenses, there has been a tendency to enact criminal rather than civil penalties. A county board recently passed legislation imposing thirty days in jail for illegal camping or allowing a dog to run loose.[16]

The state of Texas recently completed an exhaustive study of its felony sentencing patterns and found that 77 percent of all prison admissions were for nonviolent crimes.[17] The most frequent crime resulting in a prison sentence was drug possession. In the federal system, the overwhelming majority of inmates—89 percent—are convicted of nonviolent offenses.[18] We will see shortly that many of these nonviolent offenders do not need to be in prison at all, yet each one may consume tens of thousands of tax dollars per year.

One reason nonviolent offenders are crowding our prisons is because we continue to broaden the definition of crime. Historically, the term applied only to those acts that violated the rules of civilized conduct—murder, theft, and the like. Today, we classify as "criminal" conduct that which is merely undesirable or that which breaks an administrative rule (e.g., laws that ban panhandling). The increasing failure to recognize the distinction between the truly wrong and the minor infraction—and to address minor infractions outside the formal and expensive criminal justice system—at least partly explains why our jails and prisons are overcrowded.

Many state corrections leaders and prison wardens have voiced objections to the fact that nonviolent offenders take up so much space in their facilities. Bishop L. Robinson, Maryland's public safety chief, recently recommended that 32 percent of the prisoners in his state could be paroled immediately or put into alternative

Persons Admitted and in Custody
How Many? How Violent?

	POPULATION	VIOLENT	NON-VIOLENT	ANNUAL ADMISSIONS	VIOLENT	NON-VIOLENT
JAILS	490,442	23%	77%	9,796,000	n/a	n/a
STATE PRISONS	958,704	47%	53%	431,279	27%	73%
FEDERAL PRISONS	100,438	11%	89%	38,542	6%	94%
JUVENILE	93,851	15%	85%	823,449	n/a	n/a
TOTAL*	1.5 million	35%	65%	11.1 million	n/a	n/a

Note: Data are the most recent available. Population figures represent the number of persons under jurisdiction in each category.
*Totals have been adjusted to account for double counting of individuals under more than one jurisdiction.
n/a=not available
Sources: U.S. Department of Justice, Bureau of Justice Statistics; Federal Bureau of Prisons; Office of Juvenile Justice and Delinquency Prevention.

programs.[19] James A. Gondles, executive director of the American Correctional Association, agreed with Robinson. "It's not a question of being soft," he said. "It's a question of solving a problem before it eats us alive."[20] One consequence of this policy is that the system occasionally releases violent criminals early because prison space is crammed with new nonviolent offenders.

The charts above and on page 18 demonstrate how few people in the system are violent. The charts make the crucial distinction between the *population* of the system and *admissions* into the system. A facility's *population* is the number of people in that facility on any given day. *Admissions* count the number of people entering the facility during a certain period of time, usually a year. Admissions shows the dynamic nature of the system, with people entering and exiting continually. For example, a short-term holding pen in a county jail may hold 10 people on any given day, but admit 2,000 people over the course of a year.

Bait and Switch

A policy that pretends to fight violence by locking up mostly nonviolent offenders is an inefficient use of taxpayer resources. The scam works like the classic "bait and switch" marketing ploy, in which customers are "baited" into a store by an advertisement for an item at an extremely low price. Once in the store, the salesperson "switches" the customer to a higher-priced product that the scheme was designed to promote. In the criminal justice field, the "bait" is citizen fear of violent crime. The "switch" occurs when public officials fight crime by building more prisons *but then fill the new cells with nonviolent offenders.* This scheme profits those who wish to appear "tough" on crime but in reality are failing to make America safe. One consequence of this policy is that the criminal justice system spends tens of billions of dollars on prisons and then underfunds effective drug treatment, educational programs, and violence prevention programs by asserting that there is not enough money.

Criminologists Franklin Zimring and Gordon Hawkins first applied the term "bait and switch" to this aspect of criminal justice policy. Under the bait and switch, people who commit lesser infrac-

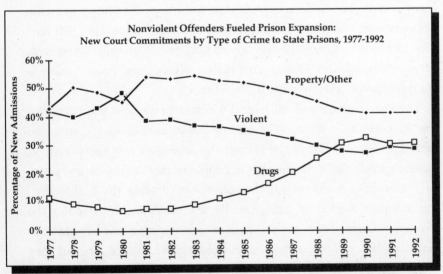

Nonviolent Offenders Fueled Prison Expansion:
New Court Commitments by Type of Crime to State Prisons, 1977-1992

Sources: U.S. Department of Justice, Bureau of Justice Statistics (May 1993), *Prisoners in 1992.* p. 10, Appendix Table 1; Department of Justice, Bureau of Justice Statistics (June 1994), *Prisoners in 1993,* p. 10, Appendix Table 1.

tions have borne the brunt of the anti-crime fervor by getting sent to prison at much higher rates and serving much longer sentences. But as the data show, violent crime is undiminished even as we engage in the largest increase in incarceration in American history.

The Bait and Switch in Practice in California

California is a good example of the "bait and switch" in practice and is illustrative of similar trends around the country. In 1980, 60 percent of the 24,569 inmates in the state had been committed to prison for acts of violence—a relatively efficient use of prison space.[21] California increased its prison population by 400 percent between 1980 and 1993 (to 125,605 inmates),[22] *yet only 27 percent of the additional prison space confined people convicted of violent offenses.*[23] The remaining 73 percent were convicted of nonviolent crimes. Today, California has more persons incarcerated for drug offenses than the entire prison population in 1980. If crime policy was intended to combat violence, then its effectiveness in California dropped considerably as the prison population expanded.

"Three Strikes and You're Out"

"Three strikes and you're out" is one of the most popular crime control initiatives. Proposals vary state by state, but the general idea behind "three strikes" is to increase the prison sentence for a second offense and require life in custody without parole for a third offense. Larry Fisher, age thirty-five, recently robbed a sandwich shop near Seattle of $135 by holding a finger in his pocket and pretending it was a gun. In the previous eight years he was responsible for two other minor robberies. Under the traditional sentencing system, Fisher would have spent about two years in prison for the sandwich shop robbery. Under the new "three strikes and you're out" legislation now in effect in Washington state, he faced life in prison with no possibility of parole for this third offense.[24]

Michael Garcia shoplifted a package of meat valued at $5.62 from a grocery store in Los Angeles.[25] At the time, Garcia was temporarily out of work and his mother's Social Security check had failed to arrive. Garcia stuck the package of chuck steak down his pants: one piece for his mother, one for his retarded brother, and one for himself. For this offense, he faces twenty-five years to life in prison under California's "three strikes" legislation. His other "strikes" also involved small sums of money and no physical injury; they were integrally related to a heroin addiction he had never been able to control. In fact, Garcia's parole agent said, "Michael is not a bad guy. He had some problems with dope use, but he's not dangerous."[26] The agent said he would have sent Garcia to a residential drug treatment program, but a slot was not available.

"Three Strikes and You're Out" Is Untested

We all acknowledge that the crime problem in most cities is severe, and that safety is the primary concern. People want tough sentences for repeat offenders, regardless of whether they are violent or nonviolent. But "three strikes and you're out"—though a great slogan—is untested and potentially disastrous. It threatens to drain billions of tax dollars to incarcerate lesser offenders for long periods of time.

The current popularity of "three strikes" legislation is in no way related to its record of success. Cases such as those of Larry Fisher and Michael Garcia appear to be typical. A survey by the legislature in California, the state to pass one of the strictest and broadest "three strikes" provisions, shows that few people sentenced under the new scheme are repeat violent offenders. Fully 70 percent of all second- and third-strike cases filed in California in 1994 were "nonviolent and nonserious offenses."[27] In Los Angeles County, only 4 percent of second and third felony convictions were cases of murder, rape, kidnapping, or carjacking. Although "three strikes" proposals typically arise from fear of violent crime, they often ensnare nonviolent offenders. The "three strikes" proposal is essentially a political ploy. Many voters who are frustrated with violent crime supported the proposal, but as we see again and again in the criminal justice system, it is doubtful they will get their money's worth. "Three strikes" proposals cast a very wide net, and most of the people caught in it do not require the kind of punishment the proposals mandate.

The Costs Run into the Billions

The costs of "three strikes" schemes are staggering. Every year an inmate spends in prison—be it under a "three strikes" law or a regular sentence—costs taxpayers an average of $22,000. As the prisoners get older, the cost of maintenance rises, ultimately reaching an average of $69,000 per year per prisoner for those over the age of fifty-five. In other words, the cost of imprisoning a person under the "three strikes" law will eventually *triple*. A study by a Stanford University professor estimated that the cost of a life term for an average California prisoner is $1.5 million.[28] Multiplied by the expected increase in prison population between now and the year 2020, the study projected total costs to California taxpayers in the hundreds of billions of dollars. While almost every other discretionary line item in the California budget is being slashed—including funds for higher education—the state still ranks first in the country in money spent to build and operate prisons.

The Rand Corporation found that the new "three strikes" law will cost between $4.5 and $6.5 billion every year to implement.[29] This is five times more than the state originally estimated. "Three strikes" will consume every dollar of new money the state expects to receive during the next six to eight years and will drain money from health and education spending. The Rand researchers concluded that the cost of the new legislation is so high that it will be impossible to implement fully. As a result, it is likely that the law will be applied haphazardly across the state. Such partial implementation can lead to dangerous, unplanned results, such as petty offenders spending decades in prison for lesser crimes while dangerous offenders are released early for lack of space.

Other unanticipated consequences already are starting to develop. One report concluded that plea bargaining is down because more felony offenders are opting to go to trial rather than risk getting a strike under the new legislation.[30] The increase in the number of trials is creating massive backlogs in the judicial system and causing court and attorney costs to skyrocket. Moreover, uneven enforcement of the law paves the way for racial and ethnic disparities to develop. Data from the Los Angeles Public Defender's office suggests that minorities with roughly the same criminal history as whites are being charged under "three strikes" at seventeen times the rate of whites.[31]

Truth in Sentencing

Prison populations in many states will increase more rapidly in coming years because of a proliferation of so-called "truth in sentencing" laws. Truth in sentencing requires the prisoner to serve the full sentence without being released early on parole. The laws are the result of public frustration with sentencing systems that do not tell the "truth" about sentence length—certainly a valid concern for all Americans who want to know how their tax dollars are being spent.

Tired of being told one thing and seeing another, the public has supported truth in sentencing enthusiastically without understanding the dramatic impact it will have on prison populations. Such laws take advantage of legitimate public frustration to instantly double and even triple prison sentences for all offenders. What the public is *not* told is that truth in sentencing will dramatically increase the amount of money going into prisons, largely to incarcerate the more numerous nonviolent offenders for longer periods of time.

The Old System of Indeterminate Sentencing

Under the old "indeterminate" sentencing system, a judge could hand down a sentence within a permissible range: Once found guilty, a person might receive a maximum of ten years in prison with the expectation that he would be released after five years if he conformed to the rules of the prison. The prospect of early release was designed to induce good behavior so inmates would be easier to manage and more likely to succeed after release. If inmates violated rules while in prison or on parole, they could be additionally punished by incarceration for the remainder of the original sentence plus any sentences for new charges. Judges usually doubled the maximum potential sentence so that the actual time served was about what the judge wished it to be and the threat of additional sentence was substantial.

This was not a straightforward way to sentence offenders. But it did serve the managerial needs of the prison system by affording parole boards the discretion to release inmates when ready or when conditions became overcrowded.

Two Main Attacks on the Old System

Indeterminate sentencing schemes have been subjected to two attacks in recent years. First, it is said that offenders only spend a portion of their actual sentences behind bars. This makes it appear that the offender gets off easy.

Although it is true that offenders often serve only a portion of the sentence, it does not follow that the offenders get off easy. Judges in indeterminate sentencing systems customarily impose longer sentences, expecting an early release.

Second, if released inmates commit another crime after being paroled, politicians charge that the crime could have been avoided if the inmate had served his full term. While this is a valid point in some cases, under the old sentencing regime the second half of the prison term is not designed to incapacitate because it is not supposed to be served. It is designed only to intimidate the inmate into better behavior. This political attack is often coupled with claims that parolees are running the streets and victimizing innocent citizens. Such claims are usually unwarranted. People paroled from prison or serving probationary sentences commit only 4 percent of offenses known to police each year for the most serious violent crimes of murder, rape, robbery, and assault.[32]

Truth in Sentencing as the Answer

In order to cure these supposed flaws, many politicians wish to require inmates to serve all or almost all (usually 85 percent) of the full sentence no matter how well they behave in prison. Under these truth in sentencing proposals, a person sentenced to ten years in prison would not be eligible for release after the four to six years customary under indeterminate sentencing systems, but would have to serve at least eight and one-half years. This single change in parole policy would effectively double most prison sentences.

Although there might be reasons to tighten the old indeterminate system, it does not appear that careful tightening is the purpose of the new proposals. Truth in sentencing tends to mix violent and nonviolent offenders, and particularly for nonviolent offenders, it often increases sentences far beyond what is needed to ensure public safety.

Truth in sentencing has become such a powerful slogan that the federal government is trying to impose it on unwilling states. Most of the $10 billion in federal money available to states for prison construction under the 1994 federal crime bill will only be granted on the condition that states adopt truth in sentencing. This represents a significant shift in the traditional balance between the state and federal governments and a significant federalization of a traditionally local issue.

The Economic Cost of Truth in Sentencing

If the longer sentences are not carefully targeted to reach only the offenders who deserve them, they can be a terrible drain on public funds. Virginia, which is considering adoption of a new truth in sentencing plan, is a case in point. The Virginia plan to abolish parole and establish truth in sentencing originally called for construction of twenty-five new prisons at a cost of nearly $2 billion.[33] The state legislature estimated that the new prisons would cost $500 million per year to operate, double what the state pays for its current system. There was little discussion about how to pay for the plan, although Governor George Allen Jr. pointed toward parks and schools as possible sources of revenue.[34]

Governor Allen claimed that the plan was necessitated by the "rapid rise of violent crime" in the state, even though violent crime fell in the two years preceding introduction of the plan.[35] He claimed that "putting dangerous predators back on the streets" is a leading cause of criminal victimization, despite the fact that only 9 percent of robberies, 4 percent of murders, and 2 percent of rapes and aggravated assaults in Virginia are committed by people on parole.[36] Most importantly, the governor claimed that the plan targeted "violent career criminals," although his own projections showed that the plan would capture almost four times more nonviolent offenders than violent offenders.

Mandatory Minimum Sentences

Mandatory minimums were a sentencing reform popular among elected officials during the height of the "war" on drugs in the late 1980s. The effect of mandatory minimum sentences on the criminal justice system has been long-term, and is still being felt by thousands of nonviolent drug offenders, many of whom are spending a decade or more behind bars for relatively modest offenses. The Rockefeller drug laws in New York, passed in the 1970s, have been so harsh on drug offenders that current Republican governor George Pataki has sought to repeal some of their provisions.

Mandatory minimums always require offenders to spend time in prison for *at least* a certain number of years. They are similar to truth in sentencing laws in that they increase the length of sentence, but they differ in that they allow parole after the minimum number of years is served. In the federal system, there are currently more than 100 provisions for mandatory minimums. Most states have mandatory minimum sentencing as well. The following illustrates the injustice and waste of tax dollars that can result from mandatory minimum sentences:

•In Mobile, Alabama, Nicole Richardson fell in love at age twenty with a small-time drug dealer who worked out of a local bar. One day, an undercover agent asked her where he could buy some drugs. She told him to talk to her boyfriend. For that degree of involvement, she was sentenced to ten years in prison with no possibility of parole. Her boyfriend had information on other drug dealers to trade. After cooperating with authorities, he received a prison sentence of five years.

•Michael Irish was a carpenter from Portland, Oregon, whose life savings had been wiped out to pay for the medical bills of his cancer-stricken wife.[37] Irish, who had no criminal history, was caught and convicted of unloading boxes of hashish from a boat. Under the mandatory minimum law, he was sentenced to twelve years in prison with no possibility of parole—an incarceration that will cost at least $250,000.

• As a young man, Bill Keagle had served six years in prison for burglary. After release, he married and adopted his wife's two children. When he was laid off, he sold some guns he had used for target shooting to a pawnshop. He did not know that possession of those guns put him in violation of the federal Armed Career Criminal Act. Although his prior crimes were old and nonviolent, they caused him to be sentenced to fifteen years in prison under a mandatory minimum provision.

Stories like these are so numerous they have undermined much confidence in mandatory minimum sentences. Ninety percent of federal judges and 75 percent of state judges think mandatory minimum sentences are unsound.[38] On the U.S. Supreme Court, Chief Justice William Rehnquist and Associate Justice Anthony Kennedy are among those who have spoken against mandatory minimums.[39] They have been joined by the United States Sentencing Commission, the American Bar Association, and the National Association of Veteran Police Officers.[40]

Mandatory minimums create a number of problems.[41] First, they apply to everybody regardless of whether the punishment fits the crime or the offender. Second, mandatory minimums create what is known as sentencing "cliffs" for drug offenses. For example, possession of five grams of crack is punished with *no more than* one year in prison; possession of 5.01 grams of crack is punished with *no less than* five years in prison.

Third, mandatory sentences do not produce an equal sentence for everybody who commits the same offense. If a drug defendant decides to cooperate with the prosecution and turns in other people, the prosecutor will often choose not to charge that person with a crime carrying a mandatory minimum sentence, thus allowing the defendant to get out of prison early. Through this process, high-level drug dealers with the most information often get off with light sentences, while low-level dealers receive the longer mandatory minimum sentence.

The Relationship Between Poverty, Family Breakdown, and Criminal Justice

The Commission members feel strongly that crime is an act of personal choice and that an effective criminal justice system holds individuals accountable for their criminal behavior. Nevertheless, those who wish to prevent crime before it occurs cannot ignore the fact that the majority of the people filling our prisons come from impoverished backgrounds and lack a formal education.[42] Research shows that children from low-income families who are placed in early childhood development programs such as Head Start have lower rates of crime and higher rates of marriage than those who are not in the program.[43] We need to recognize that investing money in early childhood development produces a safer and healthier society over the long run. Unfortunately, the United States is the wealthiest nation on earth but has the highest child poverty rates of any industrialized country. More than fifteen million children live in poverty

Some Mandatory Minimum Sentences (Federal)

Type of Drug	Five Years Without Parole
LSD	1 gram
Marijuana	100 plants or 100 kilos
Crack cocaine	5 grams
Powder cocaine	500 grams
Heroine	100 grams
Methamphetamine	10 grams
PCP	10 grams

in the United States, and up to twelve million children are malnourished.[44]

Research consistently demonstrates that a disproportionate amount of violent street crime occurs in areas that have the lowest incomes and the most desperate living conditions.[45] Furthermore, medical research suggests that children who are malnourished are more apt to engage in high-risk behavior when they get older.[46] Regardless of what one thinks of our high rates of incarceration, it is also clear that they have had a negative impact on family stability. In some cities, more than half of all young men are under criminal justice supervision on any given day. With so many men in prison, the pool of people available for marriage has dwindled. This is a two-edged sword: while it is good for public safety to take a violent criminal off the streets, it is bad for public safety to incarcerate so many petty offenders that family life is disrupted. It is two-parent families that are least likely to live in poverty and more likely to cushion young people from the temptation to adopt a criminal lifestyle.[47] Eleven percent of children who live in a two-parent family live in poverty, while 60 percent of children who live with a single parent live in poverty.[48]

It troubles the Commission that the size of the American prison population and the number of people living in poverty both increased dramatically in the 1980s. Worse, the growth of each seemed to feed off the growth of the other. This is because funding for prison expansion came largely at the expense of programs designed to alleviate poverty.

Reducing Poverty Can Reduce Levels of Crime

Poverty is not an excuse for crime, nor is crime the exclusive province of low-income persons. But overall, countries with the highest ratio of poverty have the highest rates of crime.[49] The same correlation holds true for cities. It does not follow that an increase in poverty will translate immediately into an increase in crime. It does strongly imply that if overall poverty is reduced, then in the long run the amount of street crime associated with poverty will be reduced as well.

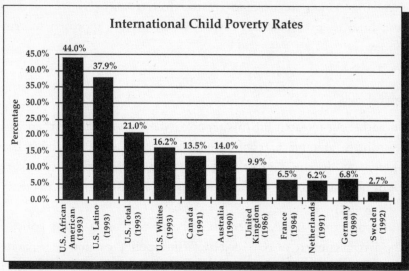

Sources: U.S. Bureau of the Census, Table 21: Poverty Status of Persons, by Age, Race, and Hispanic
Origin: 1968–1993; Rainwater, Lee, and Timothy M. Smeeding (August 1995), *Luxembourg
Income Study*, Table 3.

The increase in poverty in the United States during the 1980s was
significant. The average rate of poverty in the United States during
the decade was 17 percent higher than the average for the 1970s.[50]
But the chart above does not begin to capture the overwhelming
extent of child poverty, particularly for minorities. The poverty rate
for African-American children is an astonishing 44 percent. For
Latinos it is 38 percent, and for whites it is 16.2 percent.[51] In
Sweden, the poverty rate for children is 2.7 percent; in Canada, it is
13.5 percent; and the overall United States rate is 21.0 percent.[52]

The Tradeoff Between Prisons and Opportunity for Youth

The massive prison construction represented a commitment by our
nation to *plan for social failure* by spending billions of dollars to lock
up hundreds of thousands of people while at the same time cutting
billions of dollars for programs that would provide opportunity to
young Americans.[53] The result of our social and criminal justice policies is that today among developed countries, the United States has
the highest rates of incarceration, the widest spread of income
inequality, and the highest levels of poverty. If we are serious about

reducing crime, we need to create effective anti-poverty programs and fund them adequately as part of an overall approach to crime policy.

Conclusion

In gathering research for this report, it became clear that there is an inordinate amount of confusion about crime data. Without basic agreement on the data, it will be virtually impossible to ask the right questions so the nation can forge a consensus on how to create a safer society.

Beyond that, policymakers must begin to look at crime policy in the larger context of our society. Crime policy cannot be separated from issues of child poverty or family stability, nor can it be seen in isolation from spending in other areas of the economy. More and more, one new prison cell for an offender can mean one less classroom for a child—a process that in effect closes off options for young people, thereby justifying the need for more prisons. Our crime-fighting policies must work to make the country safer and do so in the most cost-effective manner possible.

TWO

PRISONS

Since 1980, the United States has engaged in the largest and most frenetic correctional buildup of any country in the history of the world. During this time the number of Americans imprisoned has tripled to 1.5 million. About 50 million criminal records—enough to cover nearly one-fifth of the entire U.S. population—are stuffed into police files. Hundreds of billions of dollars have poured from taxpayers' checking accounts into penal institutions and the businesses that service them. Several million people have come to depend on the criminal justice system for employment.

The hidden side of the growth of the criminal justice system is its direct effect on how much less money Americans spend on education, parks, libraries, recreation centers, highways, and universities. With a significant percentage of the potential male workforce in prison, our high rates of incarceration also act as a drag on economic growth. One estimate has the nation's jobless rate rising from 5.9 percent to 7.5 percent if male prisoners were counted as part of the labor force.[1]

One would think that the extraordinary expansion of the criminal justice system would have made at least a small dent in the crime

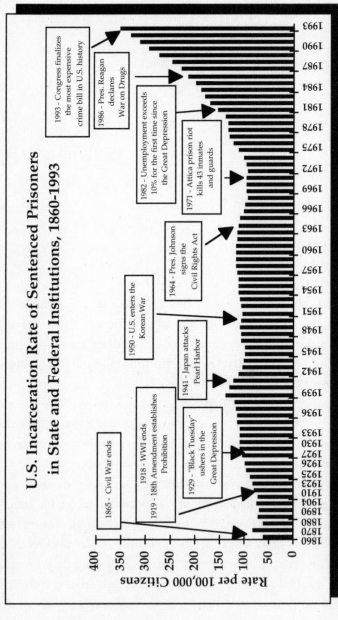

U.S. Incarceration Rate of Sentenced Prisoners in State and Federal Institutions, 1860-1993

1865 - Civil War ends

1918 - WWI ends

1919 - 18th Amendment establishes Prohibition

1929 - "Black Tuesday" ushers in the Great Depression

1941 - Japan attacks Pearl Harbor

1950 - U.S. enters the Korean War

1964 - Pres. Johnson signs the Civil Rights Act

1971 - Attica prison riot kills 43 inmates and guards

1982 - Unemployment exceeds 10% for the first time since the Great Depression

1986 - Pres. Reagan declares War on Drugs

1993 - Congress finalizes the most expensive crime bill in U.S. history

Rate per 100,000 Citizens

Sources: U.S. Department of Justice, Bureau of Justice Statistics (1994), *Sourcebook of Criminal Justice Statistics—1993,* p. 600; U.S. Department of Justice, Bureau of Justice Statistics (June 1994), *Prisoners in 1993,* p. 2; U.S. Department of Justice, Bureau of Justice Statistics (December 1986), *Historical Corrections Statistics in the United States, 1850–1984,* p. 34.

rate. The increase in the prison population did not reduce crime, nor did it make Americans feel safer. In fact, some criminologists have argued that the overuse of the penal system for so many small-time offenders has actually created more crime than it has prevented, a topic we will explore shortly.

The Numbers

In order to appreciate this development, it is necessary to examine the size and recent growth of the criminal justice system.

More Than 1.5 Million Americans Are Behind Bars

The United States now has 1.5 million people behind bars—one million in state and federal prisons and another half million in local jails.[2] Compared to other countries, this is by far the highest rate of incarceration relative to population in the Western world. The population of Americans incarcerated on any given day would qualify as the sixth-largest city in the country and is equal to the total combined populations of Seattle, Cleveland, and Denver. The Rikers Island Correctional Facilities in New York City and the Los Angeles

Who Is in Jail and Prison

	Jails	Prisons (State)	Prisons (Federal)
Number of Inmates	490,442	958,704	100,438
Jurisdiction	Cities, counties	States	U. S. Government
Characteristics of Facility	Usually holds persons awaiting trial and sentenced under 1 year.	Usually holds persons sentenced to 1 year or more.	Persons convicted of federal offenses regardless of sentence length.
Characteristics of Inmate Population	Two-thirds in custody for nonviolent offenses. Half are awaiting trial. 10 million admissions to jails every year.	53% of inmates are serving sentences for nonviolent offenses.	89% of inmates sentenced for nonviolent offenses. Nearly 2 of 3 inmates convicted of a drug offense.

Sources: **U.S. Department of Justice, Bureau of Justice Statistics (August 1995),** *Prisoners in 1994,* **p. 3, Table 2; U.S. Department of Justice, Federal Bureau of Prisons (September 4, 1995),** *Monday Morning Highlights;* **U.S. Department of Justice, Bureau of Justice Statistics (April 1995),** *Jails and Jail Inmates 1993–94.*

Change in the State and Federal Prison and Local Jail Populations, 1980–1994				
Year	State & Federal Prisons	Jails	Total	Annual Percent Change	Percent Change Since 1980
1980	329,821	163,994	493,815	n/a	n/a
1981	369,930	195,085	565,015	14.4%	14.4%
1982	413,806	209,582	623,388	10.3%	26.2%
1983	436,855	223,551	660,406	5.9%	33.7%
1984	462,002	234,500	696,502	5.5%	41.0%
1985	502,507	256,615	759,122	9.0%	53.7%
1986	544,972	274,444	819,416	7.9%	65.9%
1987	585,084	295,873	880,957	7.5%	78.4%
1988	627,600	343,569	971,169	10.2%	96.7%
1989	712,364	395,553	1,107,917	14.1%	124.4%
1990	773,919	405,320	1,179,239	6.4%	138.8%
1991	825,619	426,479	1,252,098	6.2%	153.6%
1992	883,656	444,584	1,328,240	6.1%	169.0%
1993	948,881	459,804	1,408,685	6.1%	185.3%
1994	1,053,738	490,442	1,544,180	9.6%	212.7%

Note: A small number of inmates who are held in local jails under state sentence are included in both the prison and jail counts. As a result, the totals are slightly inflated.

Source: U.S. Department of Justice, Bureau of Justice Statistics.

County Jail system are the two largest penal colonies in the world and by themselves have budgets larger than many cities.

Five Million Americans Are Under Correctional Supervision

In addition to the 1.5 million Americans behind bars, there are also an additional 3.6 million persons on probation or parole.[3] There are thus over 5 million citizens—or almost 3 percent of the U.S. adult population—under the supervision of the criminal justice system. One in thirty-eight adults in our country, and one in twenty-one men, live under the supervision of the criminal justice system.[4]

Over 11 Million People Admitted to Locked Facilities

Even this staggering sum does not reflect the reach of the criminal justice system. Each year, prisons and jails across the country admit 11 million individuals for booking. Most of these admissions are in local jails at the city or county level and lead to at least one night of incarceration.[5] The number of people admitted to a locked facility in a single year surpasses the combined populations of Alaska, Delaware,

Hawaii, Idaho, Maine, Montana, Nevada, New Hampshire, North Dakota, Rhode Island, South Dakota, Vermont, and Wyoming. Enough people are locked up every two days to fill the New Orleans Superdome to capacity.

Most People Admitted to Jail for Minor Offenses

Nationally, many citizens arrested and imprisoned in county jails have committed public order or misdemeanor offenses—crimes such as drunkenness, being a nuisance, traffic violations, shoplifting, and drug possession.[6] The average length of stay in local jails for these offenses is a few days. The jail in one Florida city is typical of national trends. Of the thousands of people booked each year into the Duval County (Jacksonville) Jail, 70 percent faced misdemeanor

The Reach of the Criminal Justice System

Adult Correctional Populations	Adults (18 and over) Pop.=192.6 million	Male Adults (18 and over) Pop.=92.4 million	African-American Male Adults (18 and over) Pop.=10.1 million	Young, African-American Male Adults (18 - 34) Pop.=4.5 million
Incarcerated on any given day	1 in 128	1 in 68	1 in 17	1 in 10
Under correctional supervision on any given day	1 in 38	1 in 21	1 in 6	1 in 3
Admitted to prisons or jails in the course of a year	1 in 25	1 in 14	1 in 4	1 in 3

Note: Population estimates are as of July 1, 1994.
Sources: U.S. Department of Justice, Bureau of Justice Statistics; U.S. Bureau of the Census.

Felony and Misdemeanor Offenses

Felony:	Offense punishable by *more than one year* in custody
Misdemeanor:	Offense punishable by *less than one year* in custody

charges and only 5 percent were convicted of a felony.[7] The jail held people for offenses that included letting a dog on the beach without a leash and shoplifting candy bars.

Fifty Million Criminal Records

Police create a criminal record each time an individual is arrested and fingerprinted, be it for trespassing or murder. It is the huge number of arrests for nonviolent crimes that explains why 50 million criminal records are on file in the United States.[8] Some individuals have a criminal record in more than one state or have committed more than one offense, so there are *not* 50 million separate people with criminal records. Nevertheless, we estimate there are at least 30 million individuals in the United States with a criminal record on file—or about one-ninth of the entire U.S. population. Since most of the 50 million criminal records are of men (80 percent of arrests are of men), and there are 92.6 million adult males in the country, we conservatively estimate that one-fourth of all men in the United States have a criminal record on file with the police.

Toward a Prison Population of 7.5 Million

One research organization has projected that the prison population will rise to 7.5 million if several "get tough" measures are implemented on a national scale.[9] The projection—made by the National Council on Crime and Delinquency, a respected research organization in San Francisco—is based upon the enactment of anti-crime proposals such as "three strikes and you're out," truth in sentencing, adding 100,000 police officers, increasing the conviction rate, and increasing the proportion of defendants who get sentenced to prison. Under this scenario, annual criminal justice costs in America will increase to almost $221 billion. In comparison, the entire defense budget for 1995 was $269 billion.[10]

Prison and jail construction in the United States continues at a rapid pace despite evidence that the increase in rates of incarceration has failed to reduce crime. More than 600 new prisons have been constructed in the United States since 1980 at a cost of tens of billions of dollars, and this does not include modifications of existing

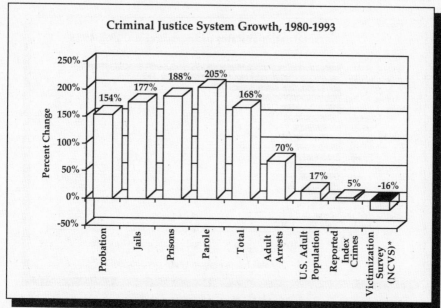

Criminal Justice System Growth, 1980-1993

*NCVS percent change is from 1980 to 1992 due to the redesign of the 1993 survey.

Sources: U.S. Department of Justice, Bureau of Justice Statistics (1994), *Criminal Victimization in the United States: 1973–1992 Trends;* U.S. Department of Justice, Federal Bureau of Investigation (1994), *Crime in the United States—1993* and (1981) *Crime in the United States—1980;* U.S. Department of Justice, Bureau of Justice Statistics Press Release (September 11, 1994), *Parole and Probation Populations Reach New Highs;* U.S. Bureau of the Census (February 1993), *U.S. Population Estimates, By Age, Sex, Race, and Hispanic Origin: 1980 to 1991;* U.S. Bureau of the Census (March 1994), *U.S. Population Estimates, By Age, Sex, Race, and Hispanic Origin: 1990 to 1993.*

facilities.[11] The 1994 federal crime bill allocated nearly $10 billion for states to build prisons.[12] Many states, including Texas and California, are carrying out ambitious prison-building programs.

Comparing Imprisonment Across Countries

One way to understand the scale of imprisonment in the United States is to compare it to other industrialized nations with similar rates of crime. The United States leads the Western world by imprisoning 555 out of every 100,000 of its citizens.[13] The imprisonment rate in the United States is about five times the rate of Canada and Australia and seven times the rate of most European democracies. Yet as we have seen, the overall crime rate in America is no higher than it is in comparable nations. The reason more people are in

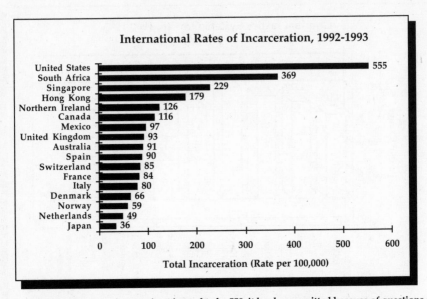

International Rates of Incarceration, 1992-1993

Country	Rate
United States	555
South Africa	369
Singapore	229
Hong Kong	179
Northern Ireland	126
Canada	116
Mexico	97
United Kingdom	93
Australia	91
Spain	90
Switzerland	85
France	84
Italy	80
Denmark	66
Norway	59
Netherlands	49
Japan	36

Total Incarceration (Rate per 100,000)

Note: Russia's incarceration rate is estimated to be 558; it has been omitted because of questions of reliability. The incarceration rates include both prison and jail populations.

Sources: Mauer, Marc (September 1994), *Americans Behind Bars: The International Use of Incarceration, 1992–1993* (Washington D.C.: The Sentencing Project); Austin, James (January 1994), *An Overview of Incarceration Trends in the United States and Their Impact on Crime* (San Francisco: The National Council on Crime and Delinquency).

prison in the United States is because our sentences are so much longer for lesser crimes. In most other countries, people who commit nonviolent offenses receive shorter prison terms or noncustodial sanctions such as fines or community service.

African-Americans in the Criminal Justice System

A race crisis of disastrous proportions is unfolding in the American criminal justice system. A racial breakdown of the inmate population in the United States reveals that African-Americans are incarcerated at a rate more than six times that of whites—1,947 per 100,000 citizens compared to 306 per 100,000 citizens for whites.[14] This disparity exists for two reasons: African-Americans tend to get arrested at higher rates than whites *and* they tend to be treated more harshly than whites as they move through the criminal justice system. That said, it is still true that the majority of violent crime nationwide is

LOCATIONS OF LOCKED FACILITIES IN CALIFORNIA

C	County Jails
F	Federal Prisons
J	Juvenile Detention Centers
S	State Prisons

LOCATIONS OF LOCKED FACILITIES IN FLORIDA

C County Jails
F Federal Prisons
S State Prisons

LOCATIONS OF LOCKED FACILITIES IN TEXAS

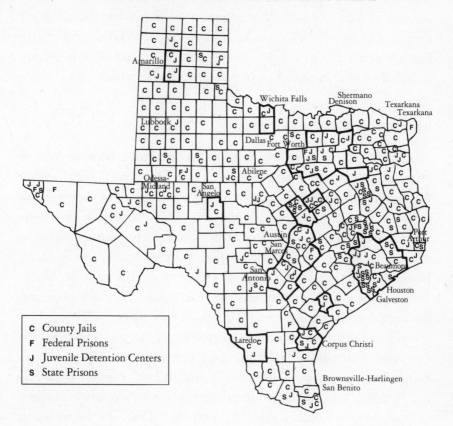

c   County Jails
F   Federal Prisons
J   Juvenile Detention Centers
s   State Prisons

committed by whites. This issue will be discussed in detail in the chapter on race. For now, it is important to remember that in many cities one-third of all African-American men aged eighteen to thirty-four are under the supervision of the criminal justice system—either in jail or prison, on probation or parole, or awaiting trial.[15]

Rates of Imprisonment and Crime

Academic research has shown little or no correlation between rates of crime and the number of people in prison. States with high rates of imprisonment may or may not have high rates of crime, while states with low rates of crime may or may not have high rates of imprisonment. North Dakota and South Dakota, which are virtually identical in terms of demographics and geography, provide an example. South Dakota imprisons its citizens at three times the rate of North Dakota, but crime between the two states is roughly the same and has been for several decades.[16] This point can also be illustrated by comparing the homicide and incarceration rates in most states. Louisiana, for example, puts more of its citizens in prison per capita than almost any other state—yet it also had the highest homicide rate in 1994. Oklahoma had the third highest incarceration rate but ranked twentieth in its rate of homicide.[17] Dramatic increases in incarceration are not necessarily followed by declines in crime.

The link between crime and imprisonment creates a great deal of confusion. Because increasing rates of imprisonment will sometimes occur at the same time as declining rates of crime (though sometimes not), those who use the data selectively can make it appear that prisons work to lower crime. In California, the prison population rose in 19 of the past 21 years. In 15 of those 19 years, violent crime rose as well. This would seem to indicate that prisons did not reduce violent crime in California. Yet some elected officials point to the few years that crime fell and claim that additional prison construction is necessary to reduce crime.

This kind of claim is becoming more frequent in the debate over crime policy, particularly since crime rates have declined slightly in each of the last three years. Though we are gratified crime is dropping, it is impossible to point to an increase in the prison population as the primary reason. In fact, nobody can conclusively explain this drop by pointing to one factor. Many experts believe the decline has resulted from a combination of demographic changes (there are fewer criminally active young males), more effective law enforcement, and greater stability in the drug trade (which leads to less violence among drug gangs).

The Effects of Incarceration

Sending such a high number of Americans through the jailhouse door each year has wide ramifications. Anyone who has been hand-cuffed by police knows how deeply humiliating the experience can be. Imagine the effects of spending even a night in the bizarre and violent subculture of most jails. Literature abounds with examples of people trau-matized by the experience. Each person booked is finger-printed and photographed for their criminal record (the record remains with them even if the charges are later drop-ped). Basic survival tactics are necessary to endure even a short stay. Inmates learn to strike first and seek strength in gangs often comprised of dan-gerous offenders. Sexual assaults are frequent and usually go unpunished.[18] The prison experience is one in which the code is survival of the fittest, in which weakness is a crime, and

Prison Incarceration Rate by State, 1994

Rank	State	Rate (per 100,000)
1	Texas	636
2	Louisiana	530
3	Oklahoma	508
4	South Carolina	494
5	Nevada	460
6	Arizona	459
7	Georgia	456
8	Alabama	450
9	Michigan	428
10	Mississippi	408
11	Florida	406
12	Maryland	395
13	Virginia	395
14	Delaware	393
15	California	384
16	Ohio	377
17	New York	367
18	Arkansas	353
19	Missouri	338
20	North Carolina	322
21	Connecticut	321
22	Alaska	317
23	Illinois	310
24	New Jersey	310
25	Colorado	289
26	Kentucky	288
27	Tennessee	277
28	Indiana	258
29	Idaho	258
30	Wyoming	254
31	Kansas	249
32	South Dakota	240
33	Pennsylvania	235
34	New Mexico	220
35	Hawaii	202
36	Washington	201
37	Montana	194
38	Iowa	192
39	Wisconsin	187
40	Rhode Island	186
41	New Hampshire	177
42	Oregon	175
43	Massachusetts	171
44	Vermont	168
45	Nebraska	159
46	Utah	155
47	Maine	118
48	West Virginia	106
49	Minnesota	100
50	North Dakota	78

Source: U.S. Department of Justice, Bureau of Justice Statistics (August 1995), Prisoners in 1994, p. 3, Table 2.

in which the expression of vulnerable feelings can jeopardize the survival of the prisoner. As ever more young men and women are socialized to the cell blocks and then are returned to the streets, the violent subculture of the correctional facility increasingly acts as a vector for spreading crime in our communities. Prisons and jails thus have a dual effect: They protect society from criminals, but they also contribute to crime by transferring their violent subculture to our community once inmates are released.

In many communities, spending time locked up is such a natural part of life that correctional facilities have lost their ability to scare people into good behavior. In California, 40 percent of youths in custody have a parent who has done time. Experts on the inner city point out that many young men do not mind going to prison because they see it as a glamorous rite of passage that earns respect and status.[19] The *New York Times* described a scene on the South Side of Chicago where neighborhood youth surrounded an ex-inmate who came home "as if he were a rap star passing out concert tickets."[20]

Commission member Joanne Page has worked with ex-offenders for years as the director of The Fortune Society in New York City. She compares the impact of incarceration to post-traumatic stress disorder, which often afflicts soldiers who return home from war. Many offenders emerge from prison afraid to trust, fearful of the unknown, and with their vision of the world shaped by the meaning that behaviors have in the prison context. For a recently released prisoner, experiences like being jostled on the subway, having someone reach across them in the bathroom to take a paper towel, or staring can be taken as the precursor to a physical attack. Professionals who work with ex-offenders have said it appears prison damages a person's mid-range response to the environment, leaving the choice of gritting one's teeth and enduring, or full-fledged attack to protect oneself from perceived danger. In a relationship with a loved one, this socialization means that problems will not easily be talked through, but are more likely to result in a blowup or an absence of communication. In a job situation, this means tensions are more likely to result in a loss of temper or in the failure to show up for work.

Jail and Prison Conditions

A few elected officials have sought to rid correctional facilities of amenities such as television and air conditioning.[21] These demands have an intuitive appeal because no taxpayer wants to fund a comfortable lifestyle for prisoners. Yet the reality in prison is different from the one described by many of those who want to toughen conditions. Three out of four inmates in the United States are housed in overcrowded facilities where the living space for two people is the size of a walk-in closet.[22] Some inmates suffer physical abuse in prison: In the high-security wing of an Oregon state prison, an inmate was stripped naked, placed in full mechanical restraints, and locked in a "quiet cell" with the lights on for twenty-four hours a day.[23] He was not permitted out-of-cell exercise for five years. Others suffer sexual abuse: It has been estimated that almost one-quarter of all inmates are victims of a sexual assault each year during incarceration.[24] Other prison systems are corrupt: Between 1989 and 1994, fifty correctional staff in the District of Columbia were convicted of serious crime, eighteen of them for smuggling drugs into prison for inmates.[25] Many prisons are clean and well-administered, but no prison is luxurious. In some, life is so wretched that the courts have ordered authorities to improve conditions or face jail time themselves. For example, in 1994, thirty-nine states plus the District of Columbia were under court order to reduce overcrowding or improve prison conditions.[26] It is partly because of these conditions that many offenders have such a difficult time making the transition to freedom.

The debate over prison conditions is often used to distract voters from the real problems facing the criminal justice system. In Mississippi, a law was passed banning individual air conditioners for inmates even though not a single inmate had an air conditioner.[27] A Louisiana law forbids inmates from taking classes in karate or martial arts, even though there were no such training classes available. The governor of Connecticut blasted a prison for providing "country club" landscaping on the outside of the facility. In reality, the planting had been done at the request of nearby residents annoyed by the ugly prison wall.[28] It appears that other new laws are intended to humiliate inmates. Mississippi recently began requiring inmates to wear striped prison suits with the word "convict" on the back. In Alabama, the governor recently reinstituted prison chain gangs. Inmates shackled together in groups of five "work" on state roadways chipping away at rocks, with no apparent purpose except to convince passersby something is being done about the crime problem.

For those concerned with public safety as well as vengeance, the issue of jail and prison conditions becomes more complicated. We all want inmates to feel the sting of punishment and loss of freedom. On the other hand, it does not serve public safety to so frustrate inmates that they return to the streets embittered and angry. Jail and prison conditions exert a significant influence on whether an inmate becomes productive upon release or resumes criminal behavior. More than nine out of ten inmates currently in prison will be released at some point.[29] Although prisons cannot become "country clubs" without losing their deterrent effect, they also cannot become gulags without jeopardizing public safety. The best correctional facilities strike a balance between punishment and the opportunity for inmates to become self-sufficient, particularly as they get closer to release.

One way to strike this balance and save tax dollars is to make offenders more responsible for their upkeep. One of the best-kept secrets in American corrections is that most inmates *want* to work, but prison jobs are scarce. Work opportunities should be provided for all inmates, and that work should be geared toward maintaining the institution at minimal cost to taxpayers. At one prison in Washington state, inmates produce blue jeans, and most of the profits are put back into the facility. In a prison in Denmark, inmates were given a budget to purchase food and then made to cook it in small kitchens in their living units.[30] Inmates quickly formed cooperatives where they pooled their money and cooked together. In the end, prisoners learned social skills and the prison saved money on food and staffing. Life skills for youthful offenders are also critical: A juvenile facility in Utah requires youths to write checks and balance a checkbook if they want to purchase food from the canteen. Before they can obtain a prison job, the youths have to prepare a résumé and be formally interviewed. We squander money by not allowing prisoners the chance to work productively. Simple measures such as work can lower costs and teach inmates the skills they will need to function on the outside.

Rates of Incarceration: The Effect on the Family

Although we know that a stable family is one of the strongest bulwarks against a life of crime, so many men in our inner cities are incarcerated that it has become increasingly difficult there to create and sustain a two-parent family. For many young women in the inner city, there is a scarcity of available men of marriage age because so many are going in and out of jails and prisons. Moreover, about three out of four women in prison have children. Only 22 percent of these women say they can count on the fathers of their children to care for them while they are incarcerated.[31] In some inner-city areas, virtually every resident has a close relative and over 50 percent have a parent who is in prison, on probation, on parole, in jail, or in hiding because there is a warrant out for their arrest.[32]

Many advocates of continued prison construction argue that longer sentences are necessary to protect families from crime. It is certainly appropriate to remove violent offenders from our streets. But the flip side of our crime policy is that the injudicious use of prison to incarcerate so many nonviolent offenders can undermine family structure by removing a large portion of the male population from community life. This reality must be weighed carefully by those who make criminal justice policy.

The Costs

States all over the country are trimming and reorganizing their budgets, but taxpayers continue to pour money into prison construction and operations in a way that competes with funding for education and other quality-of-life programs. Five states have a corrections budget of over one billion dollars.[33] California, which has the largest prison system of any state, spends $3.6 billion per year on prison operations and another $500 million per year on new prison con-

Trends in State Spending, 1976-1989

Spending Category	Percent Change
Corrections	+95%
Medicaid	+85%
Health and hospitals	+5%
Elementary-secondary education	-2%
Higher education	-6%
Highways	-23%
Welfare (non-Medicare)	-41%

Source: Gold, Steve (July 1990), *The State Fiscal Agenda for the 1990's,* p. 16.

struction.[34] Nationwide, spending on corrections at the state level has increased faster than any other spending category. Preliminary data for fiscal year 1996 show average increases in appropriations for corrections over the previous year to be 13.3 percent, more than twice the increase for education.[35] Prison has become a modern public works program: in Texas, the government spent more than $1 billion to add over 76,000 prison beds in two years and in 1995 planned to hire 12,000 employees to staff its new prisons. Spending on corrections at a national level has risen three times as fast as military spending over the last twenty years.

In order to fund jails and prisons, state and local governments have been forced to divert money from education and welfare spending.[36] California is typical of the trend. Fifteen years ago, 3 percent of the state budget in California went to prisons while 18 percent was allocated for higher education. In 1994, the state spent 8 percent of its budget on prisons and 8 percent on higher education. Between 1994 and 1995 the *overrun* in corrections spending (an 11.1 percent actual increase compared to a 7.1 percent budgeted increase) was more than the entire increase in higher education (2.3 percent).[37] From 1979 to 1990, state government expenditures nationwide rose 325 percent for prison operations and 612 percent for prison construction.[38] Some states that have built prisons find they cannot afford to run them. In South Carolina, two prisons that cost $80 million recently stood empty because of a shortage of money.[39]

The Costs of Incarceration

Many correctional facilities are built without a full understanding of the actual costs involved. What follows is a summarized breakdown of prison costs. It helps explain why many prisons—just like many projects for the Department of Defense—end up costing the public more than originally planned.

Construction Costs

The average cost of building a new cell is $54,000.[40] Because states usually pay for prison construction by borrowing money, debt service often doubles or even triples the original construction costs. With interest on the debt, the real cost of a new cell is usually well over $100,000.

Operating Costs

The capital outlay for prison construction represents only the beginning of a long-term financial commitment. According to the Justice Department, every $100 million a legislature spends on new prison construction commits the taxpayers of the state to $1.6 billion in expenditures over the next three decades.[41] The cost of operating a state prison bed averages $22,000 per prisoner per year, and this cost often does not include food and medical services that are provided by private companies under contract with the prison.[42] In the federal system, all of the taxes paid each year by three average families is equal to the cost it takes to keep one inmate in prison for one year.[43] In Delaware, all of the annual taxes paid by eighteen average residents are needed to house one prisoner for a single year.[44]

Many costs of the criminal justice system are hidden because they do not appear on criminal justice budgets. They include:

Off-Budget Items

The budget for a corrections agency often does not count the large sums of money paid to for-profit businesses that provide services to

Per Capita Corrections Spending, 1992

Rank	State	Corrections Expenditures, 1992	State Population, 1992	Per Capita Expenditures
1	Alaska	$ 135,804,000	587,000	231.4
2	Delaware	109,140,000	690,000	158.2
3	Connecticut	420,815,000	3,279,000	128.3
4	Maryland	555,635,000	4,914,000	113.1
5	New York	2,008,174,000	18,095,000	111.0
6	Massachusetts	645,378,000	5,999,000	107.6
7	Washington	544,770,000	5,146,000	105.9
8	California	3,226,256,000	30,909,000	104.4
9	Rhode Island	101,022,000	1,002,000	100.8
10	Nevada	127,967,000	1,331,000	96.1
11	Hawaii	104,655,000	1,153,000	90.8
12	Michigan	854,828,000	9,423,000	90.7
13	Virginia	579,591,000	6,389,000	90.7
14	Arizona	343,958,000	3,835,000	89.7
15	Georgia	601,073,000	6,765,000	88.9
16	New Jersey	659,074,000	7,813,000	84.4
17	South Carolina	297,225,000	3,595,000	82.7
18	New Mexico	128,427,000	1,581,000	81.2
19	North Carolina	551,411,000	6,838,000	80.6
20	Florida	1,036,611,000	13,510,000	76.7
21	Colorado	265,445,000	3,463,000	76.7
22	Tennessee	380,028,000	5,021,000	75.7
23	Texas	1,336,280,000	17,667,000	75.6
24	Kansas	189,460,000	2,518,000	75.2
25	Oregon	209,026,000	2,975,000	70.3

26	Wisconsin	338,479,000	4,997,000	67.7
27	Louisiana	275,992,000	4,273,000	64.6
28	Ohio	691,342,000	11,005,000	62.8
29	Oklahoma	200,789,000	3,206,000	62.6
30	Iowa	166,751,000	2,808,000	59.4
31	Vermont	33,664,000	571,000	59.0
32	Indiana	321,025,000	5,652,000	56.8
33	Kentucky	209,874,000	3,753,000	55.9
34	Maine	67,339,000	1,237,000	54.4
35	Idaho	57,671,000	1,066,000	54.1
36	Illinois	625,412,000	11,610,000	53.9
37	Utah	96,951,000	1,811,000	53.5
38	Wyoming	23,914,000	464,000	51.5
39	Pennsylvania	588,169,000	11,990,000	49.1
40	Nebraska	73,336,000	1,604,000	45.7
41	Montana	$37,479,000	823,000	45.5
42	Alabama	182,698,000	4,131,000	44.2
43	Arkansas	105,591,000	2,395,000	44.1
44	Minnesota	193,832,000	4,474,000	43.3
45	South Dakota	29,928,000	709,000	42.2
46	New Hampshire	45,698,000	1,114,000	41.0
47	Missouri	201,873,000	5,193,000	38.9
48	Mississippi	87,310,000	2,613,000	33.4
49	North Dakota	16,118,000	635,000	25.4
50	West Virginia	36,491,000	1,807,000	20.2

Sources: U.S. Bureau of the Census Press Release (December 28, 1994). Table 1: Estimates of the Population of States: July 1, 1990 to July 1, 1994; U.S. Bureau of the Census (1993), *Government Finances, 1992*, p. 28, Table 12.

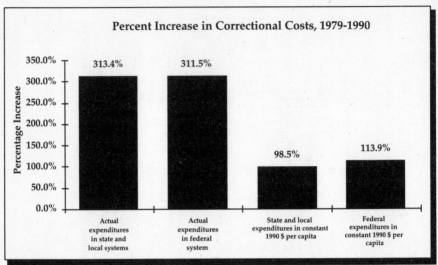

Percent Increase in Correctional Costs, 1979-1990

Note: Measuring expenditures in constant 1990 dollars per capita corrects for both population growth and inflation.

Source: U.S. Department of Justice, Bureau of Justice Statistics (1993), *Sourcebook of Criminal Justice Statistics—1992,* p. 3, Table 1.3.

the prison. These services can include everything from the cafeteria to medical care. An independent audit of the Indiana prison system found the actual expenditures to be one-third higher than the costs reported by the corrections authority.[45] In 1986, the Correctional Association of New York found that the corrections budget would increase by 29 percent if off-budget items were counted.[46] Off-budget items increase the cost of incarceration by about 25 percent or $8 billion annually.[47]

Construction Overruns

The cost of prison construction is often much higher than promised. A survey of 15 states found that cost overruns came in at an average of *40 percent* over the original budget. In many states, this adds tens of millions of dollars to the final tab.[48]

Child Support

Inmates have nearly a million children. Many of these children are in foster care or are supported by taxpayers in some manner.

Lost Tax Revenues

Because they are often barred from working, inmates cannot contribute to the government revenues that their incarceration depletes.

Public Health Costs

Prisons and jails are high-risk settings for the spread of infectious diseases, largely because of the close quarters and poor ventilation. By the end of 1992, there were more than 48,000 tuberculosis cases reported in the state and federal prison systems.[49] The rate of AIDS infection in the prison population is nearly fourteen times higher than that of the general population.[50] New York recently committed $250 million over four years to treat the growing population of AIDS-infected inmates.[51]

The High Cost of Elderly Prisoners

One effect of longer sentences is that many prisons now house an increasing number of elderly inmates who require medical care at enormous cost to taxpayers (see charts on page 54). With the passage of "three strikes" laws in California and other states, the number of elderly inmates is expected to rise sharply in the coming years. In California alone, it is estimated that the "three strikes" law will increase the number of geriatric inmates from 5,000 in 1994 to 126,400 in the year 2020. In 1993, there were 25,000 inmates over 55 years of age in state and federal prisons.[52]

The chance that a typical elderly prisoner will commit a violent crime upon release is almost nil. Yet we have seen that because of health care costs, the upkeep of an elderly inmate can run triple that of a younger inmate.[53] The Louisiana State Penitentiary in Angola has an "old folks" ward where inmates are allowed to roam about with virtually no restrictions. Others lay in bed because of severe medical conditions. Frank Blackburn, who served as warden of the prison, said he "personally knew of 25 to 50 longtermers that I would release immediately because there is no doubt they are rehabilitated. . . . There are just too many people in prison today as tax burdens who do not need to be there."[54]

Medical Problems of Elderly Inmates
• 80% have at least one chronic health condition • 38% suffer from hypertension • 28% suffer from heart disease • 16% suffer from cataracts

Source: **Zimbardo, Philip G. (November 1994),** *Transforming California's Prisons into Expensive Old Age Homes for Felons: Enormous Hidden Costs and Consequences for California's Taxpayers* **(San Francisco, CA: Center on Juvenile and Criminal Justice).**

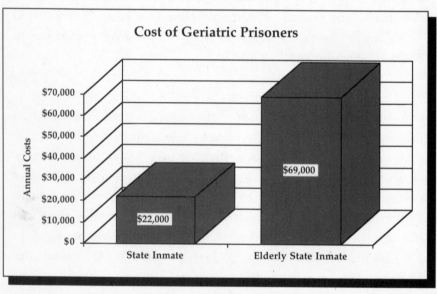

Cost of Geriatric Prisoners

Sources: **Camp, Camille G., and George M. Camp (1994),** *The Corrections Yearbook—1994; Adult Corrections,* **pp. 48–49; U.S. Department of Justice, Bureau of Justice Statistics (August 1995),** *Prisoners in 1994,* **p. 4, Table 3.**

Other Costs of Crime

Lost business revenues from inner-city crime have been estimated to cost $50 billion annually.[55] Health care costs associated with injuries caused by crime have been estimated at $5 billion annually.[56] Individuals and business spend about $65 billion each year on private security systems.[57] This so-called "security tax" is added to the actual taxes spent to finance the formal justice system—a cost incurred at least partly by the failure of the criminal justice system to achieve its ends.

Sentencing

Many Americans believe that convicted criminals get off easy, and they are partially right. Some offenders get off lightly for serious crimes while others pay too great a price for lesser offenses. A vivid illustration of this phenomenon can be seen by comparing the time served of murderers to that of first-time drug offenders in the federal system. In 1992, federal prisons held about 1,800 people convicted of murder for an average time served of 4½ years.[58] That same year, federal prisons held 12,727 nonviolent first-time drug offenders for an average time served of 6½ years.[59] No other nation treats people who commit nonviolent crimes as harshly as the United States.[60] A national survey of prison wardens revealed that the wardens felt that on average, half of the offenders under their supervision could be released without endangering public safety.[61]

Intermediate Sanctions Between Prison and Probation

Intermediate sanctions provide a means of responding strongly to a criminal act without having to rely on prisons as the primary means of punishment. For nonviolent offenders and some lesser violent offenders, it is useful to consider a wide variety of punishment options other than prison. Many are less expensive and more effective at reducing recidivism than locking up an offender in a small cell. The principle of choosing an appropriate punishment from a variety of options makes sense because most Americans do it in their daily lives. When a child disobeys his parents, they may order him to go to his room. For other infractions, he may be grounded for a night or lose his allowance. Parents recognize these as different punishments that can be tailored to the infraction. There is no reason that courts should not have as many options in sentencing offenders as parents do in disciplining their children.

More importantly for American taxpayers, non-prison sanctions are often less expensive than prison as long as they do not pose an increased risk to public safety. Each time an offender is sentenced to prison, it costs on average $22,000 per year. Including hidden costs of incarceration—construction overruns and debt service—the average inmate consumes an amount significantly higher than the salary of the typical American worker. Most non-prison sanctions cost less than half as much as prison. Taxpayers can pocket the savings.

Following is a list of currently available noncustodial punishments. None of these programs is pleasant for the offender. While all involve hardship and some encroachment on liberty, they also are designed to advance the interests of society by making it less likely that the offender will commit new crimes. Typically, the programs require the offender to work, pay fines, repay victims, and undergo substance abuse treatment if necessary. These punishments can be combined with traditional prison sentences. The reader should keep these non-prison sanctions in mind as we examine the criminal justice system. These intermediate sanctions include:

Probation
This is the most common sanction in the criminal justice system. About three million people are on probation. Probation is largely considered ineffectual because there are not enough probation officers to assist offenders to find jobs or, if necessary, receive treatment for a drug addiction. We explore this sanction in more detail in Chapter 8.

Intensive Probation
This usually includes five meetings per week with each offender, costs about one-seventh of prison, and usually leads to much lower rates of offending down the road.

Day Reporting Centers
Usually a part of probation, reporting centers are a place where offenders must check in on a daily basis, provide a schedule of the day's planned activities, and participate in programs. Offenders are subject to random telephone checks to ensure they are where they are supposed to be.

Halfway Houses
Halfway houses are used as a transition between prison and freedom. Most offenders who live there work and pay rent. They are usually

allowed to leave only to report to their job, and they must return promptly at the end of the workday. The residents are under much closer control and supervision than people living entirely on their own, but they have a far greater degree of independence and cost taxpayers far less than people in prison. Treatment services and educational programs are usually provided.

Boot Camps

One of the most publicized intermediate sentencing options, boot camps require offenders to undergo military-style training designed to foster a sense of discipline and respect for authority. What is often missing from most boot camps are services to assist the offender to adjust to life on the outside. When military boot camp is completed, the new soldier is at least assured of a job. In boot camps for inmates, there usually are not even services to help the offender look for a job. It is unrealistic to expect that a few weeks of rigorous physical training will prepare offenders to avoid or overcome the problems that led to their conviction.

Boot camps cost less than prison, and their rates of recidivism (i.e., the number of offenders who commit new crimes upon release) are no worse than those of prison.[62] There is reason to believe that better techniques will yield better results—especially if training is combined with intensive aftercare.

Fines and Restitution

These are especially appropriate for property offenses. The money collected can be used to help fund the court system and to repay crime victims for the costs of their hardship. Less affluent offenders can pay a proportional amount.

Community Service

Community service requires offenders to work without pay for a designated number of hours, usually for public or nonprofit organizations. Tasks can include cleaning up streets and public parks, maintenance work in old age homes, and clerical work in public offices. Offenders with professional skills can be ordered to put their skills

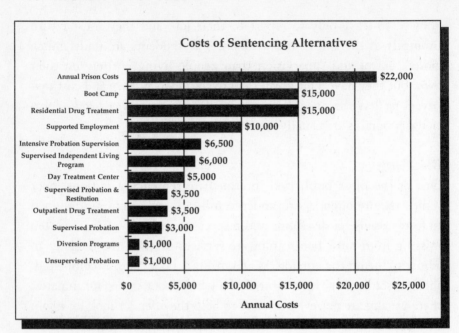

Costs of Sentencing Alternatives

	Annual Costs
Annual Prison Costs	$22,000
Boot Camp	$15,000
Residential Drug Treatment	$15,000
Supported Employment	$10,000
Intensive Probation Supervision	$6,500
Supervised Independent Living Program	$6,000
Day Treatment Center	$5,000
Supervised Probation & Restitution	$3,500
Outpatient Drug Treatment	$3,500
Supervised Probation	$3,000
Diversion Programs	$1,000
Unsupervised Probation	$1,000

to work for those who ordinarily could not afford them. The community receives services while the offender works off the punishment and, it is hoped, develops a sense of right and wrong.

Home Detention
Much cheaper than prison, this requires the offender to remain at home except for carefully controlled excursions to work or treatment.

Drug Treatment
For those with an addiction, successful drug treatment can return enormous savings to taxpayers over the long term. A study by the state of California found that each dollar spent on drug treatment saved seven dollars in reduced crime and health care costs.

What Polling Data Reveal About Crime Policy

Our attitudes toward punishment are widely considered by elected officials and the media to be far more punitive than they actually are. Most polls that gauge attitudes toward crime ask simplistic questions that produce predictable conclusions about cries for "vengeance" against criminals. More serious polling reveals a much more complex set of public concerns about crime. While we naturally want to punish offenders and hold them responsible for their actions, we also want to be *smart* about that punishment so money is not wasted and criminals do not reoffend when released.[63]

Most Americans agree with the notion that serious violent offenders need to be incarcerated to protect public safety. But public attitudes toward imprisoning nonviolent offenders and less violent offenders are decidedly different. When the issues are broadly presented, most Americans are willing to consider alternative approaches to criminal justice policy that rely much less on prison as the first response to crime control.

Research of public opinion about crime clearly demonstrates the following:

Polling Questions Can Distort Findings

We are bombarded with simplistic polling questions on crime that virtually guarantee an answer that will "prove" public support for more prisons. Consider the following polling question, which for years has been used to gauge public attitudes toward sentencing: "Are sentences too harsh, about right, or not harsh enough?" Most people consistently respond to this question by saying that sentences are *not harsh enough*.

We live in a nation where polls like these make for political platforms. From this simple response, some pollsters have suggested, and many politicians have been quick to adopt, policies that lengthen prison sentences.

This interpretation of the polling data fails to consider three additional findings from more in-depth polls. First, when answering a question like this, most of us automatically think of violent offenders who have criminal histories. Second, the public has little idea of the actual severity of sentencing practices. Most of us actually *underestimate* the length of sentences for crimes, especially those for nonviolent offenders. Finally, this question fails to take into account limited public awareness of punishments other than prison—punishments that are often more effective at preventing crime and less costly to implement.

The Public Prefers a Balanced Approach to Crime Control

Polling techniques that present crime issues squarely demonstrate that there is much less support for prison than is commonly believed. Most Americans prefer punishments outside of prison for many types of nonviolent offenders *if they are available*. Such sanctions include boot camps, intensive probation, house arrest, community service, and restitution.[64] The nonprofit Public Agenda Foundation conducted focus groups in Alabama and Delaware to determine what would happen to public attitudes if people were given information about punishments other than prison.[65] In the first phase of the research, groups of people were given brief descriptions of crimes and then asked to choose between prison and probation for the offenders. At that point, most people in the group heavily favored prison.

The participants then viewed a videotape describing five sanctions outside of prison: intensively supervised probation; restitution; community service; house arrest; and boot camp. After receiving information about sentencing alternatives, the group was asked to "re-sen-

**Support for Incarceration Before and After
Receiving Information About Sentencing Alternatives**

Offense	Alabama		Delaware	
	Before	After	Before	After
Theft (5th Offense)	90%	46%	83%	47%
Armed Robbery	78	47	72	47
Shoplifting	74	22	71	19
Burglary	68	19	70	22
Drunk Driving	13	2	16	4
Embezzlement	71	30	71	31

Source: Doble, John, and Josh Klein (1989). *Punishing Criminals, The Public's View—An Alabama Survey* (New York: The Edna McConnell Clark Foundation).

tence" the offender. *Support for imprisonment declined dramatically for a number of offenses*. A juvenile with no prior convictions who committed an armed robbery was sent to prison 80 percent of the time in the first phase, but only 38 percent of the time after the alternatives were discussed. In Delaware, participants in the first phase of the study wanted to incarcerate seventeen out of twenty-three offenders. This dropped to only five out of twenty-three in the second phase. In Alabama, incarceration was favored in eighteen out of twenty-three cases in the first phase and in only four cases afterward.

Conclusion

One has to wonder whether a further expansion of the criminal justice system will reduce crime. Crime is a complex phenomenon that derives from a combination of personal choice, family circumstance, economic condition, and much more. We should not expect the criminal justice system to correct all antisocial behavior or to solve all (or even any) of our social problems—it is simply too blunt an instrument for such complicated tasks. We cannot expect the criminal justice system to create strong families, deliver jobs, or provide hope to young people. The only service that we should expect from the criminal justice system is the one it was set up to deliver—crime control that makes all Americans safe. And in the course of delivering that service, we should expect that our tax dollars will not be wasted.

Imprisonment is a politically appealing response to fear because a person who is locked up obviously cannot commit a crime against a person on the outside. But the simplicity can be deceptive. Take the example of the typical small-time drug dealer. This offender has helped fuel the jail and prison expansion in recent years, yet it is also this offender who is most easily replaceable in the drug trade. Somebody else almost always steps in to take the place of the dealer when he or she goes to prison. Incarcerating the second drug dealer costs just as much as incarcerating the first. By the time the criminal justice system has passed through several generations of drug dealers, billions of dollars have been spent and the corner is still scattered with empty vials of crack cocaine.

Our rate of incarceration is the highest in the world. Two percent of the potential male workforce is behind bars. In some urban areas, close to half of the young African-American men are in the criminal justice system. Yet crime nationally has not been reduced significantly, and most of us do not *feel* safer. In the next chapter, we try to find out why there appears to be so little correlation between rates of imprisonment and our feeling of security.

THREE

FEAR, POLITICS, AND THE PRISON-INDUSTRIAL COMPLEX

Recently, during an election year, residents of a tranquil town in rural Virginia were polled on their most important concerns. At the time, one of the leading candidates was attracting media interest with his proposal that parole be abolished for all violent offenders. There had not been a homicide for over two decades in the town. There was virtually no violent street crime. Yet the majority of citizens listed fear of violent crime as their most pressing concern.

What happened in this town is a metaphor for what is happening in much of America. Crime is a real threat, but at least some of the tremendous fear Americans have is the product of a variety of factors that have little or nothing to do with crime itself. These factors include media reporting on crime issues and the role of government and private industry in stoking citizen fear.

This chapter explores the critical distinction between *crime* and *fear of crime* because it is fear of crime, rather than crime itself, that currently drives policy in the United States. The failure to build criminal justice policy from facts rather than fear helps explain why our policies fail in their mission to make Americans safe.

The New York "Crime Wave"

In 1976, there were widespread reports in New York City of a ferocious crime wave being waged against the elderly. For six weeks the daily newspapers and the local television stations reported a surge of muggings, murders, and rapes of elderly people. The perpetrators were reported to be African-American or Latino youth with long criminal records who lived near enclaves of elderly whites who were too poor to move away from the inner city.

Soon, the public outcry reached hysterical proportions. The mayor, who was preparing for reelection, lashed out at the juvenile justice system. The police intensified plainclothes operations in the affected areas. Communities convened meetings to advise the elderly on how to avoid crime. Police tipped off journalists about impending arrests, which were often shown at the top of the hour on the nightly news. Not to be left behind, state legislators introduced bills transferring jurisdiction to adult court of any juvenile who victimized an elderly person.

The crime wave dramatically affected the public perception of crime. A poll at the time showed that 60 percent of the public felt that assaults against elderly people in their home areas had been going up. About half of persons aged fifty or over said they were more fearful on the streets than they had been a year earlier. Elderly people hesitated to leave home.

There is only one problem with this story: *The crime wave against the elderly did not happen.* A follow-up study demonstrated that crime against the elderly either had not increased, or to the degree that it had, increased no more than all other categories of crime. Indeed, murder of the elderly dropped 19 percent during the course of the so-called crime wave—despite the fact that the crime wave began with media reports of several gruesome murders of elderly people.[1]

No one is suggesting that members of the police and the media in New York fabricated the elderly crime wave or conspired to manipulate the public. But this type of reporting about crime has happened with enough regularity in recent years to deserve examination. Many of the so-called crime waves coincide with election years and demands by law enforcement officials to increase their budgets. These budget increases often remain after the reported crime wave has passed.

Moreover, the phenomenon of a crime wave has been a significant part of recent American political history. In 1964, Republican presidential nominee Barry Goldwater courted the conservative vote by linking "violence in our streets" to civil rights demonstrators and liberal politicians. In 1968, Richard Nixon became the first modern politician to successfully use a "get tough" stance on crime issues in a presidential campaign. Since then, fear of crime has been used by candidates of both major parties largely to court suburban "swing" voters, who often have the lowest risk of being a victim of street crime. Crime as a campaign tactic achieved the most notoriety in 1988 with the Willie Horton television advertisement. Horton was an African-American man who raped a white woman while on furlough from a Massachusetts prison. His story and visual image have been credited by many analysts with destroying the campaign momentum of Democratic presidential nominee Michael Dukakis.

The false alarms also illustrate how the media and law enforcement can exercise a powerful and distorting influence on the public perception of crime. In a 1994 public opinion poll, 73 percent of the American people believed that crime had risen nationwide, when, in fact, it had declined by three percentage points.[2] The discrepancy between public beliefs about crime and the reality of crime rates raises serious questions about how crime information is transmitted to the public.

Five Crime Myths

There are at least five major myths about crime that exercise a powerful influence over criminal justice policy, despite the fact that they are demonstrably false.[3] They are:

Myth 1: Street Crime Is Increasing
Reality: As studies have shown, street crime dropped slightly in 1993 and 1994. In the last twenty years, robbery has dropped 17

percent, forcible rape dropped 30 percent, and murder has stayed the same. Overall, rates for most categories of crime have been either stable or slightly declining.

Myth 2: Street Crime Is More Violent Today

Reality: Street crime is no more violent today than it has been in other periods in American history. The serious violent crime rate for the United States stands 16 percent below its peak level of the mid-1970s. In the mid-1800s, several cities were convulsed by urban riots far deadlier than those in Los Angeles in 1992. Juvenile gangs commonly beat and mutilated Chinese immigrants in San Francisco in the late 1800s. Homicide was the eleventh leading cause of death in 1952. Today, it is tenth. Moreover, the overwhelming majority of contemporary crime is nonviolent. Injuries occur in just 3 percent of all reported crime.

Myth 3: More Police Officers Are Being Killed

Reality: Policing is highly stressful, but it is not the most dangerous line of work. Farmers are twice as likely as police officers to be killed on the job. Largely because of bulletproof vests, killings of law enforcement officers dropped by half between 1973 and 1993. Police officers spend most of their time doing routine administrative tasks or in peaceful contact with civilians. Most officers spend their entire careers without fighting a street battle with firearms.

Myth 4: Street Crime Costs More Than Corporate Crime

Reality: Corporate crime, like the savings and loan scandal, costs Americans far more than street crime. According to the Justice Department, all personal crimes and household crimes cost approximately $19.1 billion in 1991. The comparable cost of white-collar crime is between $130 billion and $472 billion—seven to twenty-five times as much as street crime. Moreover, many more people die from pollution than from homicide. There are six times as many work-related deaths as homicides.

Myth 5: Criminals Are Different from the Rest of Us
Reality: Actually, criminals are not that different from the rest of us. Many Americans admit to having committed a crime punishable by a jail sentence sometime in their lives. These crimes include failing to report income, filing a false expense report, drunk driving, illegal drug use, stealing, and spousal assault.[4]

A Brief History of Crime and Politics: A Quest for Evil

Part of our confusion over crime policy results from media reports of crime scares that end up having little or no basis in fact. Relying on the work of three criminologists, the *Los Angeles Times* published an investigation into crime scares that were reported by the media, widely believed by the public, but proven to be false or grossly exaggerated.[5] Among the false crime scares:

The Campaign to Find Missing Children
In the mid-1980s, a young Florida child named Adam Walsh was tragically abducted and murdered by a stranger. The case received extensive national publicity and the boy's father became the host of a national television show. Pictures of missing children soon appeared on milk cartons to draw attention to an alleged nationwide epidemic of kidnappings. "Victim experts" speculated that strangers victimized anywhere from 800,000 to 1.2 million children each year. In response to the reports, parents warned their children to steer clear of strangers. In one school district, police wanted to put an ID number on the teeth of all children so their bodies could be identified in the event of murder.[6]

A subsequent investigation by the *Denver Post* revealed that 95 percent of those "missing children" were actually runaway teens, or were taken by parents in custody disputes. Current reports indicate that there are only about 50 to 150 actual abductions per year by strangers—numbers that have not changed since the late 1970s. The awful fact remains that most murdered children are killed by their parents. Clearly, the milk carton campaign exaggerated the threat of abduction to children by strangers.

The Threat of Serial Killers

In the mid-1980s, the character of serial murderers like Ted Bundy was explored by numerous television programs and print media. Most programs stressed the theme that serial murder was an epidemic in America that had grown exponentially since the 1970s, that its perpetrators drifted from state to state, and that it resulted in severe forms of bodily mutilation. The media reports repeated the claims of a Justice Department official that as many as 4,000 Americans a year, or about 20 percent of all homicide victims, were murdered by serial killers. The myth grew when a drifter and convicted murderer, Henry Lee Lucas, confessed to 300 murders over many states and guaranteed himself national publicity by claiming responsibility for the murder of Adam Walsh. His claims were later disproved.

It turned out that the numbers of serial murders reported by the federal government were fake. In effect, the government interpretation made every one of the 4,000 or so unsolved murders in the United States the work of a "serial killer." It was later shown that there were only about fifty to sixty murders per year by serial killers between 1971 and 1987—far short of the 4,000 that was regularly reported by the media.[7] A spokesman for the FBI said the agency no longer makes public estimates of the number of serial killers and their victims. "With the more experience and development we have in this area, you start to realize that you really don't know, and you can't throw numbers around like that," said Les Davis, the FBI spokesman.[8] But it was already too late.

Who Influences Public Opinion

The threat of crime exercises such a powerful grip on human emotion that people are willing to spend large sums of money if they believe it will make them safer. It is the overriding importance of personal safety that makes crime an area of public policy more susceptible than most to pandering.

The Commission focused on five entities that exploit this opportunity: the popular media, the government, political campaigning, special-interest groups, and private industry. By beginning to understand how each of these entities operates, efforts can be made to understand how criminal justice policy is made.

Popular Media: Overheated, Overhyped

While poll results indicate that feelings about crime and punishment are more complex than is commonly understood, such complexity is only rarely translated into media coverage. Although crime frequently soars to the top of the nation's list of major problems, those who follow public opinion have concluded that it is driven more by the media treatment of crime than by changes in crime rates.

Crime Dominates the Network News

Most Americans get their news from television, so a major issue is the volume of crime and violence displayed in the visual media. Coverage of crime on the three major network television news shows tripled from 571 stories in 1991 to 1,632 stories in 1993—despite the fact that crime declined slightly over that period.[9] In 1993, crime was the leading story on the network news. It surpassed the economy, health care, and the war in Bosnia.

Television Drama Shows Are Beset by Violence

An analysis of 10 network and cable channels in 1992 showed 1,846 incidents of violence *in 1 day*.[10] The Annenberg School of Communication at the University of Pennsylvania found that seven out of ten prime-time shows in the past ten years depicted violence. They also found that the level of violence in children's programming on Saturday mornings has increased dramatically in recent years.[11] There has been significant debate about the effects of television violence on children—but its effects on the entire population have not been fully measured.

Television Entertainment and Violence

Not satisfied with crime as news, many television programs have converted crime into entertainment. In 1980, at the dawn of the current prison expansion, there were no "real-life" crime shows on the networks. In 1993, there were seven major programs devoted exclusively to presenting real-life crime cases. Among them are *America's Most Wanted, Top Cops, American Detective*, and *Unsolved Mysteries*. In addition, shows such as *Rescue 911, Inside Edition*, and *Hard Copy* presented numerous crime stories in addition to the regular diet of such stories on *60 Minutes, 20/20*, and *48 Hours*. Full-length crime dramas also have become enormously popular. In 1994, for example, the three major networks broadcast versions of the Amy Fisher story about events leading to the shooting of the wife of her lover, Joey Buttafuoco. Each of these programs ranked among the top-rated shows for that week. A producer for *American Detective* recently disclosed how the production staff was ordered to scour the nation for the most sensational and gory examples of crime to reenact on the show. To focus the staff on the desired themes, the supervisor of the show posted the following words on the office bulletin board: DEATH, STAB, SHOOT, STRANGULATION, CLUB, SUICIDE.[12]

The emphasis in the television media on violent images does not present an accurate picture of crime in America.[13] A major question is what effect these inaccurate images have on public perceptions of crime. The vast majority of crime in America is nonviolent and does not involve physical injury, but of course these incidents don't sell papers or boost Nielsen ratings. As a result, people continue to think of *violence* when responding to polling questions about crime.[14] When politicians want to toughen sentences as part of anti-crime strategy, many people support them enthusiastically because they mistakenly believe it will be mostly violent offenders filling the cells—the same types of offenders most often portrayed on television.

Television shows and paperback crime novels tend to depict crime in a way that diminishes public support for rehabilitation. As typified by the plots on shows such as *Murder One* and *Murder She Wrote*, a common portrait of a criminal on television is a greedy person who acts in premeditated fashion to commit a violent crime.[15] These plots tend to highlight the moral depravity of the offender rather than the difficult life conditions in which most crime actually occurs. The viewer is left with the impression that most offenders "ought to know better" than to commit crimes and therefore do not deserve compassion or rehabilitation.[16] Because such portraits tend to ignore the critical connection between social conditions and high crime rates, the logical way to respond to this portrait of crime is to expand law enforcement and toughen punishment.

The "Mean World" Syndrome

Research demonstrates that heavy viewing of violence-laden television can influence how people arrive at their views on crime. George Gerbner, a leading authority on television violence, coined the term "mean world" syndrome to describe how heavy viewers of television violence increasingly feel that their own lives are under siege. As a result, these viewers tend to support more punitive anti-crime measures. Such viewers are far more likely to overestimate their chances of involvement in violence, to believe that their neighborhoods are unsafe, to state that fear of crime is a very serious personal problem, and to assume that crime is rising, regardless of the facts.[17] One study of television shows concluded that "heavy viewers . . . exhibit an exaggerated fear of victimization and a perception that people cannot be trusted."[18] Heavy viewers are also more likely to buy anti-crime devices such as locks and guns.

The Print Media

Newspapers also tend to present a distorted view by focusing most of their attention on sensational crimes rather than the vastly more numerous nonviolent offenses. A study of crime news in Colorado newspapers found ". . . a marked lack of association between the percentages change in total Colorado crime and in newspaper coverage. . . . The findings of this study bear out the hypothesis that there is no consistent relationship between the amount of crime news in newspapers and local crime rates."[19] Another study by the *New Orleans Times-Picayune* found that stories about murder and robbery accounted for 45 percent of crime coverage in the paper but only 12 percent of actual crime.[20] In the course of gathering material for this report, Commission members noticed many examples of reporting that exaggerated the extent and threat of violent crime. Consider these two illustrative examples.

The Juvenile Crime Wave That Never Happened

A headline that fanned the flames of public hysteria over juvenile violence appeared on the front page of the *San Francisco Chronicle* on January 24, 1994. The headline read: "Teenage Crime Wave in S.F.—Homicide Arrests Up 87%." To get the 87 percent figure, the police compared the number of homicides referred to the juvenile probation department in 1992 (16) to the number of *attempted* homicides referred in 1993 (30). Attempted homicide, however, is a completely different category of crime than homicide. The number of juveniles arrested for homicide had increased 0 percent in 1993, not the 87 percent that appeared in the headline and the story.

The lead paragraph of the story also claimed that juvenile violent crime "continues to shoot through the roof" and cited a 77 percent increase in the juvenile robbery rate as evidence. The story was repeated that night on several local television stations. This statistic was also wrong. Juvenile robbery had increased 23 percent, not 77 percent; moreover, *it had only increased 4 percent over a two-year period*. To get the 77 percent figure, the police compared 240 arrests in 1992 to 444 referrals to the city probation department in 1993. Arrests and referrals to probation have virtually nothing to do with each other, making any statistical comparison of the two completely invalid.

San Francisco Police Chief Anthony Ribera later admitted that the statistics were wrong and proposed forming an audit committee to prevent similar mistakes from recurring.[21] Nevertheless, the correction of the original article ran unimpressively on an inside page of the newspaper the following week.

The "Orgy" of Violent Crime That Never Occurred

Another example of overblown media coverage occurred in *U.S. News & World Report* on January 17, 1994.[22] The magazine introduced its cover story on "Violence in America" with the following line: "A scary orgy of violent crime is fueling another public call to action." Despite the impression left by *U.S. News*, the incidence of violent crime had not risen in the last twenty years. Yet that did not stop the magazine from talking about a "wave of violence" and the "relentless growth" of crime.

The magazine came to this conclusion by using the Uniform Crime Reports (UCR) published by the FBI that—as we discussed in Chapter One—tend for a variety of reasons to overstate increases in crime rates. If the magazine had used the more reliable National Crime Victimization Survey (NCVS), then it would not have been able to claim a rising epidemic of violence in America. NCVS data indicate crime has fallen slightly over the last twenty years. Moreover, crime is actually falling in the suburbs. According to the NCVS, a suburban resident was 13 percent more likely to be a victim of violent crime twenty years ago than today. Crimes such as theft and burglary have fallen significantly in both the suburbs and rural areas. The Commission believes this flawed reporting is the result of a mistaken assumption by some members of the media that the UCR accurately measures crime rates.

The media watchdog group Fairness and Accuracy in Reporting chided *U.S. News* for overemphasizing a theme that often is repeated in the popular media: that of *invading sanctuaries*. This theme suggests that communities once considered safe are now being hit by a spreading epidemic of violent crime. The theme of invading sanctuaries runs through the *U.S. News* article: "The nature of some of the crime is changing," said the magazine, "making some people more vulnerable and bringing the worst kinds of problems into communities that many thought were safe." In reality, violent crime has been dropping in the neighborhoods that the magazine suggests were once sanctuaries of safety. We have shown that crimes such as theft and burglary have declined significantly in both suburbs and rural areas over the past two decades.[23]

The Federal Government: The Department of Justice and the Artificial Case for More Incarceration

Citizens who look to the government for leadership on crime issues may be disappointed. The federal government often puts out reports that make current policies appear successful or make popular policies appear necessary.

Exaggerating the Threat of Violence

The U.S. Department of Justice, for example, helps to foster the illusion that almost all Americans caught in the web of the criminal justice system are truly dangerous. A 1991 analysis of state prison inmates published by the Department made the following assertion: *94 percent of inmates had been convicted of a violent crime or had a previous sentence to probation or incarceration.*[24] This statistic has been cited by journalists, think tanks, and politicians at every level of government to justify the rapid expansion of the prison population.[25]

The claim is highly misleading. Consider the following claim: "94 percent of the people in America are more than nine feet tall or less than six feet tall." A reader not already aware of the scarcity of nine-foot people might think that America is full of them. The six-foot part of the disjunction does the work and the nine-foot part contributes little. A similar structure infects the government statement that 94 percent of inmates were convicted of a violent crime *or* had been convicted previously. The magic is in the word "or." It permits the government to consolidate two very different classifications into a single claim. The result is an exaggeration of the extent to which violent criminals populate our prisons.

In fact, government statistics demonstrate that fewer than half of the state prison inmates were convicted of violent crimes. In state prisons, *nearly three times as many offenders had never been convicted of a violent crime as had ever been convicted of one.* Had the government intended to accurately convey what the numbers disclosed, it could have said: *Most prisoners are not violent now and have not been violent in the past.*

The perception of the violent recidivist stalking the public provides a misguided view of the true repeat offender and plays into the "bait and switch" aspect of crime policy. People on probation or parole in any given year account for only 3 percent to 5 percent of all violent offenses known to police that occur each year.[26] A Justice Department study found that only 17.9 percent of state inmates are violent recidivists—that is, they are incarcerated for a violent offense and had committed a prior violent offense.[27] There is a huge difference between 94 percent and 17.9 percent.

The Artificial Case for More Incarceration

In 1992, at the end of the tenure of Attorney General William Barr, the Department of Justice published *The Case for More Incarceration*. The document was produced as part of a determined campaign by the Department of Justice to convince states and cities to build more prisons. It is worth looking at in detail because it is a classic example of how crime data can be misused.[28]

In support of its push for more prisons, the Department of Justice cited data from a 1987 government study that claimed the imprisonment of one inmate "saves" society $430,000 per year.[29] If this figure were true, society would be getting a 17-to-1 rate of return on its investment in prisons based on how much it costs to incarcerate one person for one year. This is a rate of return almost unheard of in the history of private business, much less government, and it invited scrutiny by a number of experts. It turns out that the study arrived at the $430,000 figure by *assuming* that each prisoner (if not incarcerated) would commit 187 street crimes *per year* at a "cost" to the victim of $2,300 per crime. This cost was estimated to result from the value of stolen property or the medical expenses associated with personal injury. Even assuming the cost is accurate, the claim that each inmate would commit 187 street crimes per year is regarded by almost all criminologists as a gross exaggeration. The researchers who came up with the original claim have since retracted it.[30]

Criminologists Franklin Zimring and Gordon Hawkins carefully analyzed the claim of $430,000 in cost savings.[31] They concluded that if the assumptions underlying the study were true, crime in the United States would have disappeared several years ago. Zimring and Hawkins worked the calculation like this: the study estimated there are about 42.5 million crimes reported each year in the United States. If each prisoner commits 187 crimes per year, you would only need to lock up a total of 230,000 additional criminals to wipe out all 42.5 million crimes! Prison populations increased by over

230,000 inmates between the time the Department of Justice collected the data and published the report, yet crime was as prevalent as ever. In fact, there are still between 30 and 40 million crimes reported each year with the prison population now at 1.5 million. Despite the fact that the government study was discredited, Attorney General Barr continued to use it to convince states to build more prisons.

Barr was so eager to pitch his plan for increased prison space that in 1992 the Justice Department flew dozens of state officials at taxpayer expense to a conference in Washington, D.C. After the conference, many participants expressed resentment at the attempt by the federal government to influence their crime policies. One account of the conference said, "A number of officials expressed anger about the format . . . saying the choice of speakers and topics reflected a tightly orchestrated attempt by the Justice Department to stifle dissent."[32] Chase Riveland, Secretary of Corrections for the state of Washington, said: "I would strongly dispute the Attorney General's contention that 94 percent of the people in our correctional systems are violent and/or recidivist. That's not true. In the state of Washington, the bulk of our people are not violent offenders."[33] The former Director of Corrections of Pennsylvania expressed similar sentiments. "The federal government does not have the same cost constraints as the states," said Joseph D. Lehman. "I think it's irresponsible for the Justice Department to put out this message here that we are going to solve the crime problem by building more prisons."[34]

The Hype Over the Threat of Random Murder

Another example of statistical maneuvering by the government is the claim that murder is so random that all Americans now have a "realistic" chance of being a victim of homicide. The murder rate has remained stable in the United States for the last twenty years, so in its latest Uniform Crime Report the FBI could not simply claim that the threat of homicide is increasing. The FBI concluded instead that "something has changed in the constitution of murder to bring about the unparalleled level of concern and fear confronting the Nation."[35] The FBI settled upon increased *randomness* in killing as the cause of alarm, and this is the claim that hit the headlines. *USA Today*, for example, ran a headline that said, "Random Killings Hit a High." The subtitle claimed, "All Have 'Realistic' Chance of Being Victim, Says FBI."[36]

Random killings by strangers are among the most frightening of crimes. Even insignificant fluctuations in the statistics can mean a deep personal tragedy for an innocent victim and his or her family. Yet despite the claim by the government, random murders are not increasing. The following table was created using the government's data starting with the first year the figures were tabulated.

Murder Victim/Offender Relationship					
	1976	1980	1985	1990	1993
Murder Rate	8.8	10.2	7.9	9.0	9.5
% by stranger	13.8%	13.3%	14.5%	14.0%	14.0%
% unknown to police	24.9%	35.8%	26.9%	35.0%	39.3%

Note: Rate is per 100,000.
Source: U.S. Department of Justice, Federal Bureau of Investigation. Data provided by the Criminal Justice Information Services Division.

The data reveal that the murder rate and the percentage of murders committed by strangers have been relatively stable in recent years. The increase is in the number of killings committed by assailants whose identity is unknown to authorities—a trend that most criminologists believe is related to the drug trade, where the killer is unknown to the police but is likely known to the victim. It is fair to claim that the vast majority of such drug-related murders are not *random* even though the assailant is *unknown* to the police.

With all that in mind, consider the report's conclusion: "Every American now has a realistic chance of murder victimization in view of the random nature the crime has assumed. This notion is somewhat supported by the fact that a majority of the Nation's murder victims are now killed by strangers or unknown persons." There is that magical "or" again. The FBI combines stranger murders, which are constant, with unknown murders, which are increasing, to support a claim that does not accurately represent reality.

The FBI claim that "every" American suddenly has a "realistic" chance of being murdered is puzzling. While the number of homicides is higher than one might hope, it does *not* present every American with a new "realistic" chance of being murdered. Occupation is also a factor. Convenience store clerks, for example, are much more likely to be murdered than accountants. Tragically, it is young minority males in the inner city who run a completely disproportionate risk of being killed by street crime. One might even make a case that unless you belong to this high-risk group or have a high-risk job, your odds of being murdered have actually *decreased* in recent years.

The Government Downplays the Role of Race

In the fall of 1994, newspapers and television stations around the country gave prominent attention to a Justice Department report that the number of state prisoners had exceeded one million for the first time in history. In putting out the numbers, the Department of Justice aggregated racial population statistics in a way that disguised the fact that minority men are being imprisoned at a much higher rate than whites.

In its press release, the Department of Justice misleadingly asserted that the incarceration rate "doubled for both black and white inmates" during the ten-year period in which the state prison population doubled from 500,000 to 1 million.[37] This statement makes it appear that the prison expansion affected whites and African-Americans equally. The Department of Justice made this claim *by counting all Hispanic inmates in the white population.* Hispanics are a minority group that in every other government survey is counted separately. Under the Department's counting technique, the African-American incarceration rate increased 98 percent and the white incarceration rate (including Hispanics) increased 75 percent, so it is just possible to claim that they both roughly "doubled." Yet in the white category, a substantial portion of the increase is accounted for by Hispanic inmates. In reality, African-Americans have been incarcerated at a rate six times that of whites.[38]

One indication that the Department of Justice is less than forth-right is that it sometimes downplays its own research when it cuts against official government policy on crime. Research regarding the Drug Abuse Resistance Through Education (DARE) program is a case in point.

DARE, which originated in the Los Angeles Police Department, is now in about 70% of the public schools in the country. DARE was designed to educate children about the perils of drug use and it developed a complete curriculum with education professionals. Although drug education is a sound idea and children seem to like the DARE program, the effectiveness of DARE was never researched by the government.[39] For that reason, the governemnt commissioned a survey in 1991 to see whether DARE had an effect upon adolescent drug use. The survey found positive attitudinal changes but questioned the long term behavioral changes brought about by the program. Because it had invested heabily in DARE, the Justice Department refused to release the survey, claiming htat the research methodology was flawed.[40] A peer-reviewed scholarly journal eventually published the study,[41] though some questioned whether the American taxpayers, drug educators, and DARE officers themselves would have been better served had the information been made available earlier.

Similarly, release of a 1994 government study that indicated that federal prisons housed a substantial portion of nonviolent offenders for long terms was postponed for several weeks.[42] The study contained information that could have been used to shorten sentences for nonviolent drug offenders at a time when "get tough" crime issues were being hotly debated in Congress. Though much information on crime released by the government is useful, the Commission has a concern that a significant portion of it is subject to political influence.

Private Political Campaigns: The Packaging of Fear

In addition to being the leading story on network newscasts, crime is often the most common theme in political advertisements among both major political parties.[43] Since the Willie Horton ad during the 1988 presidential campaign, almost all politicians have recognized that the crime issue can be turned to an electoral advantage. In the summer of 1995, the campaign to reelect President Clinton already was running television advertisements for the 1996 election touting the president's record on crime issues. In the 1994 election cycle, many of the political advertisements emphasized the threat of violent crime. In California's 1994 election, Republican candidates for Insurance Commissioner and State Superintendent of Schools ran television advertisements describing themselves as tough on violent crime—even though neither of those offices deal directly with criminal justice policy. Many political ads played into the prevailing myths of a rising crime rate to justify promises to end parole and build more prison cells.

The Texas Gubernatorial Campaign

Crime in Texas dropped in 1992 and 1993, but that did not stop candidate George W. Bush, Jr. from attacking incumbent Governor Ann Richards for being soft on crime. One would think that Richards would have been invulnerable to such an attack. During her term, she was an ardent supporter of the death penalty, oversaw one of the largest periods of prison construction in state history, and cut parole for violent offenders. But political advertising turned the crime issue against her. In 1994, Bush ran an ad with grainy black-and-white footage showing a man abducting a woman in a parking garage, his gun pointed at her head (the people in the ad were the sound man and makeup artist of a production company). Moments later, a police officer was shown putting a blanket over a dead body. The ad then blasted Richards for releasing 7,700 offenders before their terms had expired. Exit polls revealed that Richards lost the election partly because of the Bush ads on crime.[44]

The Florida Gubernatorial Campaign

In Florida, incumbent Governor Lawton Chiles faced a similar challenge.[45] His opponent, Jeb Bush, ran a television ad featuring a woman who blamed Chiles for failing to execute the man who killed her daughter in 1981. "Her killer is still on Death Row, and we're still waiting for justice," the mother says in the advertisement. "We don't get it from Lawton Chiles because he's too liberal on crime." In fact, by law Chiles could not sign the death warrant for the killer because the case was still being processed in the courts. Chiles responded with an ad in which he charged that the Bush campaign "should be ashamed" for not telling the truth. Chiles correctly noted that as many convicted killers had been put to death during his term as during the term of his Republican predecessor. Chiles narrowly won the race.

The Maryland Gubernatorial Campaign

The 1994 race for governor in Maryland was typical of races around the country in which candidates tried to outdo each other by appearing tough on crime. Maryland already had an overcrowded prison system and the eleventh-highest rate of incarceration in the country, but six of the seven leading candidates for governor in 1994 promised to cut parole to keep thousands of people in prison.[46] To carry out the plan, taxpayers would have had to spend at least $500 million to build new prison space and hundreds of millions of additional dollars each year more to operate it. None of the candidates promised to raise taxes or specified which programs would be cut to fund the expansion. The bill for such an effort would fall due in the next decade, when the winner would be out of office and the state was projected to have a budget deficit of $1 billion. Ironically, these promises came in the same year that the state legislature had already *doubled* the minimum time a violent offender must serve before being eligible for parole. Just one candidate, William Sheperd, opposed the plans for prison expansion. "We do not need a Gulag Maryland," said Sheperd, who was soundly defeated in his party's primary.

Special-Interest Groups

Many special-interest groups focus on crime. One group, the National Rifle Association (NRA), is a leading example of an organization that tries to convince the public to support prison expansion. Although known primarily for its vigorous opposition to gun control legislation, the NRA in recent years has entered the battle over crime policy with a flourish. Its agenda appears to be to divert public fear of violent crime away from support of gun control legislation and toward tougher law enforcement and prison expansion. The clout of the NRA is enormous: It counts 3.4 million members and a budget of approximately $140 million, and has the largest single political action committee in the nation.[47] It may have more influence over crime policy than any other private organization, so its claims are worth analyzing in detail.

On the eve of the vote on the 1994 federal crime bill, the NRA bought full-page advertisements in major newspapers urging Congress to increase its allocation for new prison construction from $13 billion to $21 billion and to eliminate crime prevention programs. The ads were part of a public relations initiative called *CrimeStrike,* whose stated purpose was to create a "citizen's movement" to "put real justice back in our criminal justice system" and to "keep violent criminals off our streets." The NRA bankrolled the first "three strikes" initiative in Washington, helped fund a similar, successful ballot initiative in California, and financed a successful campaign to convince the Texas legislature to spend $1 billion on new prisons.

The NRA's Case for More Prisons
The basis for much of the NRA claim that we need more prisons is a report produced by *CrimeStrike* in 1994 called "The Case for Building More Prisons." This paper misuses criminal justice data in a manner strikingly similar to "The Case for More Incarceration," published by the Department of Justice in 1992. The NRA paper included the now-famous "X" graph (see top figure on page 83) that creates an optical illusion to "prove" that imprisonment reduces crime.[48] The NRA data was analyzed by Marc Mauer of The Sentencing Project in Washington, D.C. Mauer concluded that the NRA made several false assumptions in its study. This NRA chart is an excellent example of how crime data can mislead.

Disproportionate Scaling
To produce the desired visual effect of the "X" (one line a sharply increasing imprisonment rate and the other a sharply declining crime rate), the NRA used two different scales that had nothing to

do with each other. The right-hand scale used to show incarceration rates allows for a 350 percent increase over the height of the graph. The left-hand scale showing crime rates allows for only a 56 percent increase over the height of the graph. The result is an optical illusion

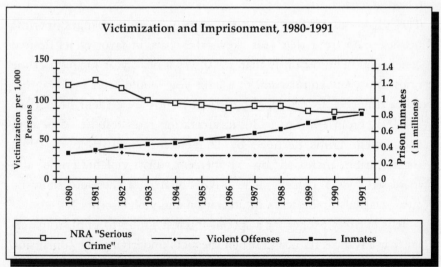

The NRA Case for Building More Prisons

Source: National Rifle Association (1994), *The Case for Building More Prisons,* p. 2.

Victimization and Imprisonment, 1980-1991

Source: The Sentencing Project (1994), *Did the Growth of Imprisonment During the 1980's Work?: The NRA and the Misuse of Criminal Justice Statistics,* p. 2.

that exaggerates changes in crime rates against the change in the prison population. Accurate scaling would have produced a completely different visual effect, one with lines that are flatter and do not support the preordained conclusion.

Selective Use of Data

To prove that "serious" victimization dropped from 1980 to 1991, the NRA chose to include in its measure the four violent crimes (murder, rape, robbery, and assault) and also the nonviolent offense of burglary. The inclusion of burglary makes no sense until one realizes that burglary is the crime that decreased the most in the 1980s. By mixing in the nonviolent crime of burglary, the NRA could make it look as if violent crime had dropped significantly when in fact it did not. Indeed, burglary alone accounts for 91 percent of the supposed decrease in violent crime documented in the NRA chart. If burglary were not included, one would find that the serious violent crime rate declined by only 4 percent from 1980 to 1991 despite a 150 percent increase in the number of inmates. If, for example, the NRA had elected to include auto theft instead of burglary in its chart, the crime rate would have *increased*.

Choice of Time Frame

The NRA uses 1980 as a starting point to measure changes in crime because data from that year skews the chart in favor of its desired conclusion. The reason is that 1980 was a peak year for high crime rates; thus, any comparison to a later year would tend to show that crime dropped. In reality, two distinct trends are evident from 1980 to 1991. From 1980 to 1986, incarceration rates rose by 65 percent and violent crime declined by 16 percent. From 1986 to 1991, incarceration increased by 51 percent, but violent crime also increased by 15 percent. The NRA's own data therefore show no clear relationship between incarceration and violent crime.

It is entirely proper for a special-interest group to publish material that advances its goals. When the facts underlying the conclusion are distorted so severely, however, the ethics become more problematic.

The Prison-Industrial Complex

If crime has decreased, one might ask why Americans are constantly warned of perils lurking around the corner. Part of the answer lies in the media attention devoted to firearms violence among young people. Another part of the answer lies in an unexplored corner of the American economic-political landscape. In this corner, fear of crime drives investment and crime control is a source of profit. We call this corner the "prison-industrial complex." Like the military-industrial complex that dominated defense policy during the Cold War, this crucible of private companies and government exercises a powerful influence on crime policy.

The government and private security companies now spend almost as much money on crime control each year as the Pentagon spends on national defense. In the last twenty years, spending on crime control has increased at over twice the rate of defense spending.[49] One hundred billion dollars of public money is spent on law enforcement every year. An additional $65 billion is spent on private security. There is nothing unusual or improper in a private business or individual making money from a government program. But there is an ethical difference when the source of private profit is the growing number of prisoners on the public dole—especially given the evident failure of crime policy to carry out its duties in the most cost-effective manner. From the use of "The Club" to reduce auto theft to home security devices sold by Radio Shack and Sears, crime has become big business, and it is growing rapidly.

The Prison-Industrial Complex in Action

In the upper-floor suites of a hotel in the nation's capital, executives from some of America's leading defense contractors recently dazzled a stream of visiting police officers with their latest technology. One company displayed the "Night Enforcer"—a high-tech pair of night-vision goggles like those used in the Gulf War. Another exhibited an electronic listening device that attaches to lightposts, detects the sound of a gunshot, and then transmits the exact location of the sound to a central computer at police headquarters. A third company marketed a wristwatch that was used to monitor vital signs of army troops on the field of battle. With defense industry cutbacks, these companies had come to Washington in search of new markets to help police fight the war on crime. They are frontline members of the prison-industrial complex.

Technology Can Improve Crime Fighting and Save Lives

There is no doubt that some efforts by private companies to improve crime-fighting technology are beneficial. Bulletproof vests have saved the lives of an estimated 1,500 law enforcement officers since being introduced in the early 1970s. Computer technology can speed up the filing of crime reports from police cars, savings thousands of work-hours and freeing up more police to patrol the streets. Equipment is being developed to force cars to stop, lessening the need for high-speed chases that cause injury and lawsuits. One company has developed a sticky foam that can freeze suspects who are about to attack or flee.

As laudable as these developments are, they still require caution and vigilance. As we have seen countless times in the area of national defense—a few years ago small bolts sold to the Pentagon cost taxpayers several hundred dollars each—the goals of private industry and the public interest can diverge. While the public is interested in safety, private industry is also concerned with profits. The continued growth of prisons is thus in the interests of the crime control industry, regardless of whether there is a need for more prisons as a matter of public safety.

The devices described above were exhibited at a two-day "Law Enforcement and Technology" conference sponsored by the Department of Justice and the private American Defense Preparedness Association.[50] The purpose of the conference was to promote greater cooperation between the defense industry and law enforcement agencies in identifying and producing crime-fighting technology. The Central Intelligence Agency has taken a leadership role in forging this cooperation. Most tellingly at the conference, not a single panel addressed the crisis in the criminal justice system, the extraordinary growth of prisons, or what impact the latest technology might have on crime control policy. The participants celebrated the glory of new crime-fighting technology without addressing the underlying causes of the criminal justice crisis.

Prisoners as Raw Material for the Prison Industry

Nils Christie, a Norwegian criminologist and the author of *Crime Control as Industry*, claims that companies that service the criminal justice system need sufficient quantities of raw materials to guarantee long-term growth. An economist looking at almost any industry might make the same simple statement. In the criminal justice field, Christie suggests a frightening scenario: that *the raw material is prisoners*, and industry will do what is necessary to guarantee a steady supply. For the supply of prisoners to grow, criminal justice policies must ensure a sufficient number of incarcerated Americans regardless of whether crime is rising or the incarceration is necessary.

Not all jails and prisons are operated by the government. Increasingly, states and counties are subcontracting the construction and operation of their correctional facilities to private companies, a trend we will examine shortly. In a 1994 article, the *Wall Street Journal* asserted that the private corrections industry uses the war against crime as a lucrative business market much the way the defense industry used the threat of Communism during the Cold War.[51] The article suggested that the prison-industrial complex, like the military-industrial complex, is based on an "iron triangle" between government bureaucracy, private industry, and politicians. The three entities create interlocking financial and political interests to push for a particular policy. In this case, that policy is the expansion of the criminal justice system.

The American prison-industrial complex involves some of the largest investment houses on Wall Street. Goldman Sachs and Co. and Smith Barney Shearson Inc. compete to underwrite jail and prison construction with private, tax-exempt bonds that do not require voter approval. Titans of the defense industry such as Westinghouse Electric and Alliant Techsystems, Inc., have created special divisions to retool their products for law enforcement. Publicly traded prison companies such as the Corrections Corporation of America and Wackenhut Corporation, as well as correctional officer unions, also exercise a powerful influence over criminal justice policy. Private companies are growing rapidly as the correctional population expands, and they are aggressively "exporting" their formula for private jails and prisons to other countries.

The Private Correctional Industry

With more than $250 million in annual revenues, the twenty-one companies that operate private jails and prisons occupy a central position in the prison-industrial complex.[52] They manage 88 prisons under contract with governments that incarcerate about 50,000 inmates. These businesses have experienced a phenomenal rate of growth, given that in 1984 only 2,500 inmates were in private prisons.[53] Though private facilities incarcerate a small portion of the overall correctional population, *the rate of growth of private facilities is currently more than four times the rate of growth of state facilities*.[54] And there is ample reason to believe that as the number of inmates increases—as well as the cost of maintaining them—states will increasingly turn to private companies as a way to save money.

Private Facilities Claim to Operate More Efficiently

The idea behind private jails and prisons is to remove the operation of a facility from government so it can be run cheaper and more efficiently by a private company.[55] The government pays the company a fixed amount for each day a prisoner is incarcerated, generally about $40. Partly because of lower salaries (private prisons tend to use non-union labor), private facilities claim to operate with a cost savings of 10 to 20 percent over state-run institutions.

Criticisms of Private Facilities

Detractors of private facilities argue that as a matter of public policy, control over an individual's life should not be contracted out to the lowest bidder. Because of the fixed sum paid for each prisoner, in order to maximize profits there is inherent pressure to provide a minimum of services. In so doing, programs such as drug treatment that are proven to lower recidivism might be scrapped solely because they are even slightly more costly. Privatization also raises questions about

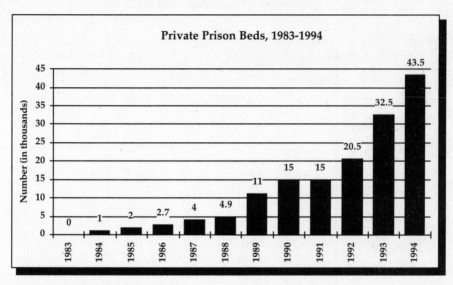

Source: Thomas, Charles W. (June 30, 1994), *Private Adult Correctional Facility Census.*

liability. To what extent, for example, should a private correctional officer with uncertain training be allowed to use force against a prisoner? If an inmate is injured, is it the private company or the government that is responsible? Finally, critics point out that the public usually has diminished control over the financing of private facilities.

The Corrections Corporation of America

Healthy profits await companies able to win contracts from state corrections agencies. The largest private prison company, the Corrections Corporation of America (CCA), had profits in 1993 of $4 million on $100 million of revenue—a 57 percent increase from the previous year.[56] The founders and officers of CCA include people with major political influence among both Democrats and Republicans.[57] Among them are Doctor Crants, who gave $5,000 to the national Democratic party, and Thomas Beasley, former chair of the Tennessee Republican party. Also on the board is T. Don Hutto, former commissioner of corrections for Arkansas and Virginia. A prestigious law firm, Covington & Burling, represents the company's Washington interests.

Founded in 1983, the CCA controls 30 percent of the private cor-

Private Prison Companies in the U.S.

Management Firm	Rated Capacity of Facilities Now in Operation	Expansion Anticipated Within 12-18 Months	Rated Capacity of Facilities Under Contract	Prisoner Population on 6/30/94	Percent Occupancy for Facilities in Operation	American Market Share
Alternative Programs, Inc.	240	0	240	240	100.00%	0.60%
The Bobby Ross Group	872	0	872	872	99.54%	2.16%
Capital Correctional Resources	836	0	836	796	95.22%	2.07%
Concept, Inc.	1,926	2,500	4,426	1,876	97.40%	10.98%
Cornell Cox, Inc.	794	0	794	752	94.71%	1.97%
Corrections Corporation of America	8,593	4,463	13,056	8,251	96.02%	29.88%
Corrections Partners, Inc.	584	1,088	1,672	562	96.23%	4.15%
Corrections Services, Inc.	32	0	32	29	90.63%	0.08%
Dove Development Corporation	762	0	762	633	83.07%	1.89%
Eden Detention Center	499	200	699	565	113.23%	1.73%
Esmor Correctional Services, Inc.	870	300	1,170	845	97.13%	2.90%
Group 4 - ICS	300	0	300	300	100.00%	n/a
The GRW Corporation	244	0	244	244	100.00%	0.61%
Management & Training Corp.	450	1,950	2,400	425	94.44%	5.96%
Mid-Tex Detention, Inc.	736	500	1,236	744	101.09%	3.07%
North American Corrections	489	144	633	489	100.00%	1.57%
U.S. Corrections Corporation	1,650	1,268	2,918	1,465	88.79%	7.24%
The Villa at Greeley, Inc.	0	400	400	0	n/a	0.99%
Wackenhut Corrections Corp.	6,568	4,250	10,818	5,593	85.16%	22.14%
TOTALS	26,445	17,063	43,508	24,667	93.31%	100.00%

Source: Thomas, Charles W. (June 30, 1994), *Private Adult Correctional Facility Census.*

rections market and is traded on the New York Stock Exchange. Most of its contracts are in Texas, Tennessee, and Louisiana, but it recently launched marketing efforts in the Northeast. In two years, the company expects its profits to double as it increases the number of prison beds it controls from 13,000 to 25,000.[58] Its financial officer recently described the 1994 federal crime bill, which allocated $9.7 billion for prison construction, as "very favorable to us."[59]

The CCA has engaged in extensive marketing to increase the size of the private correctional market and to strengthen its position within that market. In its annual report, it describes itself as the "industry leader in promulgating the benefits of privatization of prisons and other correction and detention facilities . . . the Company from time to time retains registered lobbyists who assist the Company with promoting legislation to allow privatization of correctional facilities."[60] Ted Goins, an investment analyst at Branch, Cabell, & Co. in Richmond, listed CCA as a "theme stock" for the 1990s. In his report on the CCA, Goins cited the federal crime bill and constraints on government spending as reasons "we expect a dramatic increase in the number of prisoners being served by private companies." As a result, Goins gave CCA "a strong buy rating to our clients familiar with the risks of investing in smaller capitalized companies."[61]

Esmor Correctional Services

Esmor Correctional Services, Inc., a publicly traded company based in New York, illustrates the pitfalls of the private corrections industry. Six years ago in New York City, Esmor turned a small hotel near Kennedy Airport into a prison under contract with the federal Immigration and Naturalization Service (INS). The hotel was used to detain the overflow of illegal immigrants who arrived at the airport. Esmor parlayed that one contract into a chain of ten detention centers and boot camps in several states. By 1995, it had grown into the fifth-largest private corrections company in the country, with $36 million in annual revenue.

Esmor recently won a bidding war with other private corrections companies to manage a 300-bed detention center for illegal immigrants in Elizabeth, New Jersey. Esmor was awarded the contract for $54 million, a full $20 million less than the next highest bid. Once awarded the contract, the company hired correctional staff with little or no experience, served a substandard diet to the inmates, and shackled detainees in leg irons when they met their lawyers. Despite repeated warnings from lawyers and staff that inmate frustration was rising, the company did virtually nothing to correct the problems. In the summer of 1995, the detention center exploded in violence. The uprising injured twenty detainees and caused damage in excess of $100,000.

According to staff at the facility, in order to keep costs in line with the low bid, the company cut corners and created the conditions for the disturbance. One correctional officer told a local newspaper he was placed on duty with no training and no prior experience in corrections or security. His wages were $8.60 per hour. Carl Frick, who served as the facility's first warden, said Esmor officials had instructed him to lie to INS officials about conditions at the facility. He said he was instructed to renegotiate a food service contract because $1.12 per day was considered too expensive for an inmate's meals. "They don't want to run a jail," said Frick, referring to the Esmor officials. "They want to run a motel as cheaply as possible. Money, money, money, that's all that was important to them. It was ridiculous." The local county prosecutor mocked Esmor as "privatization at its worst" and called for the closing of the detention center until the problems could be fixed.

What to Do with Private Prisons

Despite the problems with Esmor, it appears that some private corrections companies manage inmates better than some state-run facilities. In the previous chapter, we saw that a large number of state-run prisons are overcrowded and offer little opportunity for inmates to gain the skills needed to function on the outside. If private companies can operate facilities with sufficient control but also adequate care for the needs of inmates, then they should be allowed to make realistic bids on correctional projects. Their performance should be assessed by how well inmates do after release.

The trend toward using prisoners as a source of profit must be thought through carefully. Private companies have a built-in incentive to cut corners when providing drug treatment and other services to inmates that can lower the chance crime will be committed after release. Private companies also have a financial interest in supporting measures that will increase the need for construction of correctional facilities, regardless of whether those measures are needed. We should consider whether private companies should be allowed to lobby legislators to pass laws that will expand the inmate population. State and local governments should subject the performance of private facilities to a rigorous external review by an independent body.

Industries Benefit from Prison Expansion

In addition to private corrections companies, many other companies are positioned to profit from the billions of dollars flowing into local and state-run corrections systems. Private firms provide an untold number of goods and services to facilities, including food service, personnel management, architectural design, medical services, drug detection, vocational assessment, and transportation.[62] Companies also sell protective vests for correctional officers, closed-circuit television systems, fencing, flame-retardant bedding, clogproof waste disposal systems, furniture, clothes, perimeter security systems, and a host of other products.[63] The American Jail Association holds an annual convention for companies to market their products. Last year, advertisements for the convention asked people to "Tap into the Sixty-Five Billion Local Jails Market." "The local jail market is very lucrative!" the flier said. "Jails are BIG BUSINESS!!"

Correctional Medical Services of St. Louis provides medical care to 150,000 inmates—three times as many as it served in 1987.[64] The fiscal outlook for Correctional Medical Services is promising because longer sentences create older inmates and thus more demand for medical services. Advertising for prison products and services in *Corrections Today*, the industry trade magazine, has tripled since 1980. Finally, the Census Bureau reports that the hiring and training of correctional officers is the "fastest-growing function . . . out of everything the government does."[65] More than 523,000 full-time employees worked in corrections in 1992—more than all the people employed by any Fortune 500 company except General Motors.[66]

Correctional Facilities as a Rural Growth Industry

Another side of the "iron triangle" of the prison-industrial complex is communities that look to prisons as a source of economic growth. Even though most offenders come from cities, since 1980, the bulk of new prison construction has taken place in economically depressed rural communities—so much so that demographers consider the punishment of crime to be a leading rural growth industry.[67] Rural areas house such a large portion of the prison population that *5 percent of the national increase in rural population from 1980 to 1990 is accounted for by prisoners.*[68] In rural counties acquiring a jail or prison, the new inmate population amounted to nearly half of all population growth during the 1980s.

Correctional Facilities Considered a Bonanza for Economic Development
Many small towns compete to convince state officials that their community will be the best location for prison facilities that could last for as long as a century.[69] A typical prison might have several hundred staff members and a payroll of several million dollars. Free labor from prison work crews can alleviate the strains on small-town budgets; in Florida, for example, prisoners paint public buildings and clean roads and parks.[70] Economic benefits come not only from payroll, but also from construction, purchases from local vendors, and increased tax revenues from employees moving into the area. Also, jails and prisons are tax-exempt.

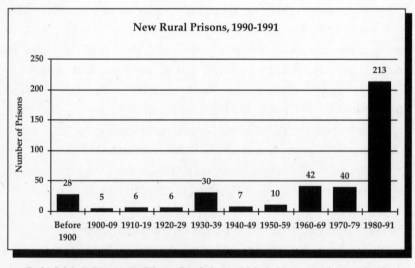

New Rural Prisons, 1990-1991

Source: Beale, Calvin L. (June 1993), "Prisons, Population, and Jobs in Nonmetro America," *Rural Development Perspectives, v*ol. 8, no. 3, p. 16.

Low Community Opposition in Rural Areas

Opposition to the construction of new prisons is often lowest in rural areas that are in need of economic development. In 1984, twenty-three state correctional departments reported local opposition to prison construction; four years later, that number had dropped to five, and twenty-four departments reported only community support.[71] In Texas, fifty towns recently solicited a new prison from the Texas Department of Criminal Justice. Some towns "bombarded the board . . . with incentives that range from country club memberships for wardens to longhorn cattle for the prison grounds." A town in Illinois put together a rap song and bought television time as part of a public relations blitz for state legislators.[72] In Minnesota, the small town of Appleton (pop. 1,500) issued $28.5 million in bonds to build a new prison *before* it had a commitment that its cells would be needed.[73] Ernie Van Sant, chief of prison construction for the California Department of Corrections, suggested a reason why so many towns want prisons: "We are not an industrial developer. We don't use a lot of chemicals. We're somewhat recession-proof."[74] In areas where the industrial or agricultural base is in decline, prisons present a bright alternative.

Economic Benefits Are Often Not as High as Anticipated

Many local leaders have ended up disappointed with the economic impact of new prisons. A quarter of all California towns with a state prison have a median family income below the federal poverty line.[75] The prison complex in Susanville, a small town in northeastern California, recently doubled its capacity to 10,000 inmates. The subsequent influx of family members of the inmates has strained social services, diminished the quality of education by increasing class size, increased crime, and divided residents over the need for the prison. A study of the effects of a new prison in Washington state found that it changed the character of the town: Residents started locking their doors and social problems increased.[76] The private prison in Appleton, Minnesota, remained empty months after it opened because the state could not afford to send prisoners there. Nevertheless, the town still had to pay exorbitant sums to staff the vacant prison in the hope that other states would rent the cells to absorb their overflow of prisoners.

Signs of Corruption

A recent investigation by the *Los Angeles Times* revealed that the state of California has paid exorbitant sums to rural landowners for property where it builds prisons.[77] Sellers included major farming corporations, a timber company, a bank, and wealthy businesspeople. Many of the individuals who sold property for prison construction were also campaign donors. In one egregious case, a 5,000-acre farm was bought in 1990 for $374 per acre. Two weeks later, the owners asked the California Department of Corrections to buy the land as a site for a new prison. After the intervention of a local legislator who co-authored the "three strikes" legislation, the state paid $3,500 an acre for the farm—almost ten times the original purchase price. The state then spent another $3 million to clean up pesticides and other toxins from the land. It turned out that the owners of the farm had donated money to the political campaigns of the state legislator who intervened on their behalf.

The Rise of the Correctional Officers

A byproduct of the expansion of the prison-industrial complex is the increasing influence of unions of prison guards over criminal justice policy. As the number of inmates has grown, so has the number of guards needed to watch over them.[78] The doubling and tripling of correctional officers in most states has created enormous clout for the unions that represent them. In Illinois, for example, the union of prison guards pushed through legislation to ban the privatization of prisons and to stiffen sanctions against inmates found carrying weapons.[79] The Michigan Corrections Organization has opposed proposals to lower the rate of incarceration by making prisoners eligible for boot camps.[80] "It's becoming a dollar-driven corrections policy in the state," says Mel Grieshaber, the legislative coordinator for the union.[81]

Nowhere are prison guards more active and powerful than in California. The guards' union in California, the California Correctional

Peace Officers Association, boasts that thirty-eight of forty-four bills it pushed in the state legislature under the last three governors were enacted.[82] The union has grown in a decade from 4,000 to 23,000 correctional officers, parole agents, and prison counselors. It has achieved an extraordinary pay and benefit plan under which the average salary for a correctional officer is $55,000 a year, far above the $43,000 paid to public school teachers and more than a tenured associate professor with a Ph.D. in the California state university system.

Collecting about $8 million a year in dues, the union has become the second-largest campaign donor in the state.[83] It spends about $1 million during each election cycle to support candidates for governor and the legislature who promote prison expansion. Its contributions are twice as large as those of the California Teachers Association, which has ten times as many members. In 1992, the union gave its largest contribution—over $80,000—to a relatively unknown candidate who ran against an outspoken critic of prison expansion who was chairperson of the Ways and Means Committee. The unknown candidate lost. The union donated the second-highest amount in support of the "three strikes and you're out" ballot initiative and spent more than $1 million on behalf of Governor Pete Wilson's last campaign. "We think we put Wilson over the top," said union president Don Novey.

Conclusion

There is nothing more viscerally disturbing than the fear of being the victim of a violent crime. Much of that fear has a legitimate basis in fact, for violent street crime is a real threat, particularly in the inner city. Yet fear of crime rather than crime itself drives much criminal justice policy in the United States. Fear of crime and crime are not the same thing. Policies based on fear are not the same as policies based on fact.

Particularly troubling is the part of our fear that does not stem from the threat of crime, but is instead created by the way crime data is presented. This often convinces us to spend tax dollars so that we *feel* like we are lowering the fear even though we are not lowering the crime. Also alarming is the fact that some entities—business and government among them—*profit financially or politically when fear is high*. The more fear can be inflamed, the more intense public passion about crime becomes and the easier it is to gain votes by proposing harsher sentences and more prisons. It is also easier for private companies to get new business, for retailers to expand the market for home security devices, and for unions of correctional officers to increase their salaries. And through it all, this fear can be used to get additional "raw material" to feed the growth of jails and prisons.

FOUR

RACE AND CRIMINAL JUSTICE

Whites and African-Americans live in completely different worlds when it comes to race and the criminal justice system. Three points about race are paramount. First, arrest rates indicate that African-Americans commit more crime than whites relative to the population. Second, there are so many more African-Americans than whites in our prisons that the difference cannot be explained by higher crime among African-Americans—racial discrimination is also at work, and it penalizes African-Americans at almost every juncture in the criminal justice system. Third, whether the cause is higher crime or discrimination or both, this country is on the verge of a social catastrophe because of the sheer number of African-Americans behind bars—numbers that continue to rise with breathtaking speed and frightening implications. The reason: our criminal justice policies are preventing many African-Americans from claiming their stake in the American dream, thereby contributing to the destruction of our national ideal of racial harmony.

While crime rates for African-Americans are somewhat higher than those for whites relative to the population, crime by African-Americans is not getting any worse. Since the mid-1970s, African-

Americans have consistently accounted for about 45 percent of those arrested for murder, rape, robbery, and aggravated assault. These numbers tell us that the *proportion* of overall crime committed by African-Americans has not increased for several years. Yet since 1980, the African-American prison population has increased dramatically while the white prison population has increased far less. Something more is at work than changes in crime patterns.

The Racial Divide

African-American business executive Earl Graves Jr. recently boarded a commuter train near his suburban home outside New York City and settled into his seat to read the morning paper. When the train arrived at Grand Central Station in Manhattan and Graves walked onto the platform, two police officers grabbed his arms and shoved him against a nearby wall as hundreds of commuters streamed by. The officers snatched away Graves's briefcase and frisked him from top to bottom. The police were looking for an African-American man approximately 5'10" with short hair and a mustache. Graves is 6'4" without a mustache.[1]

The detention of Earl Graves Jr. is but one example of how the criminal justice system is opening a racial divide in America. Race and crime always have mixed explosively in American history. The first police units in the South were used largely to catch runaway slaves.[2] Until the 1960s, almost all judges were white and most law enforcement agencies failed to hire minorities. While much has improved in recent years, there is still a tendency by some to use crime to exploit racial tension for political or personal purposes. We have seen how the Willie Horton political advertisement (Horton was an African-American man convicted of raping a white woman while on furlough from a Massachusetts prison) in the 1988 presidential campaign helped boost George Bush to the presidency. Susan Smith tried to dupe an entire nation when she blamed the drowning deaths of her two children on a mythical African-American man. In the O. J. Simpson trial, race played a central role in many of the factual disputes.

After an outbreak of race riots in several cities in the summer of 1967, President Johnson appointed the Kerner Commission to find out why the disturbances occurred and what could be done to prevent them. The Kerner Commission warned in its report: "Our nation is moving toward two societies, one black, one white—separate and unequal." At least partly because of our criminal justice policies, that prediction has come true. On any given day, more than a third of the young African-American men aged 18 to 34 in some of our major cities are either in prison or under some form of criminal justice supervision. If the racial disparities in the criminal justice system are any barometer, the racial polarization that led to the riots of the 1960s has not eased. In some ways, it has worsened.

Issues of race and crime affect many racial and ethnic minorities, not just African-Americans. Commission member Coramae Richey Mann, in her book *Unequal Justice*, asserts that when a violent crime occurs the perpetrator who comes immediately to mind to white Americans tends to be a person of color. The race or ethnicity of the stereotyped perpetrator varies between African-American, Hispanic, or Native American, depending on the nature of the crime and the section of the country. In tracing the history of racial stereotyping and crime, Mann suggests that white Americans view the classic rapist as a "black man," the typical opium user as a "yellow man," the archetypal knife wielder as a "brown man," the "red man" as a drunken Indian, and people of color as collectively constituting the "crime problem."[3] In this chapter, we focus primarily on African-Americans because they are our largest minority group and they have the highest rates of imprisonment. Their experience with the criminal justice system often mirrors that of other minority groups in the cities and regions of the country where those groups are concentrated.

The Magnitude of Minority Imprisonment

We start by counting the number of African-American men behind bars because it provides a useful frame of reference for our analysis. The numbers alone do not tell us anything except how many

African-Americans are locked up. They do not tell us if those numbers are justified by rates of African-American crime. That can only be determined by comparing the numbers of African-Americans in prison with the number of African-Americans who commit crime—a topic that will be explored shortly.

The United States imprisons African-American men at a rate six times that of white men. African-Americans are incarcerated at a rate of 1,947 per 100,000 African-American citizens compared to a rate of 306 per 100,000 for white citizens.[4] African-American males make up less than 7 percent of the U.S. population, yet they comprise almost half of the prison and jail population. In 1992, 56 percent of all African-American men aged 18 to 35 in Baltimore were under some form of criminal justice supervision on any given day.[5] In the District of Columbia, the figure was 42 percent.[6] One out of every three African-American men between the ages of 20 and 29 in the entire country—including suburban and rural areas—was under some form of criminal justice supervision in 1994.[7]

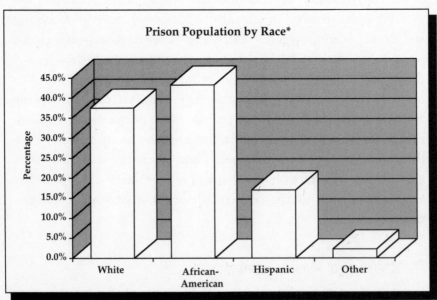

Prison Population by Race*

* Includes all facilities, juvenile and adult. Dates vary based on type of facility (1991–1993) and represent the most recent data available.
Sources: U.S. Department of Justice, Bureau of Justice Statistics and Office of Juvenile Justice and Delinquency Prevention.

State and Federal Prison Admissions by Race
1930 vs. 1992

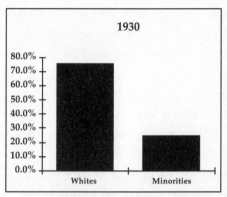

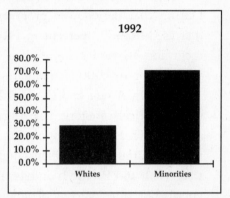

Note: Because the government determines race and not ethnicity, it counts most Hispanics with the white population. The Commission estimated the portion of Hispanics included in the white population and counted them as minorities.

Sources: U.S. Department of Justice, Bureau of Justice Statistics (May 1991), *Race of Prisoners Admitted to State and Federal Institutions, 1926–1986,* p. 14, Table 7; U.S. Department of Justice, Bureau of Justice Statistics (February 1994), *National Corrections Reporting Program— 1991,* p. 54; U.S. Department of Justice, Bureau of Justice Statistics (October 1994), *National Corrections Reporting Program—1992,* p. 12.

The difference between the numbers of minorities and whites in prison has widened as sentences for crimes have gotten longer (see chart above). In 1930, 75 percent of all prison admissions were white and 22 percent were African-American. That ratio has roughly reversed. In 1992, 29 percent of prison admissions were white, while 51 percent were African-American and 20 percent were Hispanic. Almost three out of four prison admissions today are either African-American or Hispanic. Ninety percent of the prison admissions for drug offenses are African-American or Hispanic.

Other Minority Groups

Other minority groups suffer from special problems because of criminal justice policy. Statistics on Hispanics, for example, are often unreliable because of variations in recordkeeping. Some states simply do not report data on persons of Hispanic origin, preferring instead to classify them as either black or white. The inconsistency makes statistical calculation more difficult. Nonetheless, the Bureau of

Justice Statistics (which compiles data on the criminal justice system for the federal government) estimates that Hispanics constituted the fastest-growing minority group in prison from 1980 to 1993. During that period, the proportion of inmates of Hispanic origin increased from 7.7 percent to 14.3 percent and the rate of imprisonment for Hispanics more than tripled, from 163 to 529 prison inmates per 100,000 Hispanic residents.

Similarly, Asians and Pacific Islanders are rarely tracked as a separate statistical category. Los Angeles, which has a significant Asian and Pacific Islander population, did not keep statistics on this minority group until 1991. The California Youth Authority reports that Asian and Pacific Islanders constitute six percent of incarcerated youth, but nine percent of new admissions—perhaps harbingering an increase in imprisonment. Most of the new admissions are immigrants from Southeast Asia, China, and the Phillipines, although there is little evidence these populations are more criminally active.

Native Americans suffer from jurisdictional problems relating to their status as residents of federal Indian reservations. Crimes committed on Indian reservations fall under federal jurisdiction, making Native Americans who commit ordinary crimes subject to the harsh penalties that the federal system designed for serious or interstate offenders. About six out of every ten juveniles in federal custody are Native American. In Alaska, one-third of the state prison population is native, though only 16 percent of the state population is native.

Studies Demonstrate More Minorities Than Whites in the Criminal Justice System

In 1983, criminologists Alfred Blumstein and Elizabeth Graddy found that 51 percent of nonwhite men in large cities are arrested and charged with a felony in their lifetime.[8] If the study had included the more numerous misdemeanor offenses, the proportion of nonwhite men arrested and charged would have been significantly higher. In the mid-1980s the California Attorney General's office conducted a study that found that two-thirds of nonwhite California males between the ages of 18 and 30 had been arrested.[9] An analysis of the jail system in Duval County (Jacksonville), Florida, showed that nearly one in four of all African-American men aged 18 to 34 were jailed at least once during the year 1991.[10] If the arrest and crime patterns remained the same, the analysis demonstrated that 76 percent of the African-American men living in Jacksonville in 1990 would be arrested before they reached age thirty-six. This suggests that the lifetime risk of arrest for African-Americans in many urban areas may be as high as 80 percent.

Some have suggested that racial differences in imprisonment might be due to the fact that African-Americans lag behind whites by almost every social and economic measure. In 1992, for example, 46 percent of African-American children and 39 percent of Hispanic children were born into poverty, compared to only 16 percent of white children.[11] Poverty is not an excuse for crime, nor is criminal activity limited to low-income Americans. Moreover, the vast majority of low-income people of all races are law-abiding. But we have seen that an overwhelming amount of street crime occurs in areas that have the lowest incomes.

To make this point, criminologist Elliott Currie studied two

Prominent Studies of the Criminalization of Minorities

Study	Major Findings
1995, The Sentencing Project	On an average day in America, one out of three African-American men aged 20-29 was either in prison or jail, on probation or parole.
1993, Federal Court special master in Duval County, Florida	76% of African-American men in the county would be arrested and jailed at least once before reaching the age of 36.
1992, National Council on Crime and Delinquency	One third of African-American men in Los Angeles aged 20– 29 spent time behind bars during 1991.
1992, National Center on Institutions and Alternatives	On an average day in 1991, 56% of African-American males in Baltimore, MD, between the ages of 18 and 35 were under criminal justice supervision. The figure in the District of Columbia was 42%. The odds of an African-American man in D.C. being charged with a crime at least once before the age of 35 were 70%.
1990, Rand Corporation	One-third of African-American men in Washington, D.C., were arrested and charged with a criminal offense in the three years between ages 18 and 21.
1989, The Sentencing Project	On an average day in America, one out of four African-American men aged 20–29 were either in prison or jail, on probation or parole.
1987, California Attorney General's Office	Among a representative group of people followed from the age of 18 in 1974 to age 30 in 1986, two-thirds of the nonwhite males had been arrested. 41% were arrested for a felony.
1983, Blumstein and Graddy (Carnegie-Mellon)	Between 1968 and 1972 in the country's 56 largest cities, one out of four men would be arrested for a felony in his lifetime. Only 14% of white men but 51% of nonwhite men would be arrested.

neighborhoods with roughly the same population and with the same name, Highland Park. The first Highland Park was a wealthy suburb of Chicago. The second was an impoverished community in Detroit that was largely populated by minorities. In the wealthy Highland Park in a recent year, there were no murders, no robberies, and only one rape. In the low-income Highland Park in the same year, *there were 27 murders, 55 rapes, and 796 robberies.*[12] Studies conclusively demonstrate that economic inequality affects not only the extent of crime, but its seriousness as well.[13] But no study demonstrates that poverty itself accounts for the racial disparities in prison.

A Treacherous Course for the Nation

As an exercise, the Commission decided to project what our prison system might look like in coming years if the racial disparities continue to grow.

What will happen if we continue to try to imprison our way out of the crime problem at the present rate? If the percentage of minorities in prison continues to increase at the same rate that it did from 1980 to 1993, a shocking picture emerges: almost two out of three of all young African-American men nationwide between the ages of 18 and 34 will be in prison by the year 2020.[14] For young Hispanic men in the same age range, one out of four will be in prison in the year 2020. If the growth were to continue uninterrupted at the present annual rate of increase, 4.5 million African-American men and 2.4 million Hispanic men will be incarcerated in 2020—*a prison population of minority men about five times as large as the prison population of all races combined today.* (See chart on page 107.)

This projection is obviously speculative. It would be extremely difficult for our society to sustain the financial and social cost of a prison population several times larger than the one we have now. But the projected numbers provide a stark reminder of the treacherous course the nation is taking on crime policy. As we continue to toughen sentences with "three strikes" and mandatory minimums, we inch closer to the numbers we find so shocking. In addition, these figures lead us back to the same fundamental question about the racial disparities in prison: Why do they exist?

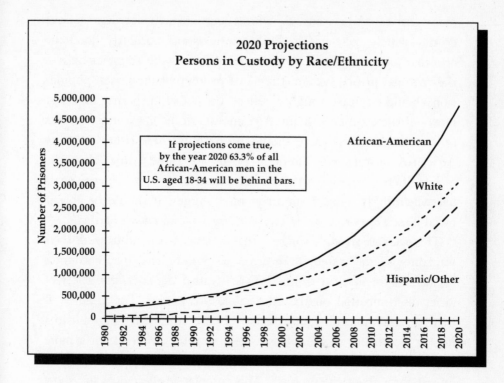

2020 Projections
Persons in Custody by Race/Ethnicity

If projections come true,
by the year 2020 63.3% of all
African-American men in the
U.S. aged 18-34 will be behind bars.

African-American

White

Hispanic/Other

Number of Prisoners

5,000,000
4,500,000
4,000,000
3,500,000
3,000,000
2,500,000
2,000,000
1,500,000
1,000,000
500,000
0

1980 1982 1984 1986 1988 1990 1992 1994 1996 1998 2000 2002 2004 2006 2008 2010 2012 2014 2016 2018 2020

Is There a Racial Bias?

One way to determine if racial bias has contributed to the minority
rate of imprisonment is to look at crime rates of African-Americans.
If African-Americans are in prison in higher proportion to their
crime rate, it suggests that they are treated more harshly by the
criminal justice system as they are processed through it. We determine crime rates for African-Americans and whites based on their
arrest rates. This assessment discounts racial bias that might have
occurred *before* arrest (some people are arrested because of a racist
police officer, not because they committed a crime), but arrest
records are the best indication we have of actual crime rates. Arrest
records are also a good frame of reference for measuring racial bias for
each subsequent stage of the criminal justice process.

Relative to population size, about five times as many African-
Americans as whites get arrested for the serious index crimes of murder, rape, robbery, and aggravated assault. About three times as

many African-Americans as whites get arrested for less serious crimes, which make up the bulk of arrests and currently flood the criminal justice system.[15] If after arrest there were *no* racial bias in the criminal justice system, the racial makeup of the prison population should at least roughly reflect the racial disparity in arrest rates—if three times as many African-Americans get *arrested* for less serious crimes, then there should be roughly three times as many African-Americans per capita in prison for those crimes. But the racial difference among African-Americans and whites in prison is overwhelmingly wider than arrest rates suggest it should be absent racial bias. *There are seven African-Americans to each white in prison.*[16]

This evidence strongly suggests that as African-Americans work their way through the system from arrest to punishment, they encounter harsher treatment than whites.[17] This is called the *cumulative* effect of racial discrimination on the criminal justice process. For instance, if there is racial discrimination when a person is arrested it can result in a harsher assessment of the offense. This, in turn, can result in a more severe charge and a more severe sentence and thus have an extended impact throughout the process.[18] This cumulative effect does not show up in all jurisdictions all the time, but it is the general pattern.[19]

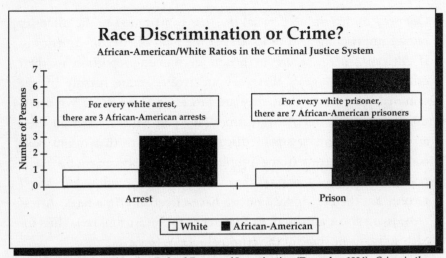

Race Discrimination or Crime?
African-American/White Ratios in the Criminal Justice System

For every white arrest, there are 3 African-American arrests

For every white prisoner, there are 7 African-American prisoners

Number of Persons

Arrest

Prison

☐ White   ■ African-American

Sources: U.S. Department of Justice, Federal Bureau of Investigation (December 1994), *Crime in the United States—1993*; U.S Department of Justice, Bureau of Justice Statistics (August 1995), *Prisoners in 1994*; U.S. Bureau of the Census (March 1994), *U.S. Population Estimates, By Age, Sex, Race, and Hispanic Origin: 1990 to 1993.*

This is not to say the criminal justice system is never fair to African-Americans. Some individuals certainly receive fair treatment, but the statistics indicate that African-Americans as a class of offenders receive harsher treatment than whites. Earl Graves Jr. would most likely agree. This fact has been borne out by studies that show whites are released more often before trial, pay less money to bail themselves out of jail, and receive significantly better deals in plea bargaining—topics we will explore shortly.[20]

Unfounded Arrests Burden African-Americans

The first place where racial disparities are usually measured is at the point of arrest. Most studies reveal what most police officers will casually admit: that race is used as a factor when the police decide to follow, detain, search, or arrest.[21] Some police officers believe that race provides a legitimate and significant basis to suspect a person of criminal behavior. To justify the use of race in forming this suspicion, these officers might point to racial disparities in arrest patterns: if minorities get arrested more often, they argue, then minorities must be committing more crime. This is a self-fulfilling statistical prophecy: racial stereotypes influence police to arrest minorities, thereby creating the arrest statistics needed to justify the racial stereotype.

A California study found that police make *unfounded* (where the suspect was innocent, or there was inadequate evidence, or there was an illegal search or seizure) arrests of African-Americans and Hispanics at sharply higher rates than those of whites.[22] For African-Americans in California, the rate of unfounded arrests was four times greater than that of whites. For Hispanics, the rate was more than double the rate of whites. The disparity was even worse in some urban areas. In Oakland, unfounded arrests of African-Americans occurred at twelve times the rate of whites. In Los Angeles, the rate was seven times as great, and in San Diego it was six times the rate of whites.

While there have been no nationwide studies of unfounded arrests, racial stereotypes can filter into the practices of police departments. The state of Maryland recently paid $50,000 to an

African-American Harvard Law School graduate and his family after state police stopped their rented Cadillac on a highway and conducted an illegal search of the car for drugs.[23] Evidence indicated that the police pulled over the family based on a "profile" of a typical drug dealer that included African-Americans driving luxury cars on the interstate highway. Police in Denver compiled a list of suspected gang members that contained the names of *two out of three African-American youths in the entire city between the ages of 12 and 24.*[24] The list had 5,500 names even though the police estimated there were only 250 gang members in the city. More than 93 percent of the names on the list were African-American or Hispanic teenagers. Police were able to stop and question those on the list even if there was no suspicion of criminal activity. Community uproar and a lawsuit eventually forced the Denver police to stop using the list.

The Decision to Prosecute or Drop the Case

Once they make an arrest, police usually refer the case to a prosecutor, who must decide whether to press charges or dismiss the matter (which might happen because of a lack of evidence, police misconduct in the gathering of evidence, or some other reason). The majority of available studies conclude that racial discrimination can and often does play a role in the prosecutorial decision.[25] One study of 1,017 homicide defendants in Florida compared the police assessment of the severity of the initial offense with the prosecutorial assessment of the severity.[26] The study found that crimes involving white victims and African-American offenders were much more likely to be upgraded in severity by the prosecutor, while crimes involving African-American victims and white offenders were more likely to be downgraded. An upgraded case leads to more serious charges, a more energized prosecution, and higher sentences. Again, this pattern does not necessarily hold true in all jurisdictions at all times. There are also nondiscriminatory factors that could help explain why prosecutorial decisions result in more severe charges for African-Americans, but overall, the studies strongly suggest that on some occasions race plays a role in prosecutorial decisions.

Minorities Pay Higher Bail Than Whites

A study by the *Hartford Courant* of 150,000 criminal cases in Connecticut found that an African-American or Hispanic man must pay on average *double* the bail of a white man for the same offense. In drug cases, the study found that the average bond for African-Americans and Hispanics in several areas of the state was *four times higher* than the bond for whites. For Hispanic women with no prior record, the average bond was 197 percent higher than the average for white women. The racial disparities in bail prompted the chief court administrator in Connecticut to charge publicly that judges were using excessive bond to punish minorities who had not been convicted.[27] And as if to compound this problem, a 1989 Connecticut study by two Trinity College professors also found that a failure to obtain release on bond increased both the likelihood of later conviction and the length of sentence.

Incarceration Before Trial

A similar study in Florida, conducted for the state Department of Corrections, found strong evidence of racial bias in the treatment of African-American defendants before trial. The sample of almost 3,000 adult offenders showed that being African-American significantly increased the likelihood of incarceration before trial. Young unemployed African-American men arrested on "public order" offenses were three times more likely to be kept in jail than unemployed whites arrested on the same charges. They were seven times more likely to be locked up than employed white arrestees.

Plea Bargaining Favors Whites

More than 90 percent of criminal cases where the defendant faces a prison sentence end in a "deal" in which the defendant pleads guilty to a lesser charge rather than face the risk of trial and a longer sentence. During negotiations between defense attorneys and prosecutors—the plea bargaining process—prosecutors have wide discretion to be tough on some and more generous with others. Evidence suggests it is minorities who get the worst deals.

A comprehensive study of racial bias in plea bargaining was carried out in California by the *San Jose Mercury News* in 1991.[28] A computer analysis of almost 700,000 criminal cases in California from 1981 to 1990 demonstrated that at virtually every stage of pretrial plea bargaining whites were more successful than minorities. All else being equal, whites did better than African-Americans and Hispanics at getting charges dropped, getting cases dismissed, avoiding harsher punishment, avoiding extra charges, and having their criminal records wiped clean. Among the findings of the California study:

•Of 71,668 adults who had no prior record and were charged with a felony, one third of whites had their charges reduced to a misdemeanor or less. Only a quarter of African-Americans and Hispanics received such reductions.

•Because of tougher plea bargaining deals, conviction for sale of drugs sent Hispanics to state prison (as opposed to county jail or probation) at twice the rate of whites. African-Americans went to state prison at rates one-third higher than whites.

•White first-time offenders were placed in community-based rehabilitation programs instead of prison at almost twice the rate of Hispanics and African-Americans.

Two offenders who entered state prison in California in 1987 illustrate how persons with the same criminal history can be treated differently.[29] Both men faced three counts of burglary and one count of receiving stolen property. Both had one prior nonviolent conviction for which they were not sentenced to prison. Neither had used a weapon and both had plea-bargained their sentences. One of the men was African-American, the other white. *The African-American inmate was convicted on the four original charges and received an eight-year prison term; the white inmate had three charges dismissed, was convicted of one count of burglary, and received sixteen months.* Not all cases have such a disparate impact. And certainly there are other factors—such as the strength of the evidence—that determine the outcome of the plea bargaining process. But in the criminal justice system, "racially biased decisions add up one by one [to form] an overall dramatic impact," according to Mark Mauer of The Sentencing Project, who analyzed the California data.[30]

The different treatment of minority defendants in the plea bargaining process can stem both from unconscious stereotyping and deliberate discrimination. "I don't think," said one California judge, "that we're talking about something where a bunch of white people sit around in white robes and hoods and there's some kind of conspiracy." A public defender added: "If a white person can put together a halfway plausible excuse, people will bend over backward to accommodate that person. It's a feeling, 'You've got a nice person screwing up,' as opposed to the feeling that 'This minority person is on a track and eventually they're going to end up in state prison.' It's an unfortunate racial stereotype that pervades the system. It's an unconscious thing." Such stereotyping is perhaps made easier by the fact that in California more than eight out of ten judges and prosecutors are white even though fewer than four out of ten defendants are white.[31] But it would be a mistake to say that this unconscious stereotyping is any less real just because it is not completely in the open. In fact, it may be even more dangerous.

Sentencing Discrimination

Although there is no definitive national study, there is evidence that African-Americans and whites are treated differently at sentencing. Florida has a statute that enables prosecutors to seek longer sentences for repeat offenders. The state legislature found that county prosecutors used this statute to lengthen sentences against African-Americans more than whites. The study found that African-Americans were more than twice as likely to have their sentences lengthened for a nonviolent offense than were whites. For violent offenses, African-Americans were 50 percent more likely to have their sentences enhanced than whites.[32] In Florida, African-Americans received longer sentences even though they had engaged in the same criminal conduct and had the same criminal history as whites.

Discrimination and the Death Penalty

Some of the most blatant racial discrimination in the area of sentencing takes place in the application of the death penalty. The most comprehensive study of the death penalty found that *killers of whites were eleven times more likely to be condemned to death than killers of African-Americans.*[33] Discrimination in the application of the death penalty can be seen most vividly by focusing on the race of the *victim.* Prosecutors nationwide—more than nine out of ten of whom are white—tend to seek the death penalty more often if the victim is white. To take one typical example, Georgia prosecutors sought the death penalty in 70 percent of the cases where the perpetrator was African-American and the victim was white. When there was a white killer and an African-American victim, the same prosecutors sought the death penalty in only 15 percent of the cases.

Racial Bias Through the Entire System

The *Harvard Law Review* in 1988 published a comprehensive legal dissection of racial discrimination in the criminal justice system.[34] It is the overall conclusion of this authoritative journal that is so persuasive: after looking at every component of the criminal justice system, it determined that there is evidence that discrimination exists against African-Americans at almost every stage of the criminal justice process. Other researchers across the political spectrum have reached the same conclusion. A 1994 study of race bias led by researcher Robert Crutchfield concluded that a "growing body of evidence suggests that justice is by no means guaranteed" for minorities in the criminal justice system.[35] Research by criminologists Alfred Blumstein and Joan Petersilia compared arrest rates to rates of incarceration and concluded that a significant portion of the racial disparities in prison is accounted for by racial discrimination.[36] According to Commission member Norval Morris, there is "measurable racial discrimination in our police practices, in our prosecutorial practices and in our sentencing." Morris concluded that the "whole law and order movement that we have heard so much about is, in operation though not in intent, anti-black and anti-underclass—not in plan, not in desire, not in intent, but in operation."[37]

Race and the War on Drugs

The "war on drugs" launched in the mid-1980s was a pivotal event in the history of African-American imprisonment in the United States. Amid much media fanfare, President Reagan launched the war on drugs by saying, "The American people want their government to get tough and go on the offensive."[38] He promised that police would attack the drug problem "with more ferocity than ever before." What he did not say was that *police enforcement of new drug laws would focus almost exclusively on low-level dealers in minority neighborhoods*. Police found more drugs in minority communities because that is where they looked for them. Had they pointed the drug war at college campuses, it is likely that our jails would now be filled overwhelmingly with university students.

African-American arrest rates for drugs during the height of the "drug war" in 1989 were five times higher than arrest rates for whites *even though whites and African-Americans were using drugs at the same rate*.[39] African-Americans make up 12 percent of the U.S. population and constitute 13 percent of all monthly drug users, but represent 35 percent of those arrested for drug possession, 55 percent of those convicted of drug possession, and 74 percent of those sentenced to prison for drug possession.[40] While the rhetoric of the drug war may have peaked, the particular "practice" of the drug war still is being carried out with considerable vigor. In *Malign Neglect*, his study on the war on drugs and its impact on minorities, criminologist Michael Tonry wrote: "Urban African-Americans have borne the brunt of the War on Drugs. They have been arrested, prosecuted, convicted, and imprisoned at increasing rates since the early 1980s, and grossly out of proportion to their numbers in the general population or among drug users."[41]

Surveys conducted by the National Institute for Drug Abuse have consistently found that arrest rates bear no relation to drug use.[42] African-Americans and whites use cocaine and marijuana at roughly the same rate, yet African-Americans suffer five times the number of arrests of whites for these drugs (see chart on page 118). Between 1985 and 1989, the number of African-American arrests for drug offenses nationwide more than doubled from 210,000 to 452,000, while the number of white arrests grew by only 27 percent.[43]

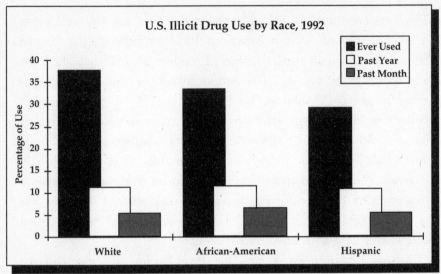

U.S. Illicit Drug Use by Race, 1992

Source: **U.S. Department of Health and Human Services (1992),** *National Household Survey on Drug Abuse.*

The war on drugs did not succeed in its goal of stemming drug use.[44] As the war heated up in the late 1980s, the street price of cocaine should have increased as police interdicted supplies and dealing became riskier. Instead, the street price of cocaine *fell*. Increased arrests and harsher sentences should have forced dealers off the streets. Instead, drug dealing in most communities remained steady or increased. Nor was there any evidence that the war on drugs succeeded in lowering drug use—drug use was in decline well before the war was declared.[45]

But the collateral effects of this "war" on minority communities were devastating. Some of the most striking evidence can be found in Baltimore. Again, remember that African-Americans and whites were using drugs at roughly the same rate all across the country. Of 12,956 arrests in that city for "drug abuse violations" in 1991, 11,107 were of African-Americans. In Columbus, Ohio, African-Americans accounted for 90 percent of the drug arrests despite comprising only 8 percent of the population. In New York City, 92 percent of drug arrests were of African-Americans or Hispanics. In St. Paul, African-Americans were

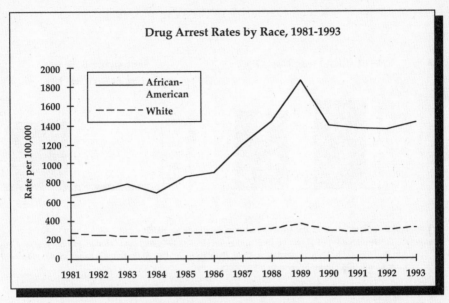

Drug Arrest Rates by Race, 1981-1993

Sources: U.S. Department of Justice, Federal Bureau of Investigation (December 1994), *Crime in the United States—1981* through *1993*; U.S. Department of Justice, Federal Bureau of Investigation (December 1993), *Age-Specific Arrest Rates and Race-Specific Arrest Rates for Selected Offenses 1965-1992*, pp. 205–207; U.S. Bureau of the Census (February 1993), *U.S. Population Estimates, By Age, Sex, Race, and Hispanic Origin: 1980 to 1991*; U.S. Bureau of the Census (March 1994), *U.S. Population Estimates, By Age, Sex, Race, and Hispanic Origin: 1990 to 1993*.

26 times as likely to be arrested on a drug charge as whites.[46] *USA Today* found that in some cities African-Americans were arrested at as much as 50 times the rate of whites for drug offenses.[47] This pattern was repeated in cities throughout the country.

This pattern helps explain the exploding rate of incarceration among African-Americans. In 1979, only 6 percent of state inmates and 25 percent of federal inmates had been convicted of drug offenses. In 1991, the proportion of state inmates convicted of drug offenses had nearly quadrupled to 21 percent, while the proportion of federal inmates so convicted had more than doubled to 58 percent. The overwhelming majority of these new prison admissions for drug offenses were minority men, because that is who the drug war targeted.[48]

Racial Disparity in the War on Drugs

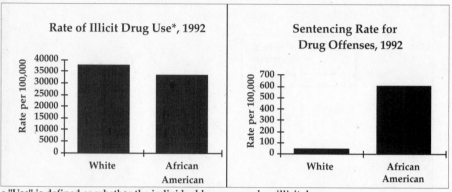

* "Use" is defined as whether the individual has *ever used* an illicit drug.

Sources: U.S. Department of Health and Human Services (1994), *National Household Survey on Drug Abuse, 1992;* U.S. Department of Justice, Bureau of Justice Statistics (October 1994), *National Corrections Reporting Program, 1992.*

Harsher Sentences for Crack Cocaine

One of the most shocking events in the sporting world in 1986 was the cocaine-induced death of University of Maryland basketball star Len Bias. The awful consequences of this tragedy are still reverberating through the criminal justice system and have contributed markedly to the explosion in African-American incarceration.

Almost immediately after Bias died, then–Speaker of the House Tip O'Neill led a charge in Congress to impose strict mandatory sentences for possessing or selling crack cocaine. Though it could be foreseen that the bill would dramatically reshape the racial composition of federal prisons, there was virtually no debate before the provisions were passed into law. Again, criminal justice policy was being made in response to a sensational media event. Almost overnight, penalties for the use of "crack" cocaine became up to 100 times harsher than the penalties for powder cocaine. Under federal law, possession of five grams of crack cocaine became a felony that carried a *mandatory minimum* sentence of five years, while possession of the same amount of powder cocaine remained a misdemeanor punishable by a *maximum* of one year. Both before and after the law was passed, about 90 percent of "crack" arrests were of African-Americans while 75 percent of arrests for powder cocaine were of whites. During the period from January 1989 to June 1990, more than eight out of every ten crack cocaine cases in federal court involved African-Americans, whereas in powder cocaine cases the percentage dropped to 33 percent.[49] The law clearly punished African-Americans for the use of crack cocaine more than whites for the use of powder cocaine. Under these laws, African-Americans were sent to prison in unprecedented numbers, to be kept there longer.

Violence and Crack Cocaine

The different sentences for crack and powder cocaine are hard to justify. Even the U.S. Sentencing Commission has recommended the disparity be eliminated. After Bias died, the media trumpeted crack cocaine as a highly addictive drug that had the potential to destroy communities and wreak wanton violence, but careful research now tells us that this was largely myth.[50] Although some claim that smoking crack cocaine produces a quicker and higher high, the evidence of meaningful pharmacological differences between crack and powder cocaine is exceedingly thin. The violence associated with crack stems more from turf battles between police and crack dealers, and among crack dealers battling to control lucrative markets, than from the narcotic effect of crack itself.

Given its impact on minorities, the drug war is a classic case where the treatment for the problem might be worse than the disease. After police raid a drug corner, drug dealers usually pick up and move their operation to another block to continue. Police could never really *stop* the drug trade, they could only *displace* it. In the process of that displacement, violence erupted as dealers jockeyed to control market share. Experts who have studied the drug war have concluded that the amount of trafficking, lawlessness, and violence in the United States increased along with the all-out attempt to capture, prosecute, and imprison traffickers and users of illicit drugs.[51] One journalist who has observed the drug war in Washington, D.C. described it this way: "The number of dealers killing each other had gotten too high . . . so an all-out drug crackdown was imposed. But a crackdown without a parallel push to curb drug demand is truly a gory endeavor with no real point, like stomping the hell out of a wasp's nest and running away simply because you don't like wasps. All the crackdown does is tear up turf and reshuffle turf and introduce additional chaos to the street, which leads to additional—and essentially gratuitous—violence sanctioned by a society ostensibly dedicated to bringing violence down."[52]

Judges React to the War on Drugs

Several judges have refused to enforce the harsher penalties for crack cocaine on the grounds that they discriminate against African-Americans. Other judges have resigned in protest.[53] Federal Judge Lyle E. Strom of Omaha ruled that African-Americans convicted in crack cases "are being treated unfairly in receiving substantially longer sentences than Caucasian males, who traditionally deal in powder cocaine."[54] In 1991, the Minnesota Supreme Court ruled that the differing sentences for crack and powder cocaine discriminated on the basis of race.[55] In the Minnesota case, expert witnesses testified that they suspected crack cocaine was more addictive, but their evidence was based mostly on anecdotal stories. Although there have been calls by some politicians to eliminate the disparity between crack and powder cocaine, it still exists in federal law and in the laws of many states.

Discrimination in Drug Treatment

The racial discrimination in the war on drugs often does not end with the sentencing of African-Americans for drug crimes. Once sent to prison, African-Americans are less likely than whites to be assigned to the small number of coveted treatment slots designed to help inmates cure their addiction. A California study showed that two-thirds of drug treatment slots went to whites despite the fact that 70 percent of inmates sentenced for drug offenses were African-American. A study in New York revealed the same pattern.[56] Yet those who receive drug treatment are much more likely to be paroled and much less likely to reoffend upon release. Because African-American addicts have less access to drug treatment, they are more likely than white addicts to stay in prison longer under harsher conditions of confinement.

Stereotyping of Minority Groups

There is a sordid history in the United States of associating minority groups with illicit drugs. In 1918, the *New York Times* helped spread a rumor about drug-crazed African-Americans when it ran a story about a "Negro cocaine fiend" who threatened public safety even though whites used the most cocaine. In the early part of the century, Chinese opium smokers bore the brunt of anti-drug fervor even though Caucasian women consumed the most opium. In the 1930s, authorities put out a scare that Mexicans were dangerous because they smoked huge quantities of marijuana even though there was no such evidence. Starting in the mid-1980s, crack cocaine was associated with disadvantaged minority residents of the inner cities. This unfortunate historical trend suggests that the war on drugs has much more to do with political posturing than wise social policy.

Other academics place the blame on the shoulders of those who designed the drug war. Michael Tonry concluded in *Malign Neglect* that it was easily foreseeable that the war on drugs would discriminate against minority communities; thus, from an ethical standpoint, policymakers who designed the war should be held accountable *as if they intended to discriminate*. Tonry makes an analogy: "Blowing up an airplane to kill a passenger is equivalent to blowing up an airplane to destroy a fake painting and thereby to defraud an insurance company, knowing that the passenger will be killed. Both are murder. Most people would find the latter killing more despicable. By analogy with the criminal law, the responsibility of the architects of contemporary crime control policies is the same as if their primary goal had been to lock up disproportionate numbers of young blacks."[57] New York Senator Daniel Patrick Moynihan echoed the same theme: "By choosing prohibition, we are choosing to have an intense crime problem concentrated among minorities."

Race and Juvenile Justice

Racial discrimination appears to have penetrated the juvenile justice system as a result of the war on drugs. In 1980, the national rate of drug arrests for white and African-American juveniles was about the same. In that year, 400 out of every 100,000 juveniles in our country were arrested on drug charges. As the drug war became more intense in the late 1980s, arrests of African-American youths surged, almost quintupled—to 1,415 per 100,000—while arrests for white youths remained stable. This occurred even though African-American and white juveniles were using drugs at the same rate.[58]

In Baltimore in 1981, a total of 15 white juveniles and 86 African-American juveniles were arrested on the charge of drug sales. By 1991, the number of white juveniles arrested on drug charges declined to 13 while the number of African-American juveniles so arrested increased to 1,304.[59] African-American juveniles in Baltimore were being arrested for drugs at roughly 100 times the arrest rate of whites of the same age—even though drug use was not higher among African-American youths.

The racial makeup of populations in juvenile detention centers also changed dramatically. The percentage of white juveniles placed in detention centers dropped 2 percent between 1984 and 1988. During the same years, the percentage of nonwhite youths detained grew 269 percent. State training schools and youth detention centers were filled disproportionately with African-Americans.[60]

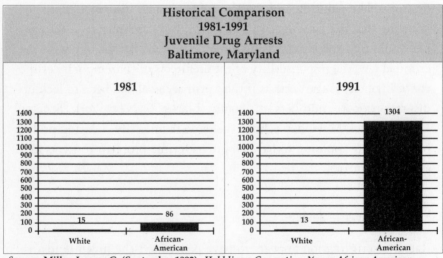

Source: **Miller, Jerome G. (September 1992),** *Hobbling a Generation: Young African American Males in the Criminal Justice of America's Cities.*

Explaining Racial Bias in the Juvenile Process

Racial discrimination can seep into the juvenile justice system at a number of entry points and have a powerful cumulative effect. This is important because such discrimination can influence who receives harsher treatment at the later stages. One drunk teenager might be warned and sent home by police, while another might be taken to a juvenile detention facility and charged with disorderly conduct or public intoxication. A 1987 study found that race was one of the most important factors when determining which juveniles were sent home and which were charged with a crime.[61] All other things being equal, minority youths faced criminal charges more often than white youths for the same offenses. Also, African-American youths are charged more often than whites with a felony when the offense could be considered a misdemeanor.[62]

Several studies have documented that minority youth are more likely to be arrested, referred to court, and placed outside the home when awaiting disposition of their cases.[63] It is extremely rare for a police officer to arrest and take to jail a middle-class white youth who gets into trouble; more often than not (unless the crime was violent), police will warn the youth and take him home to his parents. Minority youth are also more likely to be waived to adult court, where they will face longer sentences and fewer opportunities for rehabilitative programs. If removed from their homes, minority juveniles are much more likely to be placed in state reform schools rather than the better-staffed and less restrictive private group home facilities.

When he was director of the Massachusetts Department of Youth Services, Commission member Jerome Miller wrote of the cumulative effect of decisions made throughout the juvenile justice process: "I learned very early on that . . . when we got an African-American youth, virtually everything—from arrest summaries, to family history, to rap sheets, to psychiatric exams, to 'waiver' hearings as to whether he would be tried as an adult, to final sentencing—was skewed. If a middle-class white youth was sent to us as 'dangerous' he was more likely actually to be dangerous than the African-American teenager with the same label. Usually, the white kid had been afforded competent legal counsel, appropriate psychiatric and psychological testing, been tried in a variety of privately funded options, and all in all, had been dealt with more sensitively and individually at every level of the juvenile justice process. For him to be labeled dangerous, he had usually to have done something very serious indeed. By contrast, the African-American teenager was dealt with as a stereotype from the moment the handcuffs were first put on—to be easily and quickly moved along to the 'more dangerous' end of the 'violent-nonviolent' spectrum, albeit accompanied by an official record meant to validate the biased series of decisions."[64]

Unanticipated Consequences

Many criminologists have begun to ponder the unthinkable: that the criminal justice system itself, rather than guarding the peace, contributes to social instability in America. This is the main theme of *Search and Destroy,* Miller's book on African-American males and the criminal justice system. By running so many persons through jails and prisons each year, the violent ethos of the correctional facility has increasingly come to shape behavior on the streets and undermine respect for the law. Arrest records dim employment prospects for millions of young men each year. Massive levels of incarceration in some areas diminish the likelihood that young people will create and be able to sustain a family. Sociologist William Julius Wilson developed a "marriage index" that shows that the number of employed minority men per 100 minority women has been declining for several years, particularly for those under 25. With so many men in prisons and jails, family life is disrupted and another buffer to violence is lost.

Loss of Faith in Government

In 1990, an eighteen-year-old African-American man was acquitted of a felony by a jury in Washington, D.C. The jury had been comprised mostly of African-Americans. A juror later wrote a letter to the court that explained how most of the jurors believed the defendant was guilty, but they had capitulated to those who did not "want to send any more Young Black men to Jail."[65] This is one example of an unintended consequence of the massive law enforcement intervention in the inner city. When so many family members and friends have been jailed, it becomes hard to see the "criminal" as an outside force. When the "criminal" is more than half the young minority men in the city, it can force residents to choose between loyalty to their community and their civic responsibility to the justice system. This is not to say that juries from the inner city are less likely to convict a defendant because of racial reasons. To the contrary, some defense attorneys believe such juries might be *more* inclined to convict because it is their communities that suffer the most from crime. But inner-city juries are more suspicious of the police and are less likely to trust police testimony.

Nevertheless, widespread arrests in minority communities have had a negative effect upon the ethic and attitude of the wider community toward the law and its representatives.[66] Mike Davis, a writer on urban affairs who has studied the Los Angeles Police Department, claims anti-gang sweeps in that city arrest kids at random and "have tended to criminalize black youth without class distinction. Between 1987 and 1990, the combined sweeps . . . ensnared 50,000 'suspects.' Even the children of doctors and lawyers from View Park and Windsor Hills have had to 'kiss the pavement' and occasionally endure some of the humiliations that the homeboys in the flats face every day—experiences that reinforce the reputations of the gangs . . . as the heroes of an outlaw generation."

Many young people receive a chilling message of neglect from representatives of law enforcement. Earl Graves Jr. said that in addition to his frisk at Grand Central Station, he had been stopped at least a dozen times by police because of his skin color—including once in Cambridge, Massachusetts when he was a student at the Harvard Business School. Like the gang arrests in Denver, a significant portion of the millions of arrests of African-Americans each year are accompanied by name-calling, harassment, and abusive treatment.[67] The mistreatment is so pervasive that young men in the inner city know to quickly "assume the position" with their face down on a concrete sidewalk or street while they get handcuffed and searched.[68]

Employment Prospects Diminish

The effects of such treatment can have consequences that go far beyond personal humiliation. John Hagan, the recent president of the American Society of Criminology, said there is "evidence that contact with the criminal justice system has especially negative effects for underclass males." Several studies link involvement in the criminal justice system with lowered employment prospects.[69] Employers tend to pass over applicants who have a criminal record of any sort—even if the record only reflects an *arrest* for a minor infraction and even if that arrest is unfounded. Yet increasing concentrations of joblessness have been consistently associated with urban crime.[70] There are intergenerational effects as well: children of the unemployed are more likely to engage in delinquent behavior and become unemployed themselves, setting the stage for the cycle of crime to continue. By stigmatizing so many youth with arrest records for minor offenses, our crime policies can contribute to a level of unemployment in the inner city that is an obstacle to efforts to lower crime rates.

The private sector often perceives minority teenagers as crime-prone and thus fails to provide entry-level jobs to them. In the nation's capital in 1995, city officials asked 6,000 area companies to commit $1,000 each to hire 1 youngster for the summer at the minimum wage. More than 16,000 youths signed up, but only 560 companies agreed to offer jobs. "In the District, the perception is that all black youths are bad," said an official with the city employment office. "The businessmen come up with all kinds of excuses for not hiring based on what they've seen or read in the media . . ."[71] Another official said: "We know the employment community in Washington hires young people. They just don't hire our young people."[72] The corporate response across the country was dismal as well. The federal government allocated funds for 625,000 summer job slots and called on corporations for a matching commitment. As of mid-June, only a small number of corporations had responded and 500,000 teenagers still had not found summer work.

The Increase in Snitching and Informants

Another unanticipated consequence of crime policy is the expanded use of "snitches" by police in order to gather information about drug users and sellers. The increase in firearms violence in some urban minority neighborhoods in the early 1990s coincides with the development of a national anti-drug strategy based on the massive use of informers in the cities. In the federal system, the percentage of sentence reductions given to offenders who "informed" for prosecutors rose by more than five times between 1989 and 1994. Some criminologists now assert that the widespread use of informants has transferred the code against snitching and the violence it spawns from prison to the streets of urban America.[73]

The prosecutorial practice of enlisting defendants as informants in the drug war tends to inflame the violence associated with the code against snitching. While in certain situations informants are a necessary tool of law enforcement, in the drug war the practice has been used as a routine measure. It is common for federal prosecutors to threaten drug defendants with mandatory sentences unless they incriminate others. Many defendants decide to inform on their associates and friends in an effort to get a lighter prison sentence. This practice frays bonds of personal trust and corrodes the community cohesion that might otherwise act as a buffer to violence.

The Effect of Criminal Justice Policy on Voting

One of the least recognized consequences of crime policy is its impact on political power through voting. Andrew Shapiro, a leading authority on the issue, found that about four million Americans have lost their right to vote because of a criminal conviction.[74] A disproportionate number are African-American.

Sadly, many laws that take away the right to vote were passed in the early part of the century with the express purpose of undermining the political power of African-Americans. In Virginia, a legislator explained that the criminal disenfranchisement law was passed "with a view to the elimination of every Negro voter."[75] In Louisiana in 1898, the Chief Justice of the Supreme Court urged that the law be passed "to establish the supremacy of the white race."[76] What is ironic is that it is contemporary criminal justice policies that are to some degree making the wishes of segregationist legislators from the early part of the century come true. In Illinois, 63 percent of state prisoners are African-American compared to the 15 percent of the population. In Florida, where convicts on probation cannot vote, half of those under probation are Hispanic, even though Florida's general population is 12 percent Latino.[77]

Conclusion

The fact that so many minority men are in the criminal justice system raises profoundly disturbing questions. To the extent that racial disparities in prison are the result of racial bias, then that bias must be rooted out of the criminal justice system. To the extent that they are the result of higher African-American crime, then the underlying causes of that crime must be addressed. Failure to do so puts the nation at risk of a social catastrophe. The riots following the acquittal of the police officers who beat Rodney King are a vivid illustration of what can happen when race issues are ignored and minorities experience the criminal justice system as biased against them.

Many minority citizens are the subjects of a double victimization as a result of the failure of criminal justice policy. They are victimized once by the high incidence of crime. They are victimized again by being arrested and incarcerated at rates far higher than their level of criminality can justify. As a result of the treatment of young African-American males, many inner-city areas are filled with people who have a criminal record. Virtually everyone there has a relative or friend in prison, on probation, on parole, or in hiding because there is a warrant out for their arrest. Many of the men arrested have children, and those children know where their parents are. For many such children, a trip to prison to visit relatives is more common than a school field trip. Many courthouses now offer day care centers for parents who must bring their children to court. In this way, the children experience prison and the larger criminal justice system as a natural part of community life. There is no way of knowing—and nobody is making the effort to find out—what effect this tragic phenomenon will have on the life of these young people.

The reason our crime control policies have had such a destructive impact in minority communities is because of choices made largely by elected officials. It is legislators who write sentencing laws, appropriate funds for more prisons, and promise that people will feel safer. When that sense of safety fails to materialize, they propose even harsher laws and longer sentences in an open-ended cycle that threatens to destroy whatever hope the nation has of achieving racial unity. The fact that disadvantaged minority men disproportionately fill the cells for nonviolent offenses makes little difference. When politicians openly paint crime with an African-American face—as in the Willie Horton ad—or simply boast of getting "tough" on lawbreakers in urban areas, they exploit latent racial tension for political purposes. They also move our nation one step closer to a racial abyss that has little do with the creation of a safe society.

FIVE

YOUTH VIOLENCE AND JUVENILE JUSTICE

If the criminal justice system has largely been driven by the need to protect society by punishing offenders, the hallmark of the juvenile justice system is the quite different presumption that young people who commit crimes can learn to do better if placed in the right setting and given the right care. Yet most juvenile correctional facilities in the United States are designed to hold large numbers of youths in primitive conditions. Many of these juvenile facilities are over-crowded, rely on leg shackles and handcuffs to control behavior, and "graduate" youths who often go on to commit more serious crimes as they get older. Each year about 11,000 out of the 65,000 incarcerated juveniles commit suicidal acts, yet most facilities have inadequate suicide prevention programs.[1]

In recent years, as stories of teen violence have become regular features of our newspapers and television news programs, we have lost sight of the crucial distinction between adult and juvenile facilities. Until the 1980s, the biggest threats to young people were car accidents and suicide. In that decade, according to the National Center for Health Statistics, teenage males in all racial and ethnic groups became more likely to die from a bullet than from all natural causes combined (see chart below). The death rate by homicide in the 1980s of young people aged 15 to 19 increased by 61 percent. Between 1986 and 1992 alone, the number of children in the United States killed by firearms jumped 144 percent, compared to a 30 percent increase for adults.[2]

Although they are shocking at face value, these statistics mask a dramatically higher homicide rate among minorities. For African-American youths, the homicide rate is almost eight times that of the rate of whites—34.9 homicides per 100,000 population, compared to 4.4 per 100,000 population for white male youths.[3] Firearms violence kills about 1,700 African-American youth and about 1,000 white youths aged 10 to 19 each year.[4] The increase in juvenile firearms homicide has swept across racial lines: the rate at which white youths are victims of homicide doubled between 1988 and 1992, even though on a per capita basis there are far fewer white homicide victims than African-American homicide victims.[5]

Teenage homicide is the most terrifying element of a much larger

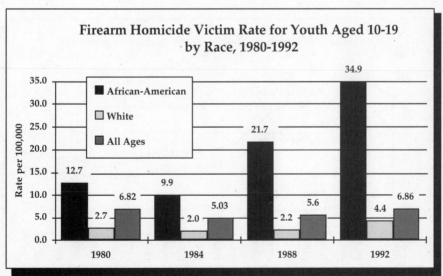

Firearm Homicide Victim Rate for Youth Aged 10-19 by Race, 1980-1992

Sources: **National Center for Health Statistics (August 23, 1994),** *Death for Selected Causes, By 5 Year Age Groups, Color and Sex: United States, 1979–92;* **U.S. Bureau of the Census (February 1993),** *U.S. Population Estimates, By Age, Sex, Race, and Hispanic Origin: 1980 to 1991;* **U.S. Bureau of the Census (March 1994),** *U.S. Population Estimates, By Age, Sex, Race, and Hispanic Origin: 1990 to 1993.*

geography of juvenile crime. Still, the overwhelming majority of the two million juvenile arrests in the United States each year have nothing to do with crimes of violence; only 6 out of 100 juvenile arrests are for violent crimes (for adults, 13 of every 100 arrests are for violent crimes).[6] The most serious crimes of rape and murder account for less than one-half of one percent of juvenile arrests.[7] (See chart on page 133). Although there has been a dramatic rise in juvenile firearms homicide, we are not in the midst of an *overall* juvenile crime wave. The total rate of arrest for juveniles has been declining in the past ten years (see chart below).

Nevertheless, because gang killings, drive-by shootings, and high school arms buildups have gained headlines nationwide, we have shaped our policies in response to them, even where there are not such severe problems. But it is unrealistic to expect that the treatment of one part of the problem will properly cure the whole. Increasingly, the juvenile justice system has focused on punishing all offenders—violent and nonviolent alike—with harsh sentences while paying lip service to rehabilitation. Our "get tough" policies are perhaps even more severe when we are dealing with children. We cele-

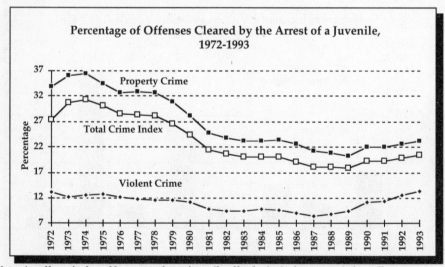

Percentage of Offenses Cleared by the Arrest of a Juvenile, 1972-1993

Note: An offense is cleared by arrest when a juvenile offender is cited to appear in juvenile court or before some other juvenile authority.
Sources: U.S. Department of Justice, Federal Bureau of Investigation, *Crime in the United States—1972 through 1993.*

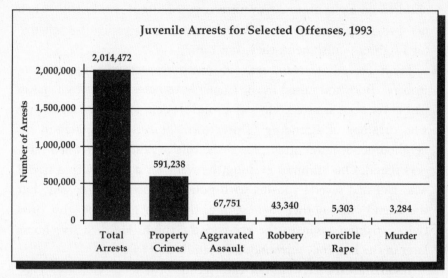

Source: **U.S. Department of Justice, Federal Bureau of Investigation (December 4, 1994),** *Crime in the United States—1993,* **p. 227.**

brate judges who allow juveniles to be tried as adults. We allow the death penalty to be imposed against teenagers. But we have failed to solve the problem of juvenile violence.

Two Victims of Juvenile Violence

In September 1994, Robert "Yummy" Sandifer was taken by fellow gang members under a Chicago expressway and was shot twice in the skull. Robert was only eleven years old. His story was so wrenching and disturbing that a national magazine placed his picture on the cover, a modern urban horror tale. Burned with cigarettes and beaten as a baby, Robert was only three when first called to the attention of child welfare authorities in Illinois. Accused of shoplifting, he made his debut in court at age eight. He was subsequently arrested six times on twenty-three different charges. Robert was shuttled between group homes and detention centers and identified as "at risk" by almost every public agency with which he had contact, but nobody stepped in to offer the help he needed. Robert tried to impress local gang members by spraying gunfire into a group of children on a playground. A fourteen-year-old girl was killed. When his own gang members feared he would talk to police in exchange for a lighter punishment, they shot him.[8]

Jason Sowell, sixteen, was in many respects the opposite of Robert.[9] Born and raised in the Coney Island area of Brooklyn, Jason had never been arrested. He was a solid student and a basketball star who dreamed of attending Georgetown University. Popular in his neighborhood, Jason often played the role of peacemaker when tempers flared. One summer evening, he went for a walk with a friend who had had several run-ins with police. Nobody is sure why, but the friend and another man struggled over a gun. The gun fired twice, striking Jason in the eye and the thigh. He died five hours later in the hospital, surrounded by family and friends.

Jason and Robert were not the victims of random violence. They were put at a higher risk of death than most children because of the circumstances of their lives. Jason lived in a neighborhood where young people carried guns. Robert grew up in a country unwilling to take the steps needed to detour him from his perilous path.

The Temptation to Increase Punishment

Some simply wish to write off these losses as tragedies of a "lost" generation who can never be brought into the mainstream of American life. We are almost relieved when more troubled youths are sent to jail, as if it erases the problem from our consciousness and confirms the expectation we had for them. Others wish that the government or private charities would build orphanages and fill them with youth who come from troubled families.

The Commission strongly believes that chronic violent offenders need to be incarcerated for as long as necessary to protect public safety. But that does not change the fact that the increase in juvenile homicide has given rise to several harsh proposals that are once again bait and switch deals that, at enormous cost, will send mostly nonviolent offenders to prison.

The temptation to punish all delinquent youth with harsher penalties because of the violent activities of a few carries real political value. During the debate over the 1994 federal crime bill, one proposal called for spending $500 million to build new juvenile institutions to hold 65,000 delinquent youths. At the time the proposal was made, *all* juvenile facilities in the United States held a total of 63,000 youths, and only about 18 percent of those had been convicted of serious violent crimes.[10] There was little discussion as to how the additional 65,000 beds would be filled, but it at least *sounded* as if something was being done about the juvenile violence problem.

This kind of proposal might appeal to the emotional frustration many Americans feel over youth violence, but it is unlikely to relieve the problem. In 1992, over half of the incarcerated children in confinement had committed property or drug crimes and were experiencing their first confinement to a state institution.[11] If 65,000 more beds were created in juvenile institutions, there is no doubt they would be filled with lesser offenders. Based on current trends, most of these would be minorities. Minority youths nationwide are already three times more likely than whites to end up in long-term detention centers.[12]

Another response to juvenile violence is the call to "waive" minors to adult criminal courts for prosecution. States that allow and

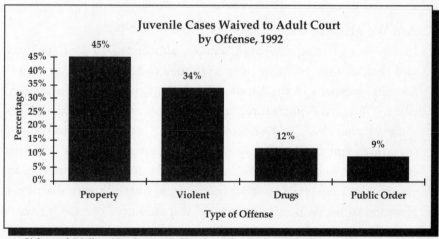

Source: Sickmund, Melissa (October 1994), *How Juveniles Get to Criminal Court,* U.S. Department of Justice, Office of Juvenile Justice and Delinquency Prevention, p. 3.

encourage such waivers have made a decision that the need to protect the public from juvenile crime outweighs the desire to provide rehabilitation and treatment to youthful offenders (it is virtually impossible for a youth to be sent to a juvenile institution from an adult court). Though the policy was originally designed to incarcerate violent juvenile offenders who committed crimes of adult severity, most youths who have been waived to adult court are convicted of nonviolent offenses rather than offenses against persons.[13] In fact, the greatest increase in juvenile waivers from 1987 to 1991 was for drug cases, which jumped 152 percent.[14] While a few repeat drug offenders might be more appropriately handled in adult court, adult waiver is not being used to target violent criminals.

Imprisoning Juveniles Is More Expensive

The cost of locking up a young offender in a secure institution can run over $100,000 per child per year. The cost at state-run facilities can range from $35,000 to $70,000 per year. Since youth need more supervision and more educational and treatment services, the cost is usually higher than for adult prisons. Many young offenders are sent to private for-profit treatment facilities at even higher cost. The justice system is spending more than $3.2 billion each year to keep children in custody.[15]

Are We Missing the Problem?

In a survey of inner-city high schools, almost one in four students said that at some point in their lives they had possessed a firearm.[16] So many weapons in the hands of adolescents has had an incendiary effect. "We have immature, impressionable children armed with some of the most sophisticated weapons," said Matt Rodriguez, superintendent of the Chicago Police Department, when asked to explain why Robert Sandifer was killed. Dr. Kathleen Kostelny, an expert on the effects of violence on children, likened the proliferation of weapons to a domestic arms race. "You only need one twelve-year-old with a gun, then other twelve-year-olds feel they need a gun," she said.

An essential element of the problem is that weapons on the streets are more lethal than in the past. In part, this reflects the nature of the drug war. As profits grew, those drug dealers with superior fire-power found they could control greater market share and intimidate their competitors; an Uzi can spray many more people with bullets than the old handgun known as the Saturday Night Special. The sophistication of weapons means that the chances of a bullet *killing* rather than *wounding* have grown substantially. Researchers have found that increases in gang killings in Chicago resulted almost exclusively from high-tech firearms available to young people, not more incidents of shooting.[17]

Why the Increase in Youth Homicide?

The increased availability of weapons does not by itself explain *why* young people have decided to use them with such frequency. Sociologists and criminologists have tried to explain the impulse to kill with a variety of theories: some cite a chemical imbalance in the brain, others cite an increase in television violence, and others claim it has to do with racism, poverty, and reduced opportunities for upward mobility. In some neighborhoods, carrying a weapon is clearly a way to gain respect and status among peers. This is espe-cially true in communities where traditional opportunities to build self-esteem—such as excelling in school or getting a job that pays a decent wage—are sorely lacking. "The inclination to violence springs from the circumstances of life among the ghetto poor—the lack of jobs that pay a living wage, the stigma of race, the fallout from rampant drug use and drug trafficking, and the resulting alien-ation and lack of hope for the future," sociologist Elijah Anderson wrote recently.[18]

Placing Juvenile Homicide in Context

The overwhelming tragedy of youth homicide must not be allowed to overtake our entire approach to juvenile justice. Juvenile courts in 1992 handled more than 1 million criminal cases, but only about 2,500 of them involved a youth accused of homicide.[19] If one sub-tracts the cases dismissed for lack of evidence, less than 1,000 youths nationwide were actually convicted of killing somebody in 1992.

There clearly is no reason to build new juvenile institutions just to house youths convicted of murder. Many of these youths already are being tried in adult court and sent to adult prison. For those who are not, there is plenty of space and ample resources to keep them in custody in the juvenile justice system. How we treat this fraction of youth killers—and how we prevent the many other juvenile offenders from heading in the current direction—is the most important policy issue in juvenile justice today.

Dealing with Juvenile Offenders

The big question is how states can design juvenile justice systems to deal with the violent offender as well as the more numerous lesser offenders. The goal of any juvenile correctional system should be to hold young people accountable for their behavior and to allow them the opportunity to develop the skills and confidence necessary to lead productive lives upon release. Over the past twenty years, a number of states, including Massachusetts, Utah, Missouri, Hawaii, Oregon, Montana, and Arkansas, have tried a more balanced approach with great success. The approach focuses on a combination of smaller facilities for violent youth and community-based programs for lesser offenders.

The majority of juvenile prisons and "training schools" in the United States are large facilities built to hold several hundred young people. About two-thirds of these large facilities house more people than they were designed to accommodate.[20] It is extremely difficult if not impossible to rehabilitate youth in such large and overcrowded institutions. When security becomes paramount—as it almost always does—conditions can degenerate into outright abuse. For purposes of security, incarcerated youth in the District of Columbia were kept in leg shackles while seated in an English class. A sign in the central administrative office of the facility said, "ALL THE KOOKIES ARE NOT IN THE JAR." In Florida, ten-year-olds sent to training school for petty thievery were hogtied (a person is hogtied when he is made to lie down on his stomach, his arms are twisted as far as they can go behind his back and toward his waist, and then both wrists are handcuffed to both ankles, forcing a painful arch in the back). After being hogtied, they were strip-searched and thrown into isolation cells—sometimes for as long as sixty days (a court declared the practice illegal in 1988, but it still occurs in some facilities around the country). In Idaho, children as young as thirteen were made to stand with noses pressed against the wall for as long as sixteen hours a day for such infractions as talking. "We're talking about kinds of physical and mental punishment that don't go on even in adult institutions," said David Lambert, an attorney who has worked to improve conditions in juvenile facilities.[21]

Some states have tried to modernize their juvenile systems by closing the large institutions and replacing them with smaller facilities that provide more intensive services. The most important feature of a modern juvenile corrections system is a wide array of treatment and educational options that can be applied to offenders individually.

Building Smaller Facilities for Chronic Offenders

Utah learned from the failure of its large juvenile training school. Three out of four "graduates" of the state's 166-bed Youth Development Center went on to commit new offenses on the outside.[22] Most of the youths were nonviolent offenders who were being turned into hard-core criminals while incarcerated. Key staff had agreed the large institutional approach was not working. "We were creating good inmates," said C. Ronald Stromberg, the superintendent of the facility. "We got the youth out of bed every morning, taught them how to pick up a tray, go through a food line three times a day, how to line up and 'march' to school, the cafeteria, and gymnasium, and we conducted head counts. When they left our facility we knew they'd be able to adapt quickly to prison life. What we were not doing was teaching them to be good, productive citizens."[23]

In the 1980s, Utah decided to close its juvenile institution. The state built two thirty-bed secure facilities. The smaller facilities were based on the premise that people would respond more positively if their surroundings were more humane. Each youth sent to a locked facility had his or her own bedroom. The common area had soft carpet and living room furniture. Meals were cooked and eaten together in living units of ten. Youths had treatment and educational plans tailored to their particular needs. Group and family counseling was available, as were services for drug treatment and sex offender therapy. The smaller facilities produced impressive results: in one four-year study, recidivism dropped by more than 70 percent. Judges expressed surprise that so many of the youths were able to lead lives free of crime.

There is no juvenile facility that can turn each and every offender into a law-abiding citizen, and Utah is no exception. Yet the success of the Utah approach in reducing criminality speaks for itself. Superintendent Stromberg noticed his staff had become more animated in the smaller facilities because they felt they were making a difference in the lives of the children. The number of fights in the facility and incidents between offenders and staff diminished markedly when the large institutional approach was scrapped. Contact with families and the transition into school and jobs also improved. "What we do know is that we are certainly doing no worse than we did under the old institutional system," Stromberg wrote in 1989.[24] Since then, Utah has kept the smaller facilities but lengthened sentences for some juvenile offenders in a new push by some elected officials to crack down on juvenile violence. But the thrust of the Utah system remains intact.

The Massachusetts Model

Massachusetts is often cited as a standard-bearer in juvenile corrections.[25] All of its large juvenile institutions were closed in the early 1970s and resources were shifted to privately run community-based programs that focused on rehabilitation. Currently, violent youths who need secure confinement are placed in one of fourteen small facilities around the state. Each of the facilities has between fifteen and thirty beds. Only about 15 percent of juvenile offenders in Massachusetts are placed in these locked facilities.

Nonviolent juvenile offenders are placed in group homes and intensive supervision programs that permit staff to individualize treatment services. Regional case managers monitor the youths as they are moved through a spectrum of care and security based on how they respond to treatment at each stage. If they do well at a given stage, restrictions are slowly lifted and the youths are able to enjoy more freedom and responsibility. If they do poorly or violate rules, restrictions are added until they improve their behavior. Most importantly, the Massachusetts system is committed to rewarding or punishing youths with certainty and speed.

Researchers have found that both violent and nonviolent youth in Massachusetts were much less likely to commit new crimes upon release than juveniles in other jurisdictions.[26] Even chronic violent offenders showed a significant decline in the incidence and severity of new offenses in the year after release from community programs. Although Massachusetts initially spent more money than most jurisdictions in developing its program for violent and serious offenders, the overall system costs are much lower over the long term because expensive secure confinement is used sparingly. It is estimated that Massachusetts saves over $11 million annually.[27]

There are a number of key elements that make the Utah and Massachusetts models effective. The success is due to the continuous case management of each youth, the availability of opportunities to build self-esteem through learning and decisionmaking, clear consequences for misconduct, enriched educational and vocational opportunities, individual and family counseling tailored to the needs of the offender, and an emphasis on making sure the child readjusts to the community *after* his sentence expires. There is nothing magical about these services. Taken together, they send a strong message to juvenile offenders that society cares about them and wants to bring them into the mainstream.

Addressing the Problem of Youth Violence

In 1993, the Office of Juvenile Justice and Delinquency Prevention (OJJDP), a division of the Department of Justice, put forth a document entitled *Comprehensive Strategy for Serious Violent and Chronic Juvenile Offenders*.[28] The prevention approach advocated by the federal government focused on minimizing risk factors (e.g., child abuse) that pushed youth toward delinquency and maximizing protective

How to Attack the Delinquency Problem	
A Plan by the Federal Government	
Individual Influences	
•Head Start	•Career Youth Development
•Mentoring	•Leadership and Personal Development
•4-H Clubs	•Recreational Activities
•Boys and Girls Clubs	•Literacy and Learning Disabilities
•Health and Mental Health	
Family Influences	
•Parent Support Groups	•Teen Abstinence/Pregnancy Prevention
•Family Crisis Intervention	•Parent and Family Skills Training
•Runaway/Homeless Youth Services	•Permanent Planning for Foster Children
•Court-Appointed Special Advocates	•Family Life Education for Teens and Parents
School Influences	
•Vocational Training	•Drug and Alcohol Prevention and Education
•Violence Prevention	•Law-Related Education
•Truancy Reduction	•Targeted Literacy Programs
Peer Group Influences	
•Gang Prevention and Intervention	•Community Volunteer Service
•Conflict Resolution—Peer Mediation	•Athletic Team Participation
•Peer Counseling and Tutoring	•Teens, Crime, and the Community
Neighborhood and Community Programs	
•Community Policing	•Neighborhood Mobilization for Community Safety
•Safe Havens for Youth	•Foster Grandparents
•Victim Programs	•Drug-Free School Zones
•Neighborhood Watch	•Job Training and Apprenticeships for Youth
•Community-Sponsored Afterschool Programs in Tutoring, Mentoring, Recreation, and Cultural Activities	

Note: **This is a summary of the plan created by the Office of Juvenile Justice and Delinquency Prevention of the Department of Justice.**

factors (e.g., family preservation programs) that encouraged youth to lead law-abiding lives. It was based on years of research by juvenile justice experts and represented an emerging consensus in the field.

The strategy of the OJJDP proposal was to strengthen those institutions that had the most influence over young people—families, schools, peer groups, and neighborhood and community programs. It recommended that policies be created that try to achieve the following objectives:

•*Strong families.* The family is the most important influence in the lives of children and the first line of defense against delinquency. Families must be given adequate resources and support to provide minimal care to children. Currently, there is not a state in the country that gives single mothers enough support to live at the federal poverty level. Day care is largely unavailable to the poor. If we are serious about having strong families, we must design programs that allow single parents the opportunity to gain job skills and become financially independent. Until that time comes, we must make sure their children do not suffer.

•*Strong core social institutions.* Schools, churches, and community organizations exercise great influence over the lives of adolescents and must be enlisted as partners in delinquency prevention efforts. Scott Harshbarger, Attorney General of Massachusetts, recently implemented a mediation program in high schools throughout the state. The number of incidents of violence dropped considerably. In other areas, churches are "adopting" at-risk youth to make sure they do not get into trouble.

•*Sound prevention strategies and programs.* Communities must take the lead in designing and building comprehensive prevention approaches that address known risk factors. Successful delinquency prevention strategies must be positive in their orientation and comprehensive in their scope. If a neighborhood needs a recreational center, it should take the lead in securing the necessary funds to build it. If it needs an after-school tutoring program, the community should help to design it. Government leaders must support such efforts with adequate funding.

•*Immediate intervention when delinquency occurs.* It is necessary to intervene immediately and aggressively with community-based treatment and rehabilitation services at the first sign of delinquent behavior, no matter how minor. If a child is missing school, intervention must take place. If he shoplifts a candy bar, intervention must occur. Too often, the system waits for a serious crime before it responds effectively. For people like Robert Sandifer and the young girl he killed, it was too late.

Successful intervention programs for first-time nonviolent offenders should be small, located near home, and maintain community participation in planning and operation. Programs can include mediation, community service, informal probation, day-treatment programs, restitution, and outpatient alcohol and drug abuse treatment.

•*Intermediate sanctions for lesser violent offenders.* Lesser violent offenders or repeat nonviolent offenders should be given intermediate sanctions that may be residential (where the youths live away from home) or home-based. Appropriate programs include drug testing, intensive probation supervision, weekend detention, inpatient alcohol and drug abuse treatment, rigorous outdoor programs, and electronic monitoring.

•*Secure confinement for violent and chronic offenders.* Serious violent offenders should be treated in a highly structured and secure environment. Large institutions should be closed and replaced with smaller facilities designed along the Massachusetts model, but adapted to local conditions. Secure sanctions are most effective in putting delinquent youths on the right course when they are coupled with comprehensive treatment and rehabilitative services.

Where Do We Go from Here?

The youth violence problem seems overwhelming only if we ignore immediate steps that can be taken to deal with it. Many respected organizations—including the federal Centers for Disease Control, the American Bar Association, and the Children's Defense Fund—have outlined violence reduction strategies based on years of research that are similar to the one put forth by the federal government. Indeed, a consensus has emerged among those in the field that the approach used by Massachusetts and Utah, if applied nationally, could reduce juvenile violence. The strategies have been at our disposal for years. What is lacking is the will to implement them.

Conclusion

The violence children endure and perpetuate in this country is a disgrace. Almost as shocking is the unwillingness of our leaders to take the practical steps necessary to do something about it. The federal strategy calls for prevention programs that reduce known risk factors for violence in the same way doctors try to reduce risk factors for disease. Risk factors for youth violence are many, but some of the most obvious are the prevalence of firearms and child abuse. Research shows that children are best able to avoid crime when they are provided with opportunities for healthy physical and mental development that involve families, schools, health care providers, police officials, and neighborhood groups. Most children already experience these opportunities as a normal feature of their lives. But for those who do not, it is our obligation as a society to see to it that they do—not only for their own benefit, but because it will make America safer.

SIX

WOMEN AND THE CRIMINAL JUSTICE SYSTEM

One of the more overlooked facts about the criminal justice system is that women suffer significantly from the failings of crime-fighting policy. Though men dominate prison populations in raw numbers, women are the fastest-growing category of prisoners nationwide. In the 1980s, taxpayers financed the construction of thirty-four prisons for women, compared to only seven in the 1960s.[1] In a 1990 survey, the American Correctional Association found that nearly half of the jurisdictions nationwide were planning to build additional jails for women.[2] Women offenders have been affected harshly by changes in sentencing laws, by the impact of the war on drugs, and by laws that allow for the termination of child custody if parents are imprisoned.

The imbalances of our crime-fighting policies are even more critical to women. None of our current strategies have stemmed the single greatest threat to the safety of women: domestic violence. The federal Centers for Disease Control reports that more women seek treatment in hospitals for injuries from domestic violence than from all muggings, car accidents, and rapes *combined*.[3] Women are far more likely to be killed by their husband or boyfriend than by a stranger.

Yet in an area where so much can be done to stem the violence, the machinery of justice is conspicuously quiet. This neglect puts millions of women, and often their children as well, in peril.

Women Behind Bars

The number of females behind bars has grown at a faster rate than men. In 1980, the number of women in prison nationwide stood at 12,331.[4] By 1990, that number had grown to 43,000. By 1994, the population of women in prison stood at 64,403—a fivefold increase since 1980.[5] If the jail population is included, about 100,000 women are behind bars on any given day in the United States.[6] In the 1980s, rates of increase in the number of women in prison surpassed male rates of increase for every year except one.

It should be no surprise that research on the racial composition of the U.S. prison population shows growing racial disparities in the punishment of women. A 1990 report by The Sentencing Project found that one in thirty-seven young African-American women aged

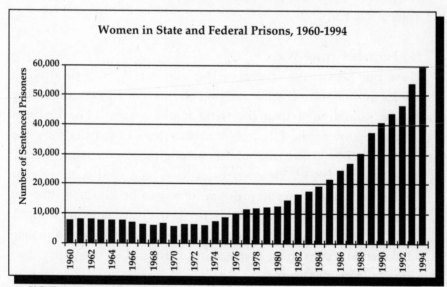

Women in State and Federal Prisons, 1960-1994

Source: U.S. Department of Justice, Bureau of Justice Statistics (1994), *Sourcebook of Criminal Justice Statistics, 1993,* p. 600; U.S. Department of Justice, Bureau of Justice Statistics (August 1995), *Prisoners in 1994,* p. 5, Table 5.

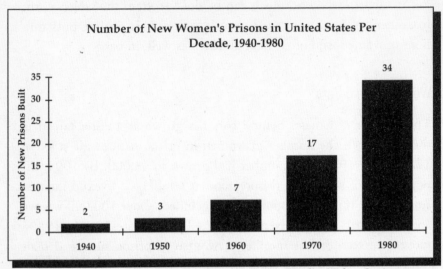

Number of New Women's Prisons in United States Per Decade, 1940-1980

Source: Chesney-Lind, Meda (1993), *Sentencing Women to Prison: Equality Without Justice;* paper presented at the Seventh National Roundtable on Women in Prison, American University, Washington , D.C., June 17–20, 1993.

18 to 29 and one in fifty-six young Hispanic women in the same age group were under criminal justice control. The rate for young white women was 1 in 100.[7]

No Female Crime Wave

These numbers make it appear that the nation is confronting a women's crime wave of epidemic proportions. Once again, the reality is more complicated than the trend might suggest. The Uniform Crime Reports of the FBI indicate that arrests of females for some violent crimes—assault and robbery among them—rose significantly from 1984 to 1993.[8] These statistics have been used to argue that the increase in women's imprisonment was to be expected. But we already know the FBI data tends to skew crime rates upward. A closer look at the evidence demonstrates that the increase in female incarceration results more from a shift in criminal justice policy than a change in women's crime.

A rise in the number of arrests of women would be a fairly reliable indicator that crime by women is increasing. If arrests rise but imprisonment rates rise even faster, then it suggests that women offenders are being treated more harshly and/or are being given longer sentences. This is precisely what is happening. Arrests for women have risen in recent years, but not nearly as fast as the level of imprisonment. Between 1984 and 1993, the population of women in prison increased 181 percent but the number of arrests increased only 37 percent.[9] Indeed, during the last three years of that period (1990 to 1993), the number of adult women arrested showed almost no change at all, but the numbers of women being sent to prison continued to increase.[10]

The "bait and switch" aspect of crime policy also helps explain the trend in women's imprisonment. The increase in arrests of women is accounted for mostly by nonviolent property offenses such as shoplifting, check forgery, welfare fraud, and drug violations. The percentage of women in state prisons for violent offenses declined from 48.9 percent in 1979 to 32.2 percent in 1991.[11] (See also chart below.) A study done in Rhode Island found that only 10 percent of the women were imprisoned for violent offenses. One-third of the

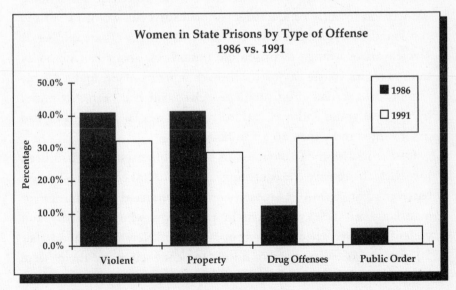

Source: U.S. Department of Justice, Bureau of Justice Statistics (1994), *Sourcebook of Criminal Justice Statistics—1993*, p. 614.

women in Rhode Island were serving time for loitering or prostitution, while another third were serving drug sentences.[12] In California, only 16 percent of the women admitted to prisons in 1992 had been convicted of violent crimes, compared to 32.7 percent in 1982.[13]

Women Are Less Likely Than Men to Commit New Crimes

Women are much less likely than men to commit a new crime upon release from prison. A study in Wisconsin followed women for two years after their release from prison.[14] They were found 44 percent less likely than their male counterparts to commit further criminal offenses. In New York, another study found that women prisoners had a much lower rate of being returned to prison than male prisoners: only 17 percent of female offenders were returned to prison, compared to 37 percent of male prisoners.[15]

Characteristics of Women in Prison

Most of us have images in our minds, stereotypes, of the women in prison, but the reality is much different. The American Correctional Association recently conducted a national survey of women in prison and found that three out of every four female prisoners are mothers.[16] Two-thirds of women in prison are minorities, about half ran away from home as youths, a quarter had attempted suicide, and a sizable number had serious drug problems. Over half had been victimized by physical abuse and over a third reported sexual abuse. Most had never earned more than $6.50 an hour.

Of the few women convicted of serious offenses, most had been involved in abusive relationships and had lashed back at their batterer. For example, most women convicted of murder or manslaughter had killed men in their lives who repeatedly and violently abused them.[17] A recent survey in New York found that 59 percent of women who killed someone close to them were being abused at the time of the offense.[18] A study of women in prison in Chicago found that 40 percent of those serving time for homicide had killed husbands or lovers who had repeatedly attacked them.[19]

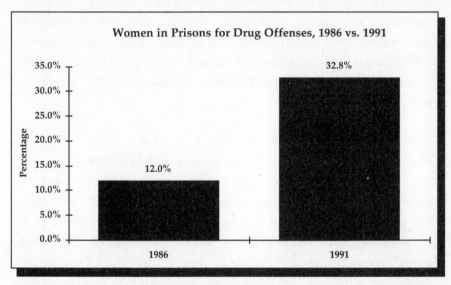

Source: U.S. Department of Justice, Bureau of Justice Statistics (1994), *Women in Prison,* p. 3, Table 2.

Women and the War on Drugs

We have talked of the effect of the "war on drugs" in driving up the prison population. In some respects, the impact of the drug war was greater on the female offenders.

Women in prison nationwide are substantially more likely than men to be serving a sentence for a drug offense.[20] Between 1987 and 1989, the number of women committed to state prison in New York for sale or possession of drugs rose 211 percent—compared to an 82 percent rise for men. A 1990 study by the Massachusetts Department of Correction found that 47 percent of sentenced women compared to 19 percent of sentenced men were incarcerated for drug offenses.[21] In Florida, drug admissions to state prison increased by 1,825 percent in the 1980s; for female drug offenders, the increase was a phenomenal 3,103 percent.[22] One out of three women in U.S. prisons in 1991 were doing time for drug offenses, compared to one in ten in 1979.[23]

Women and Sentencing

Many criminal justice practitioners operate under the mistaken assumption that judges treat women more leniently than men during sentencing. To the extent that women receive shorter sentences than men, it is largely because they tend to have shorter criminal histories and tend to play lesser roles in criminal activity.[24] A recent survey found that an estimated 51 percent of all women in state prisons had zero or one prior offense, compared to 39 percent of men.[25]

Mandatory Sentences Hurt Women More Than Men

Mandatory sentencing guidelines require judges to sentence men and women who committed the same offense to the same punishment. Under the guidelines, extenuating circumstances are often not given full consideration. This fact tends to place women at a disadvantage. One recent study found that the federal sentencing guidelines do not permit judges to consider the role of women in caring for children, the subordinate roles women play in many crimes, nor the fact that women are much less likely than men to commit new crimes after being released from prison.[26] Three years after full implementation of the federal sentencing guidelines, the absolute number of women in federal institutions nearly doubled.[27]

Mothers in Prison—Children Adrift

Disruption of family life due to parental incarceration is an increasingly serious consequence of America's criminal justice policy. Fully 78 percent of the women in prison have children. The failure to deal with the problem of children separated from their parents not only creates the risk of deep emotional wounds for millions of children, but may create more crime over the long run.

It is estimated that between one and two million children have at least one parent in prison at any given time.[28] Many more children have experienced the imprisonment of a parent at some point over the course of their young lives.[29] According to a 1993 study, these children are far more likely to become incarcerated than children of parents who never spend time behind bars.[30] The negative effects on children of parental arrest include traumatic stress, loneliness, developmental regression, loss of self-confidence, aggression, withdrawal,

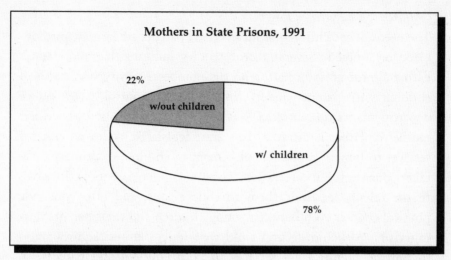

Mothers in State Prisons, 1991

22%

w/out children

w/ children

78%

Note: **Percentages include adult as well as minor children.**
Source: **U.S. Department of Justice, Bureau of Justice Statistics (1994),** *Sourcebook of Criminal Justice Statistics—1993,* **p. 616.**

depression, interpersonal violence, substance abuse, and teenage pregnancy. Only 9 percent of women inmates at the state level receive visits from their minor children, largely because most state prisons for women are geographically isolated.[31]

When a father is put behind bars, responsibility for his children is typically assumed by their mother. Ninety percent of the children of male prisoners live with their natural mother.[32] On the other hand, when the mother is imprisoned, the father does not generally assume primary care of his children. Seventy-five percent of children of female prisoners are placed with relatives other than the natural father or in foster care.[33] Separation of siblings and multiple placements are also more common for children of incarcerated mothers than they are for children of incarcerated fathers.

The desire to reunite a child with an incarcerated parent can obviously never justify the early release of a dangerous criminal. And one can certainly imagine instances when it would be better for a child to be separated from a parent who commits *any* crime. But it is in the interest of all Americans to minimize the collateral damage done to children by parental incarceration without jeopardizing public safety.

Children of Incarcerated Parents

The needs of the children of incarcerated parents are largely unrecognized or ignored. Several recent studies indicate that most states gather almost no information on the number, identity, and status of children with parents under criminal justice control.[34] Few police departments train their officers in how to handle children when their mother or father is arrested. Few state legislative codes provide for services to inmate parents or placement of children of primary caretakers during the incarceration. Local jails offer parents little access to the telephone, limit them to collect calls, and often preclude physical contact even between young children and their parents during visits. Although federal child welfare legislation requires states to provide reunification services to both children and parents, in practice these services are rarely provided to families in contact with the criminal justice system. In sum, these families have been left off the national agenda for family preservation.

Loss of Parental Rights

Parents who are confined for significant periods of time are at risk of losing their families through the termination of parental rights and adoption proceedings. This is especially true for incarcerated mothers. They frequently do not have family members available to care for their children and consequently may see their children placed in government-run foster care systems. About half the states have termination of parental rights or adoption statutes specifically written to remove children from incarcerated parents.[35] In the remainder of states, incarcerated parents can lose their children under regular termination procedures.[36] The threat of permanent loss of family is very real.

A Columbia University survey found that states have been unable to adjust their policies to deal with the growing number of parents in prison.[37] Historically, state laws pertaining to termination of parental rights and adoption were aimed at parents who voluntarily abandoned their children or mistreated them. The laws are ill-equipped to deal with the present situation, where parents are separated from their children through incarceration but strive to continue to be parents to their children. Sometimes a woman does not even know that termination proceedings have started until she receives a summons to attend a hearing. A close examination of state court decisions reveals that courts often treat incarceration alone as a sufficient reason for permanent termination.

Reducing Women's Imprisonment

The needs of public safety would be served more effectively if many women currently incarcerated for nonviolent offenses were placed in community-based programs where they could be rehabilitated and maintain ties to their families. Delaware provides a good case study of how this process can be carried out.[38]

The Women's Correctional Institution in Delaware was built to hold a maximum of sixty-six female inmates when it opened in 1975. By 1988, the prison housed an average of 145 women in severely overcrowded conditions. Later that year, sentencing consultants were hired by the state to assess the problem and to make specific recommendations to solve the overcrowding crisis. The recommendations included additional use of work release beds, increased residential drug treatment for addicts, and a day reporting program. It was also suggested that the state create a unit in the parole office to deal with problems of immediate concern to female offenders, such as obtaining child support benefits. By implementing the recommendations, Delaware soon reduced the female prison population and saved millions of dollars per year.

Though it has grown dramatically in recent years, the population of female prisoners is still small enough that a thoughtful effort to reduce the number of female inmates will likely show meaningful results. If the Delaware model were to be adopted by other states, much of the money currently devoted to building prisons for women could instead be diverted to support community-based programs.

Domestic Violence

Long considered a private matter, family violence is now understood as criminal behavior and a serious threat to public safety. And unfortunately, family violence teaches young children that violence is an acceptable way to solve problems. Children who learn this behavior are much more likely to commit acts of violence themselves.

Most experts agree that domestic violence is one of the most common crimes in the United States, yet it is extremely difficult to gather accurate information about its prevalence. Many victims do not contact police—usually out of fear that their batterer will find out and abuse them further. As a result, widely different estimates have arisen as to the number of victims of domestic violence. A leading advocacy group for victims of domestic violence claims that more than half of married women (about 27 million women) are beaten by men during their marriage and that more than one-third of married women (18 million women) are battered repeatedly.[39] On the other end, a survey conducted by the National Institute of Mental Health found that about 3 to 4 percent of all families—1.8 million—have members who engage in "severe" violence that includes kicking, punching, or using a weapon.

Whatever the estimates, domestic violence against women occurs so often that the U.S. Surgeon General in 1992 ranked abuse by husbands and partners as the leading cause of injuries to women aged 15 to 44.[40] Of the 3,055 women murdered in 1993 where the sex of the offender was known, 90 percent were killed by a man, and 29 percent of those men were husbands or boyfriends.[41] All things considered, women in this country are nine times more likely to be a victim of crime in the home than out on the streets.

Domestic abuse is not significantly confined by economic class or race. The Department of Justice has found that there is no significant difference in the domestic violence rates among racial groups.[42] Age, however, is a factor. Women aged 19 to 29 are more likely than other women to be victimized by an intimate. Also, low-income battered women are more likely to be counted in official statistics because they are more likely to seek help from public shelters and hospital emergency rooms.

Although battered women shelters are more numerous now than ever before, they still turn away the vast majority of women seeking shelter. In Massachusetts, shelters turn away five women for every two they accept and turn away four children for every one they take in.[43] Ninety-five percent of homeless shelters will not accept women with children, and those that do accept them tend not to accept battered women because the batterer places all women at risk.[44] More battered women are killed while attempting to flee the abuser than at any other time.[45]

Cycle of Violence

The cycle of violence that begins in the home tends to reach beyond the home as the children grow older. Many become abusive toward their own partners and violent toward people in general. One study found that children growing up in homes where violence occurred were five times more likely to be delinquent or unmanageable than those not subjected to family violence.[46]

Virtually all children living in a home where one parent assaults and terrorizes the other are aware of the violence. Children from violent homes are almost two times more likely to commit crimes against other people and twenty-four times more likely to commit sexual assault crimes than their counterparts from nonviolent homes. They are also six times more likely to commit suicide.[47] A different study found that males who witnessed violence between their parents were almost three times more likely to hit their wives than males raise in nonviolent households.[48] Research from the National Institute of Justice found that the odds of future criminal behavior increase by 40 percent when the person has suffered a history of child abuse.[49] The study revealed that child abuse increased the likelihood of arrest for juveniles by 53 percent. These studies, though differing in the details, make it clear that childhood abuse victims and witnesses are more likely to begin a life of crime, at a younger age, and with more serious and repeat criminal involvement.[50]

The same conclusion can be drawn by studying people locked up for serious crimes. The federal government has documented a high incidence of physical and sexual abuse in the histories of incarcerated violent juvenile offenders. In Oregon, 68 percent of the delinquent youths in treatment programs said they had either been abused themselves or had witnessed their mothers' abuse.[51] Another study found that incarcerated men abused as children were three times more likely than nonabused men to commit violent acts as adults.

Family violence has been linked to later homicidal aggression.[52] Almost all of the 2,000 inmates on death row in the United States have family histories of physical or psychological abuse.

Conclusion

Though the criminal justice system can arrest and punish perpetrators, we clearly must go outside the formal justice system to stop the cycle of violence that begins in the home. Policies should be designed to strengthen the family and improve the community response to family violence. They should help women improve their economic and educational standing so they do not depend on those who abuse them. They should fund enough shelters for victims of domestic violence and provide aggression therapy for those who perpetrate these crimes. The courts should hand down graduated sanctions for repeat abuse.

A more profound problem is that funds that could support programs to break the cycle of violence are instead being spent to build new prisons to incarcerate increasing numbers of nonviolent female offenders. Legislators in Hawaii recently proposed spending $200,000 per cell to build a new prison for women at the same time they were cutting hundreds of thousands of dollars from programs that provide services to women, including funds for shelters for victims of domestic violence.[53] New York recently spent $180,000 per bed to add 1,394 prison spaces for women at the same time thousands of women and children were turned away from shelters.[54] Additional money to build more prisons for women could be spent far better on programs designed to minimize the risk that victims of domestic violence will resort to violence to protect themselves.

SEVEN

TOWARD A NEW MODEL OF POLICING

fascinating turn of events unfolded recently in New Haven, Connecticut. On a street corner in a high-crime area—near the site of several recent gang shootings—a handful of young men stood nervously under a tree watching a stranger walk toward them. The stranger wore baggy pants, high-top sneakers, and a baseball cap. "He's cool," said one of the men under the tree, smoothing the stranger's transition into their community. In the background, New Haven Police Chief Nicholas Pastore stood watching.[1]

This was not a prelude to a drug bust, nor was the young newcomer an undercover police officer. He was T. C. Islam, a local community leader and perhaps the city's best hope for bringing peace to warring gangs. For days, members of two gangs had staged hit-and-run forays into each other's territory. Gunfire had erupted and innocent bystanders had been wounded. Infuriated residents demanded the police do something, but no SWAT team had been called in to quell the violence. "If we jumped in and did our police thing, the violence would've just escalated," Pastore explained.[2] Instead, the police asked Islam, widely known in the neighborhood and respected by members of both gangs, to broker a peace. A short time later the gangs settled their differences at a negotiating table.

It was no coincidence that the lead headline in the *New Haven Register* several months later read "Murder Rate Plunges." Under the tenure of Police Chief Pastore, crime in New Haven had dipped across the board as the city became a leading example of a modern version of an old concept in law enforcement: *community policing.* At its core, community policing is a philosophy that holds that officers should *serve* residents in a neighborhood rather than simply *police* them. In part, it represents a return to the old-style policing of the first half of the century, when officers lived in the neighborhood where they worked. Most police in large cities now live away from where they work—often in the suburbs—reaffirming in many ways that they are outsiders who occupy the inner city.

Many minority communities in America feel both *overpoliced* and *underprotected*—overpoliced because of the massive intervention of law enforcement in the inner city to fight the war on drugs, and underprotected because the drug trade flourishes with the same vitality as before, and because police are often slow to respond to 911 calls from minority neighborhoods. We believe modern community policing has at least the potential to provide neighborhoods in America with adequate police protection so that community vitality is strengthened. Nevertheless, community policing is only one of a variety of approaches to reduce crime.

Some police departments have had success recently with an updated version of the more traditional method of patrolling in squad cars and responding to citizen complaints as they are relayed by a dispatcher. Moreover, community policing has not been applied fully in most cities and clearly needs further experimentation. That said, we believe we need to learn how to police better before we add more police. If community policing can lower crime, it can also slow the growth of the prison population, allow criminal justice policy to rebound from its dependence on prison expansion, and help close the racial division created by our criminal justice policies.

Policing: Background

Given that they arrest and jail about 11 million people each year, the police occupy a frontline position in the criminal justice system.[3] They have the power to decide how to apply the law and determine the crime-fighting agenda of a community. They have wide discretion to decide who will be stopped and searched, which homes will be entered into, and which businesses will be inspected. If misused, that power can cause everything from a minor inconvenience to the destruction of life and property. If used properly, it can save lives and help make neighborhoods safer.

Police have an incredibly stressful job that offers modest monetary compensation. The dangers of carrying a weapon and enforcing the law in crime-ridden neighborhoods are well known. Most police who patrol the streets wear bulletproof vests—a device that has saved the lives of an estimated 1,500 officers since the early 1970s. Police must work all hours of the night, which puts additional pressure on family life. In most major cities, the starting salary for a police officer averages about $30,000.

There are nearly 600,000 sworn police officers working in the United States in more than 17,000 separate police departments.[4] Most police departments are in small towns and have no more than a dozen officers. Backing up the police are more than 200,000 civilian personnel.[5] The national outlay for police in 1990 was about $32 billion.[6] The 1994 federal crime control act earmarked an additional $8.9 billion for the hiring of up to 100,000 new police officers.[7]

It is uncertain whether hiring additional officers will make a significant difference in the crime rate. In our existing forces, most police officers do not spend the bulk of their time fighting street crime. In fact, about 75 percent of police time is spent on routine patrol or administrative tasks in the police station.[8]

Officers on routine patrol cruise in their squad cars until a dispatcher (after receiving a 911 call) informs them of a crime in progress or some other complaint that needs police assistance. In suburban areas, most 911 calls concern domestic violence, medical emergencies, traffic accidents, lost animals, or loud parties. And almost all calls come when it is too late to catch the perpetrator; it only takes a few seconds for a person to get away, whereas it often takes the police a few minutes to arrive at a crime scene. A reliance on 911 calls is central to the *reactive* nature of police culture in the United States—police react to crime after it occurs, rather than devising strategies to prevent crime before it occurs. On urban police forces, only 3 percent of all officers nationwide are assigned to crime prevention efforts.[9]

Traditionally, police understood their role to be enforcing the law and apprehending criminals when the law was violated. The primary measure of law enforcement was the quantity of arrests made rather than changes in crime rates. If the number of arrests in a city was high even though crime did not drop, police still considered their work to be successful. Many police departments pointed to high crime rates—as proven by an increase in arrests—to justify larger budgets, more high-technology equipment, and more officers.

Do We Need More Police?

In many cities, police complain that they are understaffed and overworked. It is an article of faith among many political leaders that more police will lead to less crime.[10] There is scant evidence this is so.

In a Kansas City study, the police divided the city into three comparable areas for research purposes.[11] In one area, patrols were doubled and sometimes tripled. In another, patrols were eliminated entirely, although the police continued to respond to 911 calls. In the third, no changes were made. After a year, the police checked to see how the crime rates differed in each of the three areas. There were no changes. The crime rates stayed the same in all three areas, and the public barely noticed the difference. Adding patrols had no effect on crime.

These findings are confirmed by comparing crime rates and police department sizes in various cities. In 1991, for example, San Diego and Kansas City had about the same ratio of police to population, yet Kansas City had twice as much crime reported to the police. On the other hand, San Diego had half as many police per capita as Cleveland, but both cities had comparable crime rates.[12]

Such figures lead criminologist Richard Moran to conclude that once a city staffs its police department, there is little additional benefit from employing more officers. "Adding more police may be good politics," he has said, "but it will do little to reduce crime and violence in America."[13] New Haven Police Chief Pastore agrees: "We don't need more police. We need to police better."[14]

Obstacles to Effective Policing in America

Most police departments are under extraordinary public pressure to reduce crime, and they operate remarkably well given the dangers officers face on the street and the scrutiny they are under by the public and the media. Nevertheless, we are struck by the fact that police departments in several major cities—New York, Los Angeles, New Orleans, and Philadelphia among them—have been saddled recently by major corruption scandals. The racist comments made by Los Angeles Police Department detective Mark Fuhrman, publicized during the O. J. Simpson trial, once again focused attention on the credibility of police nationwide.

Unfortunately, the problems of police mistreatment of citizens, corruption, and falsification of records have never been examined in a nationwide study. It is therefore difficult to determine with any precision the scope of these problems on a national level. Nevertheless, the available information makes it clear to us that some major police departments share serious institutional problems that hinder effective policing. We focus largely on two cities where extensive information recently became available because of public investigations into police activities—New York and Los Angeles.

New York City and the Mollen Commission

In New York City in 1992, Mayor David Dinkins appointed a commission headed by Judge Milton Mollen to investigate corruption in the police department. The Mollen Commission found shocking evidence that numerous police officers committed theft, protected drug traffickers, sold and used drugs, falsified police reports, lied in court, and treated citizens brutally and violently. One police witness told the commission that corrupt police officers "view the community as a candy store. I know of police officers stealing money from drug dealers, police officers stealing drugs from drug dealers, police officers selling stolen drugs back to drug dealers. I also know of police officers stealing guns and selling them."[15] The Mollen Commission concluded:

> The problem of police corruption extends far beyond the corrupt cop. It is a multi-faceted problem that has flourished in parts of our City not only because of opportunity and greed, but because of a police culture that exalts loyalty over integrity; because of the silence of honest officers who fear the consequences of "ratting" on another cop no matter how grave the crime; because of willfully blind supervisors who fear the consequences of a corruption scandal more than corruption itself; because of the demise of the principle of accountability that makes all commanders responsible for fighting corruption in their commands; because of a hostility and alienation between the police and community in certain precincts which breeds an "Us versus Them" mentality; and because for years the New York City Police Department abandoned its responsibility to insure the integrity of its members.[16]

The Mollen Commission found that corruption in the drug trade in New York was often the result of a "premeditated" effort by groups of officers. One former officer snorted cocaine off the dashboard of his patrol car and made $8,000 per week as a drug dealer. Other police officers raided drug locations almost daily for the sole purpose of garnering cash for themselves. Some of the corrupt officers beat up people so badly that a new phrase was coined to describe the activity: *tune-up*. An officer nicknamed "The Abuser"—because he loved to inflict pain—did not just steal from drug dealers on the streets. He set up a system where the dealers were required to make regular payments to him for protection. If they fell short on a payment, he would rob them with his service revolver. On one occasion, he was in uniform when he shot a dealer and stole a package of drugs. To cover up the corruption, officers filed false police reports and lied to authorities. The Mollen Commission concluded that the police department did virtually nothing to address the problem because it was more worried about bad publicity than the corruption itself.[17]

Lying and the Falsification of Records

The Mollen Commission found that the most common form of police corruption was the falsification of police records and testimony. Several officers told the Mollen Commission that the practice was so widespread in certain precincts that officers created a name for it: *testilying*.[18] To explain how they got around the law to make an arrest, officers simply made up facts. To justify unlawfully searching a person on the street, the officers would claim the person dropped a bag of drugs as they approached. To justify a raid on a drug den, officers would claim that they were tipped off by a confidential informant. To stop a car, the officers would claim it ran a red light. Even more disturbing was that supervisors tolerated and in some instances encouraged police falsification. Such lying not only violates the constitutional rights of citizens, it tarnishes the reputation of all police and makes juries less likely to rely on police testimony. It also makes it easier for criminals to escape punishment.

Just a few months after the Mollen Commission released its report, other stories of corruption came to light. Officers from a precinct in the Bronx were indicted on charges ranging from theft to insurance fraud.[19] Seventeen police officers and three sergeants were implicated, and they implicated officers in other precincts. To some degree, this indicates that New York City is effectively cleaning house. But it also suggests that corruption is so entrenched that it outlasts any particular effort at reform. In the past five years, police brutality cases have cost New York City $87 million in court judgments.[20]

Acting Under Pressure

In the summer of 1989, police stopped seventeen-year-old Charles Smith on a highway between Washington and Baltimore. They searched his car and found two grocery bags filled with marijuana. While in jail, Smith received a letter from the District of Columbia Police Department notifying him that he had been accepted as a police cadet. A few months later, Smith was out of jail and cruising the streets of the nation's capital as a police trainee.[21]

This remarkable turn of events exemplifies what can happen when police make hiring decisions in response to political pressure. In the late 1980s, the District of Columbia had more police officers per capita than almost any city in the country. Yet violence was rising and members of Congress were understandably nervous. Instead of crafting a broad-based anti-crime strategy, Congress ordered the city to either hire 1,800 additional officers or lose a $430 million payment from the federal government. The city agreed to hire the officers, but problems immediately arose. To quickly assimilate so many officers into the force, officials eliminated a written application procedure and failed to do background checks on applicants. An investigation by the *Washington Post* revealed a disturbing result: *One out of every fourteen officers hired during those years had been arrested for a criminal offense.*[22] Since 1989, 201 members of the 4,200-person police force in D.C. have been arrested and charged with a crime—some for behavior much worse than the civilian criminals they were supposedly policing. The charges range from shoplifting to forgery to rape and murder. In 1993 alone, 79 officers in D.C. were arrested—a rate of nearly 19 per 1,000 officers.

At the height of the recruiting binge, 1,000 people took a streamlined police exam that did not test arithmetic or writing skills. Only half of the 100 questions had to be answered correctly to pass. Smoking marijuana or PCP up to a dozen times would not disqualify an applicant. One in four applicants were accepted, far more than the national average of one in ten. In normal years, the psychological services unit rejected one applicant in five. But under this duress, it only rejected one in twenty. The *Washington Post* found that "class after class of recruits was rushed through cramped academy classrooms, sometimes with outdated materials, and sent to patrol city streets scared and unprepared. Some rookies did not even know the proper way to handcuff suspects."[23] Graduates of the two tainted classes accounted for more than half of the officers arrested since 1989, more than half of those involved in disciplinary proceedings, and more than half of the 185 officers prosecutors refused to put on the witness stand because they were so tainted by their own criminal problems that juries would not believe them.

Dozens of other officers in the District had criminal charges dismissed or dropped in exchange for internal discipline or resignations. But the record of criminal conduct of these officers is only the tip of the iceberg. These young men and women, barely meeting minimal selection criteria and inadequately trained, were given guns and badges and set loose on the streets. The damage done to the credibility of that badge is incalculable.

Other cities also have had problems with police officers committing crime instead of preventing it. The Philadelphia Police Department was thrown into turmoil in 1995 when a group of rogue officers confessed to planting evidence in drug cases, shaking down drug suspects and pocketing the money, and making false arrests. More than 2,000 criminal cases had to be reopened as a result of the police misconduct. In 1994 and 1995 in New Orleans, 4 police officers on a 1,400-person force were charged with murder and another 179 officers were suspended, disciplined, or fired.[24] When Officer Ronald Williams, twenty-four, was shot and killed during a robbery at a restaurant (he was working an off-duty security detail to supplement his meager salary), the main suspect turned out to be another police officer. It is perhaps no coincidence that with 425 killings in 1994, New Orleans had the highest per capita murder rate in the country.[25] "There is a lack of trust and confidence in the police in our city," said Eddie Jordan, the United States Attorney in New Orleans. "It reminds us of how thin the blue line is between civilization and anarchy."[26]

Corruption and Excessive Use of Force

After he was stopped by the Los Angeles police and California state troopers, Rodney King suffered a variety of injuries: nine skull fractures, a broken cheekbone, shattered eye socket, broken leg, partial paralysis of his face, internal bleeding, and broken teeth. While the King incident received worldwide attention, what is less known is the extent to which members of the Los Angeles Police Department (LAPD) were mistreating citizens in minority neighborhoods—and to what extent this mistreatment was occurring in other cities.[27]

Following the King incident, lawyer Warren Christopher (who later became Secretary of State) chaired a commission to determine if the Los Angeles police officers used excessive force on a regular basis. The Christopher Commission found "a significant number of LAPD officers who repetitively misuse force and persistently ignore the written policies and guidelines of the Department regarding force."[28] The Christoper Commission also found that LAPD authorities knew which officers tended to use excessive force but failed to discipline them. Performance evaluations for those officers who committed the most abuse were generally very positive.[29]

The National Perspective on Police Abuse

Police officers have a stressful job, but no level of stress can justify the mistreatment of citizens or the use of excessive force when making an arrest. Of all people in our society, it is police officers who are given the unique right to use force—including *deadly* force—against citizens.

After the Rodney King incident, police chiefs from ten major cities met and emphasized that "the problem of excessive force in American policing is real."[30] Commission member Hubert Williams, President of the Police Foundation and former police chief of Newark, said: "Police use of excessive force is a significant problem in this country, particularly in our inner cities."[31] In many cities, disrespect of minority citizens has eroded the relationship between the police and the community. More than half of all adults believe that police brutality is common in the United States and that it is more likely to affect minorities than whites.[32] In Los Angeles, the Christopher Commission found that a quarter of police officers believed "racial bias (prejudice) on the part of police officers toward minority citizens currently exists and contributes to a negative interaction between police and community."[33] More than a quarter said that this prejudice may lead to the use of excessive force. Mistrust of the police is also high among African-Americans: three-quarters of the African-Americans questioned in one national survey thought that police treated blacks less fairly than whites.[34]

Sparked by the Rodney King incident, the National Association for the Advancement of Colored People held hearings in six cities (Norfolk, Virginia; Miami; Los Angeles; Houston; St. Louis; and Indianapolis) on the issue of police brutality of minorities.[35] The subsequent report, written by the Criminal Justice Institute at Harvard Law School, represents a rare snapshot of police practices across the country. After hearing testimony from dozens of witnesses, the researchers found that for minorities *any* encounter with police "carries the risk of abuse, mistreatment or even death."[36] The report documented examples of excessive force, verbal abuse, unjustified searches, and trumped-up charges against minorities. The NAACP report also found that African-Americans were far more likely than whites to be shot by police and bitten by police dogs.

Despite the findings of the Christopher Commission, the Los Angeles Police Department has yet to completely change its practices. In April 1995, for example, an 800-member law enforcement task force conducted a series of gang sweeps in minority neighborhoods called "Operation Sunrise." The sweeps led to sixty-three arrests and received wide publicity. Yet it turned out that *just one person of those arrested was charged with a violent felony*. One police officer called the action "a big dog and pony show."[37] The audience for the show was not the residents of the neighborhood subject to the sweeps, but voters who lived in other districts. People closer to the sweeps resented the heavy hand of government. "If [police] want to get a promotion, they come get our kids," one African-American woman complained.[38]

Police mistreatment of minority citizens takes its toll on the confidence of all Americans in the justice system. During the trial of O. J. Simpson, a poll asked if people thought Simpson was guilty.[39] Seventy-eight percent of whites but only 22 percent of African-Americans answered yes. African-Americans and whites were equally split along racial lines over the not guilty verdict. In the poll taken during the trial, most African-Americans who thought Simpson innocent repeatedly referred to their distrust of police and illustrated it with examples from their own lives. They spoke of false accusations and mistreatment of themselves and their friends.

Where to Go with Policing

Those police departments with entrenched problems must reform their own institutions in order to win the respect of the communities they serve. Independent review boards with the power to investigate citizen complaints against police is one way to restore credibility and to minimize the chance that a small amount of corruption will grow into an institutional problem. Police must treat citizens with decency and improve their ability to communicate with all citizens, particularly those in the inner city, who are most victimized by crime and least trusting of law enforcement.

Before we examine community policing in detail, it is important to note that crime has dropped recently in other cities where community policing is *not* a central tenet of crime-fighting. Homicide in New York City, for example, was down 31 percent in the first six months of 1995 after police used the "squeegee strategy" to arrest thousands of low-level offenders such as the squeegee men who clean the windshields of cars at intersections. Misdemeanor arrests in New York increased dramatically, clogging the court system. Police Commissioner William Bratton and Mayor Rudolph Giuliani credited the increase in low-level arrests with the decrease in more serious crime.[40] We prefer to wait and see if the decline in homicide in New York holds before drawing a conclusion, especially because serious crime dropped in many major cities at that time, regardless of changes in police practices.

The real question is how to make the necessary changes so that policing can be responsive to citizen concerns. Under community policing, police officers are assigned by their superiors to a small neighborhood. Some are encouraged to own a home within their city and work out of a mini-station in order to gain a personal stake in the quality of life in their assigned area. The officers walk the beat and listen to the concerns of residents. By building trust between the police and residents, community policing makes people feel safer. It also makes it more likely that the officers will receive "tips" that will allow them to more effectively fight crime.

Community police officers also make arrests when necessary and act as firm as any traditional officer. They utilize traditional law enforcement techniques as part of a multi-angled attack on crime. In New Haven, for example, Chief Pastore was a leader of a task force that disbanded 10 drug gangs and jailed 200 people.[41] All police departments should still have the best technology and, if they choose, SWAT teams to deal with crisis situations. But the number and magnitude of such crisis situations, at least in theory, should diminish because of prevention efforts made by community police officers. Community policing is "more listening, more learning, more thinking as opposed to using the tools of the belt," says Pastore, a member of the Commission and one of the first police chiefs to put the philosophy into practice in an urban area.[42]

Police Work with Local Residents

Community policing recognizes that most crime control already is done informally by citizens in a neighborhood. When residents report suspicious activity to the police, leave their lights on to deter intruders, watch the house of a neighbor who is away, or make sure the local park has enough lighting, they are helping to prevent crime. Most street criminals avoid neighborhoods where residents look out for each other and take care of their surroundings. Therefore, a very effective way to fight crime is to strengthen existing crime prevention efforts and foster cooperation between the community and the government.[43]

Under community policing, residents must learn to identify and report not only crime but the precursors to crime. If they spot suspicious activity, they should notify police. If they see vandalism, they should make sure it is repaired as soon as possible. In turn, the police department must relinquish some of its control over crime prevention in the community. Officers must become community advocates and serve as a link between residents and law enforcement services.

Community Policing Strategies

There are two crucial ingredients to successful community policing: *neighborhood-oriented* policing and *problem-oriented* policing. These ingredients are subject to considerable variation as police departments adapt the philosophy to local conditions.

Neighborhood Orientation

Under neighborhood-oriented policing, small community substations or portable vans replace the central station as the hub of police activity. Decentralization makes it possible for individual officers to penetrate more deeply into the community. In addition, police officers become more visible. A more positive rapport with residents is crucial to gathering quality information. New Haven has even set up libraries in police mini-stations where children can do homework after school.

Paradoxically, increasing rapport with the community often requires the police to use careful judgment when enforcing the law. Success is achieved if fewer arrests are made *and* the crime rates are lowered. If there is a gang problem, a smart community police officer might try to organize a midnight basketball league to provide teenagers with the opportunity to engage in a constructive activity. Police must be seen as a positive presence that enables law-abiding members of the community to isolate and remove unmanageable individuals. Reducing the number of arrests for petty offenses such as loitering also frees police officers from doing the paperwork that supports each arrest. It reduces congestion throughout the criminal justice system by ensuring that only the right people enter it.

Home Ownership in High-Crime Areas

One way to integrate police officers into the neighborhood is to entice them to live there. Columbia, South Carolina pioneered this approach in 1991 by offering low-interest loans to police officers who bought houses in high-crime neighborhoods. "Now [the residents] know that officers do live among them, and that they do care," the police chief explained.[44] Large cities where many officers live in the suburbs should use low-interest loans to convince officers to live in those inner-city neighborhoods where crime is greatest.

Problem-Oriented Policing

The problem-solving dimension of community policing requires police to analyze problems and develop solutions. Police do not simply dispose of each case; they try to figure out why crime happened and how similar instances can be avoided. Problem-oriented police are much more active crime fighters and community actors. They practice what some people call "environmental criminology"—the practice of assessing the environment and adjusting it in a manner calculated to reduce crime.

The Broken Windows Theory of Policing

Central to problem-oriented policing is James Q. Wilson's theory of "broken windows."[45] Wilson has argued that if the first broken window in a building is not repaired, then people who like breaking windows will assume that nobody cares about the building and break more windows. Soon the building will have no windows. The sense of decay in the neighborhood will increase and social disorder will flourish, while the law-abiding citizens will be forced to hide indoors. The key to problem-oriented policing is to find and fix the broken windows as early as possible.

A police sergeant in Los Angeles put it this way: "When people in the district see that a gang has spray-painted its initials on all the stop signs, they decide that the gang, not the people or the police, controls the streets. When they discover that the Department of Transportation needs three months to replace the stop signs, they decide that the city isn't as powerful as the gang."[46] The spray painting is itself trivial. But as a sign to law-abiding residents that they should stay indoors and cede control of the streets to the gangs, it is important. A problem-solving police officer in Los Angeles organized neighborhood residents and Boy Scouts to paint over the graffiti soon after it went up. This simple step was an important dimension of a campaign to take back the streets.

Another example of the "broken windows" theory can be seen in the sleek and modern subway system in Washington, D.C. When the subway opened in the early 1970s, transportation officials decided to paint over all graffiti on a nightly basis to prevent the appearance of neglect. They devoted a significant portion of their budget to hiring the personnel to carry out this commitment. It was quickly noticed that the faster they painted over the graffiti, the less likely it was that vandals would paint it back. Soon, the problem of graffiti almost disappeared altogether. With no graffiti, the subway was more pleasant to ride and more people used it.

More Than Just Windows

Community policing is not limited to quality-of-life issues. It can also be used to solve serious crime problems. Police in Newport News, Virginia used problem-oriented tactics to reduce robbery and prostitution in the downtown business district.[47]

Consider first the traditional response by the Newport News Police Department to a complaint received in the middle of the night. A man called 911 from a downtown phone booth and said he had been robbed. A police officer arrived four minutes later. The man first said that he did not see the robber. After persistent questioning, however, the man admitted that he was with a prostitute he had picked up in a bar. They went to a hotel room together, where the victim learned that the prostitute was actually a man. The prostitute beat the victim up and took his wallet. The officer filled out a report and passed it to the next layer of authority. The victim wanted to let the whole matter drop. He refused to cooperate and the authorities had no choice but to abandon the case. The robber got away. Such incidents happened again and again.

When the city instituted a problem-oriented approach, things changed. Police officers identified and interviewed all twenty-eight prostitutes who worked in the downtown area. The purpose was not to make arrests but to learn how prostitutes solicit, what happens when they get arrested, and why they are not deterred. The police learned that the prostitutes worked in bars downtown because customers were easy to find. They learned that being arrested and released (or sentenced to unsupervised probation) were simply inconveniences that the prostitutes considered a cost of doing business.

Based on this information, the police formulated a response. They worked with the Alcoholic Beverage Control Board and local bar owners to move the prostitutes into the street, where they would be easier to spot. They asked judges to agree to give convicted prostitutes stiffer conditions of probation. Many of those convicted were required to stay out of the downtown area or go to jail for three months. Police made sure that convictions were obtained and sentencing sanctions enforced. In the meantime, police talked to the customers of the prostitutes and explained that half of those soliciting were actually men. The Navy arranged for the police to talk with incoming sailors to warn them that soliciting a prostitute was illegal and that those caught would be arrested.

In three months, the number of prostitutes working downtown dropped from twenty-eight to six. Robbery rates were cut in half. After eighteen months, neither robbery nor prostitution showed signs of returning to previous levels. The Newport News Police Department used the problem-oriented approach to reduce car thefts at the local shipyard by 53 percent in one year.[48] Burglaries at a low-income apartment building fell 35 percent after police worked with several city agencies to clean up trash, sweep streets, and have the landlord fix broken windows.[49]

Community Policing Has Reduced Reported Crime

Many cities throughout the nation have implemented some form of community policing programs, though few have gone as far as New Haven or Newport News. Baltimore has opened a handful of ministations. Many other cities have added officers to beat patrols. Citizens typically feel they are receiving a higher degree of service from community police officers even if crime does not drop. When community policing is implemented throughout a city, results can be dramatic. Not only did murder decrease by 36 percent in New

Haven, burglary decreased 21 percent, aggravated assault decreased 42 percent, and motor vehicle theft decreased 32 percent.[50]

Ron Hampton, executive director of the National Organization of Black Police Officers, contends that statistical measures of crime do not fully capture the benefits of the problem-oriented approach.[51] As an example, Hampton pointed to a family-oriented neighborhood in Washington, D.C., that was a home to a variety of people: doctors, lawyers, teachers, postal workers, construction workers, retirees, and young families. In the early 1990s, drug traffickers entered the neighborhood and began selling from vacant lots and on the steps of houses. They invaded the lobbies of apartment buildings to conduct business. Residents felt frustrated and helpless. The police decided to respond with a problem-oriented strategy. First, officers walked around the neighborhood and introduced themselves. Meetings were held to develop a plan to drive out the drug dealers, clean up trash, repair street lighting, and remove abandoned autos.

Once the plan was implemented, residents noticed that loitering in parking lots and on the street was greatly reduced. The drug trade was disrupted as dealers took their business elsewhere. Order slowly returned. Children began playing outside and older residents started taking evening strolls. Such improvements may not be reflected in official crime statistics. But by any measure, the quality of life in the neighborhood improved. The fact that the neighborhood *appeared* nicer to outsiders made the residents feel better about themselves and their community.

Not all police programs that fall within the rubric of community policing are as effective. Because the concept is popular with the public, many departments feel they must create at least one neighborhood-oriented crime program. When assessing a community policing program, it is important for residents to make sure it is comprehensive, that police officers and political officials support it, and that the officers solicit information from citizens and respond to actual concerns. Finally, there is no reason community policing programs cannot fit into existing police budgets. Barring start-up costs, community policing does not require more money than traditional policing. If successful, it can cost a lot less.

Some Cities That Use Neighborhood Patrols	
Baltimore, Maryland	Newark, New Jersey
Fort Worth, Texas	Newport News, Virginia
Houston, Texas	Oakland, California
Madison, Wisconsin	Philadelphia, Pennsylvania
New Haven, Connecticut	Portland, Oregon
New York, New York	San Juan, Puerto Rico

Obstacles to Community Policing

Like any bureaucracy, police departments can resist and ultimately defeat efforts to change.[52] When Nicholas Pastore tried to change practices in the New Haven Police Department, his own officers rebuked him with a "no confidence" vote. He then offered early retirement to veteran officers so he could hire new recruits who better reflected the racial and ethnic diversity of the city.[53] The philosophy of community policing challenges many of the basic assumptions of police bureaucracies and individual officers. Unless the change is carefully managed and police personnel are skillfully integrated into the new system, community policing is likely to fail.

Officers Should Be Given Proper Incentives
Police performance should be tied to the ability to identify and solve problems rather than the quantity of arrests. Rewards for strict adherence to rules must give way to rewards for innovative thinking. Performance evaluations must include an ability to relate to members of the community, an ability to solve problems with the least amount of force necessary, skill at steering addicted persons into drug treatment rather than jail, and work in the community to prevent gang membership.[54] A successful police force is one that keeps crime down, not necessarily one that keeps arrests up.

Training Needs to Improve
Similarly, training regimens must be modified to reflect new responsibilities and expectations. A 1991 study found that training con-

sumed just 1.1 percent of the average police department budget. The highest amount budgeted was 3 percent and the lowest amount was zero.[55] Many departments provide no additional training beyond that provided to recruits. Veteran officers cannot be retooled to implement community policing unless there is a budget for training.

In most training programs, recruits are made to memorize information and are taught correct solutions to predefined problems. They are encouraged to be tough and uncompromising. Much of the training focuses on the use of firearms, intermediate weapons (nightsticks, pepper spray, electronic prods), and unarmed combat. Such skills and weapons are vital for dangerous situations, but without additional training in problem-solving they will not be enough to implement the problem-oriented approach.

Police Forces Should Reflect the Communities They Serve

Police departments should as much as possible reflect the racial and ethnic composition of the communities they serve. It would be extremely difficult for an all-white police force to build trust in a primarily African-American neighborhood, or vice versa. Departments should also make efforts to assign officers to immigrant communities who are able to communicate with residents in their native language. While police departments genrally are committed to greater diversity, some have yet to make significant progress in hiring. In Los Angeles, the police force is predominantly white even though African-Americans and Hispanics comprise the majority of the city's population. Female officers also are underrepresented on police forces nationwide.

In New York City, efforts to increase diversity compete with the desire of many youths to follow their family members into the ranks of the police. Fully half of the white recruits in 1994 had a relative who was presently or previously a New York City police officer.[56] Many of them took the entrance exam as early as they could—often around age sixteen—so they could begin the process of joining the force at the entry age of twenty. Despite the desire of the department to attract more inner-city recruits, most of the new police officers were white and male and grew up in the suburbs. Though the population of New York City is more than 25 percent African-American, in 1994 the New York City Police Department was only 12 percent African-American.[57]

Conclusion

Despite the serious institutional problems facing some big-city police departments, most police officers are conscientious crime fighters who work under difficult conditions. Unfortunately, all police officers must pay a price for the major corruption scandals caused by some of their colleagues—scandals that in recent years have tarnished the reputation of law enforcement generally. One way to restore credibility is for municipal governments to create mechanisms to root out police corruption and to prevent it from arising. Cities should consider raising salaries so corruption becomes less a temptation and more qualified applicants will be attracted to police work. Police departments also must take the necessary steps to build credibility with the citizens for whom they work. Such credibility is a prerequisite to effective crime fighting. We believe it can best be accomplished by incorporating the philosophy of community policing into police departments. Before the federal government spends billions of dollars to hire more officers, it would be much wiser to first think about how existing police can be utilized more effectively.

EIGHT

THE APPARATUS OF JUSTICE: COURTS, PROSECUTION, DEFENSE, AND PROBATION

The trial of O. J. Simpson provided the nation with a compelling yet somewhat distorted view of the inner workings of the criminal justice system. It touched on several of the critical issues that hinder the creation of an effective crime policy: domestic violence, racism, police bias, and the role of the media. It also highlighted the difficulties courts have in dispensing justice to the accused and in providing crime victims with a degree of closure to their experiences. It did not, however, give a true picture of what the criminal justice system is like for the majority of people who enter it—people who, unlike O. J. Simpson, are of limited financial means and have no status as celebrities.

This chapter is devoted to understanding how some of the formal pieces of the criminal justice system are constructed and how they work. We recognize that each of the subject areas of this chapter could justify more material than will be presented here. Our goal is to briefly review each of these areas, describe how they relate to the themes in this report, and suggest ways they can be improved so the criminal justice system can function more effectively.

To begin, it is important to understand that the criminal justice "system" is not a unified system. It is comprised of a number of independent elements—the courts, the prosecution, the defense, and probation and parole departments—each of which has the capacity to move the system toward, or divert it from, the goal of making America a safer place to live. Just as important, each of these elements also has the capacity to preserve or violate the rights and freedoms of each individual who comes in contact with the criminal justice system.

Beginning with the police and their power to arrest, the decisions made at each level of the system can severely impact other elements. Yet there is no systematic process used in making decisions. Rather, each component is left to its own, often fighting for resources against other parts of the system. For example, if more police are hired there will probably be more arrests, which means more prosecutions. More prosecutions creates a burden on courts and generally results in more people on probation or in prison and on parole. It is a relentless cycle that does little to correct the many problems facing the criminal justice system.

We begin with the courts. In this chapter, we identify some of the key problems of the court system—including the roles of prosecutors and defense lawyers—and recommend ways they can make the criminal justice system more effective.

The Courts

The courts by themselves cannot stop crime. They can help deter crime through sentencing, but their mission is much broader.

Courts are charged with determining the guilt or innocence of people accused of crimes that have occurred. Their responsibility is to be fair to all citizens charged with a crime and to impose a just punishment on those found guilty. They must accomplish this task in a manner that reflects the basic human dignity to which every citizen is entitled, the gravity of the offense before the court, and the legal boundaries of our Constitution. Yet the courts often bear the brunt of criticism from people frustrated with crime policy. While the courts can do much to improve their performance, many of their problems are the result of flawed decisions made elsewhere in the system.

Courts Suffer from Excessive Caseloads

Like prisons, most court systems are overcrowded due to the rapid expansion of the criminal justice system. When new laws are passed and additional police and prosecutors are hired, more citizens are arrested and charged with crimes. But new judgeships are not automatically created, nor are new courthouses easily or quickly constructed. In San Jose, California, local officials estimate that the new "three stirkes" law will triple the number of jury trials, yet no additional resources were provided the county to handle the new caseload.

The result is often a long backlog of criminal cases. Since criminal defendants have a constitutional right to a speedy trial, civil cases—those cases involving business disputes or lawsuits between private parties—often wait years to be heard while the onslaught of criminal cases ties up most judges and courtrooms. Cases involving lesser crimes often get shunted aside: In the fall of 1995, New York City had an estimated backlog of 50,000 misdemeanor cases directly as a result of changes in arrest policies.

The Role of Plea Bargaining in the Court System

Courts have the capacity to try only a small fraction of criminal cases. More than 90 percent of all criminal felony cases end with a plea bargain. Were all criminal defendants to demand their right to a jury trial, the criminal justice system would grind to a halt. There simply are not enough courtrooms or personnel to accommodate more than a small fraction of the criminal trials that would result. Though plea bargaining is now essential to the smooth functioning of the court system, it is often criticized for bestowing lenient treatment on the guilty or coercive treatment on the innocent.

The challenge for courts is to achieve a fair result through plea bargaining. That requires that the plea bargain be based on a balanced assessment of the facts and the law. Most importantly, it

requires that the judge—the one impartial player in the courtroom—monitor the process and not allow it to be dictated by the
prosecutor, who holds enormous power during the plea negotiations.
Every plea bargain should be accompanied by a written statement of
the facts upon which the bargain is based. And to assure the public
of the fairness and legitimacy of the process, no plea bargain should
be accepted by a judge without first allowing the crime victim to
read it and comment on its accuracy.

Transfer of Sentencing Power to Prosecutors

With mandatory minimum sentences and truth in sentencing proposals, we have seen how the change in sentencing laws has lengthened the time many offenders spend in prison. Less known but
equally as important, it also has removed sentencing power from
judges and transferred it to prosecutors. For example, in a state with
mandatory sentences, the base sentence is determined in large part
by what charges the prosecutor decides to bring. If one man attacks
another man on the street, beating him badly, the prosecutor may
charge him with anything from assault to attempted murder. The
judge must sentence the defendant according to the statutory pre-
scription for the offense, regardless of any facts that may have led a
different prosecutor to charge differently or any mitigating circumstances. Before these changes, prosecutors made the charging decision and judges made the sentencing decision. The distribution of
power ensured that no single actor exerted too great an influence.

Mandatory minimums, "three strikes" provisions, sentencing
guidelines, and a host of other new statutes have resulted in
enhanced and usually severe sentences. The prosecutor's decision
whether to charge a person under those statutes—as opposed to
statutes carrying a far lesser sentence—fundamentally alters the
nature of the case. If the accused cooperates with prosecutors and
provides information on other criminal activity, then prosecutors
might reward the defendant by charging him with an offense that
does not carry a mandatory sentence. If the accused does not cooperate, or has no information to offer, prosecutors are more likely to

charge a crime that carries a mandatory sentence. The point is that much of the sentencing authority has shifted away from the judge to the prosecutor.

For courts to ensure that sentences are fair and that valuable prison space is not wasted on lesser offenders, judges must be given enough discretion to impose a punishment that reflects the severity of the crime and the circumstances of each case and each defendant. Sentencing discretion should be returned to the judge by repeal of mandatory sentencing laws. Flexible sentencing *guidelines* can adequately ensure that the will of the legislature is not superseded by the judge.

The Jury System

Most Americans dread being called for jury duty because the experience is often so unpleasant. The problem lies not with the citizens who form juries, but with the court system that creates them. Many jurors are subjected to endless waiting, insensitive questions, and discrimination by lawyers who want them removed because they do not believe a person of a particular race or gender could be sympathetic to their version of events. Juries in high-profile cases are sometimes sequestered—literally taken from their families and made to stay in a hotel—for months so they will not be tainted by publicity about the trial. Many jurors lose substantial income during a trial. Impaneling a jury can sometimes take hours, or in the case of a highly publicized trial, several days. Perhaps the worst outcome is that citizens—who should understand jury service in terms of civic responsibility—instead see the entire process debased by the maneuverings of lawyers and the inefficiency of the courts.

During jury selection—called *voir dire*—both lawyers and the judge question prospective jurors to determine if there is any bias against the defendant or the prosecution. If bias is apparent, either side can remove the juror for what is clearly a legitimate reason. Peremptory challenges permit lawyers for either side to exclude a potential juror *without stating a reason*. It is these challenges that most often are used to discriminate against citizens whom prosecutors or defense attorneys think will vote against them because of racial, religious, or personal characteristics. Even though such discrimination is illegal, the practice is common because it is so hard to prove an improper intent.

To improve the jury system, courts must first create comfortable conditions under which jurors work. Waiting time should be decreased and compensation should be increased. Policymakers should look more closely at the reasons behind peremptory challenges. And jury sequestration should only be used in extremely rare cases.

Services to Crime Victims

Courts must treat victims of crime with special regard for the pain and loss they have suffered. Victim support services should be available to provide restitution and psychological help, when appropriate, and to explain the procedural steps involved in a criminal prosecution. Too often, victims who are also witnesses are required to miss work and appear in court only to learn that the hearing or trial has been postponed or a plea agreement has been reached. Victims of crime should know the status of the case and be given notice if a plea bargain is being considered. If victims are treated with more respect, they presumably will be more likely to report crimes to the police.

The Prosecution

Perhaps more than any other actor in the criminal justice system, the prosecutor is responsible for ensuring that offenders are held accountable for their crimes. But justice does not require that *every* crime be prosecuted. If a prosecutor had the choice to pursue charges against five trespassers or one murderer, it would obviously be in the best interests of society that the murderer be prosecuted and the trespassers allowed to remain free.

Some crimes are more serious and require vigorous prosecution. Others can be handled more effectively and less expensively by a plea agreement to a lesser offense, participation in a community-based program, restitution to the victim, or outright dismissal. The goal of all prosecutors should be *a fair outcome that protects public safety,* not necessarily high conviction rates and long sentences.

In the American system of justice, the prosecutor always has had enormous discretionary power. The prosecutor decides whom to charge with a crime and which charges to bring; what evidence to divulge; what plea bargain to offer; and very often, under new sentencing laws, what prison term an offender will receive. If this responsibility is not exercised carefully, the innocent can be locked up, the guilty can go free, and the rights of all Americans can be jeopardized. Our criminal justice system must give prosecutors the tools needed to properly exercise this discretion, but not so much power that the system itself loses balance.

More Money, but Little Oversight

Prosecutors have more resources than ever before. The budget of the United States Department of Justice *quadrupled* between 1980 and 1992. The number of federal prosecutors during that time jumped from 1,621 to 3,883, an increase ten times greater than the population. Nationwide, budgets of prosecutor's offices jumped 230 percent during the 1980s to $5.5 billion.[1] (See chart on page 187.)

More Supervision of Prosecutors Needed

The increase in prosecutorial power has not been matched by improved management of the prosecutorial process. One would think the additional money for federal prosecutors would have gone to highly populated or high-crime areas, but that has not been the case.

Although Congress stated that illegal drugs and bank fraud drove the criminal justice budget increases, the areas that received the most money were neither major distribution points for illegal drugs nor major financial centers. A study by the Transactional Records Access Clearinghouse at Syracuse University found that the six districts receiving the most money from the budget increase were Hawaii, the western district of Michigan (Grand Rapids), the north-

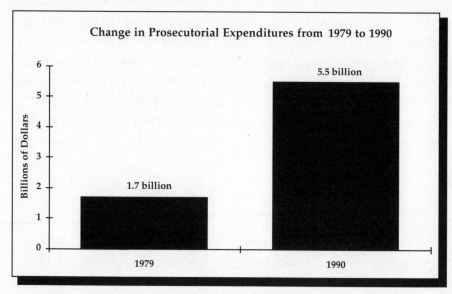

Change in Prosecutorial Expenditures from 1979 to 1990

Sources: Department of Justice, Bureau of Justice Statistics (September 1992), *Justice Expenditure and Employment, 1990,* p. 3, Table 2; Department of Justice, Bureau of Justice Statistics (August 1991), *Justice Expenditure and Employment in the U.S., 1988,* p. xix, Table F.

ern district of New York (Syracuse), Rhode Island, the northern district of West Virginia (Wheeling), and Wyoming. Those that got the least money were the places that needed it the most—Los Angeles, New York, Chicago, and other cities with significant financial activity and violent crime associated with the drug trade. The study found that the deployment of new federal prosecutors had been erratic and disorganized, with no central planning by the Department of Justice.

Personal Ambition and the Prosecutorial Duty

Prosecutors, who are usually overworked and underpaid, are often caught in a bind. Many of them know the uselessness of sending increasing numbers of lesser offenders through the criminal justice system. Yet many work conscientiously to keep the justice system running and to carry out the wishes of legislators who are mandating lengthy sentences for nonviolent offenders.

While prosecutors have considerable discretion within each case, they do not control the system as a whole. Prosecutors must follow the law as written. Usually, they are promoted on the basis of high conviction rates. Prosecutors cannot boast of how often they dismiss trivial arrests or drop charges against innocent people, though these are also important to the fair administration of justice. Some prosecutors even use high conviction rates or the trials of high-profile individuals as a stepping stone to higher office. The result can be an uncomfortable tension between personal careers and professional duties.

Defense Attorneys

When defense lawyers are mentioned, many Americans might have an image of the "dream team" of lawyers who represented O. J. Simpson. In reality, the defense team hired by Simpson operated with a level of resources that is highly unusual for an individual defendant.

The overwhelming majority of people accused of crimes cannot afford to hire their own attorney, let alone expert witnesses. In such cases, the defendant is provided *one* attorney (often called a public defender) by the government, not a team of lawyers.[2] This attorney might have the courtroom skills of the best private defense lawyers, but he or she might not. No matter what the level of skill or dedication, most public defenders have few if any resources to conduct the kinds of spirited investigations that led to the discovery of the Mark Fuhrman tapes. Nor do they have the funds to analyze DNA evidence independent of the prosecution, a process that can cost tens of thousands of dollars.

The public defender system in this country is almost at the breaking point because of a lack of funding. Public defenders may carry 350 cases or more at a time, and have several different trials scheduled for the same day. At times, the public defender might meet his or her client for the first time on the day of trial.

In Connecticut, the public defender's office handles about 75 percent of the state's major felony cases.[3] Each attorney who works in the office represents an average of 1,045 people a year. The National Advisory Commission on Criminal Justice recommends that public defenders handle no more than 150 felonies or 400 misdemeanors per year. In Connecticut, attorneys sued the state for money to satisfy the constitutional requirement that people accused of crimes be granted an adequate defense. Similar legal challenges have been brought in other states.

Some low-income defendants are represented by private attorneys paid by the government. Again, the shortage of resources has diminished the quality of defense provided. To save money, states have adopted unreasonably low fees for a case, a fact that discourages lawyers from spending more than a minimal number of hours on preparation. The federal government regularly runs out of money to pay lawyers who represent indigent clients, but not to pay the prosecutors.

Public defenders received just over 2 percent of the total spent on criminal justice by all levels of government in 1990.[4] Of the remainder, police (who serve as investigators for the prosecution) received 43 percent, prisons received 34 percent, courts received 13 percent, and the prosecution received 8 percent. The inability of the defense to keep pace with the resources of the prosecution has prompted the American Bar Association to report that the underfunding of indigent defense has created a "crisis of extraordinary proportions."[5]

The constitutional right to an attorney is meaningful only to the extent that resources are available to adequately prepare a defense. That includes access to investigators, expert witnesses, paralegals, and support staff, as well as time to research the law and prepare the legal motions. This cannot be accomplished if those who represent the indigent are required to represent hundreds of defendants at once, or if they are poorly paid and tardily reimbursed.

The inadequate support for public defenders is important because of the role they play in the scheme of checks and balances that keeps the system in working order. Defense attorneys are constitutionally assigned to protect the individual from the awesome power of the state: the right to a speedy and public trial, and the right to be informed of the nature of any accusation and to confront accusing witnesses, to be free from excessive bail, and to be secure against unreasonable searches and seizures. People often do not fully appreciate these rights until they have to use them. Public defender programs must receive the level of funding needed to invest the constitutional right to a trial with real meaning.

Probation and Parole

The roots of probation in America reach to 1841, when John Augustus, a shoemaker, visited Boston's criminal court. As a judge was about to send a drunk off to jail, Augustus intervened and offered to look after the man. Three weeks later, Augustus returned to court. The man he had taken was sober and remorseful. The Court soon gave Augustus other cases, and by 1878, Boston had instituted the nation's first full-fledged probation system for adults.

Probation today is the most commonly used sanction in the criminal justice system. In 1994, two-thirds of all people under criminal justice supervision, or about three million people, were on probation.[6] Most of the people on probation committed crimes of the lowest measurable severity—driving with a suspended license, petty larceny, and possession of small amounts of controlled substances.

Offenders who are put on probation are released to the community under the supervision of a probation officer. The supervision often consists of nothing but brief weekly or monthly meetings. Probation is usually combined with a series of orders that require the offender to stay away from a certain person or place, to abstain from using drugs or drinking alcohol, and to seek and hold a job. The average cost of probation is about $850 per offender per year. In many states, probationers are required to contribute earnings toward the cost of supervision.

Few people believe the probationary system is successful in helping to reduce crime in America. This is not surprising in light of the fundamental shift in the goals and priorities of probationary sentences. In the 1960s and 1970s, probation officers believed that their mission was to rehabilitate offenders, whom they regarded as clients. The goal was to increase community safety by supervising offenders closely and helping them adjust to community life. Probation officers helped their clients to find work, overcome drug problems, and maintain family and community responsibility. In the 1980s, probation systems reacted to the harsher political climate and recast their role in terms of punishment. They focused on catching offenders for violations and largely abandoned efforts to help the offender solve the problems that may have led to the offense.

Like other parts of the system, most probation programs are bogged down with huge caseloads. While a caseload of approximately 30 probationers is considered optimal, most probation officers carry caseloads of 200 and higher. The volume alone prevents most probation officers from getting actively involved with offenders in an individualized manner, either in a supportive or punitive capacity. Offenders who commit income tax evasion and those who commit armed robbery require different strategies. All too often a leveling phenomenon results where everyone gets a little attention, but few receive the individual supervision they need. One man under supervision in California said his supervisor would not help him find a job. He continued:

> I mean, it's not really his fault because he got three hundred other guys. And he doesn't even know me. All he knows is my number is three seven such and such. All he knows is . . . if he wants to keep his job, all he got to do is have me come in once a week, piss in the bottle. As long as the bottle don't show no drugs in it, I can stay on the streets another week. First time the piss is not good, all he gotta do is send me to jail, that's it. He put my file back over there in "inactive" and that's it.[7]

Such a system does little to protect public safety. It also does little to keep offenders out of trouble or to help them get their lives in order.

The problem is not the *concept* of probation, but the implementation. If probation officers had the resources to properly supervise and assist offenders, and if they understood their role as more than detecting violations, probation would be more effective.

Intensive Probation
Intensive probation is a program that monitors the offender much more closely than traditional probation. Offenders in this program

usually must contact their probation officer more than once per week, sometimes on a daily basis. While more expensive than ordinary probation, intensive probation permits the safe release of more serious offenders into the community. It costs an average of $2,912 per offender per year—much less than prison.[8]

An intensive probation program in Georgia was designed for serious nonviolent offenders. It assigned two probation officers to twenty-five offenders and scheduled at least five face-to-face contacts each week.[9] The total cost of a single probationer was about one-seventh the cost of operating a prison bed in Georgia. At the first evaluation, the failure rate was just 16 percent, with only 0.8 percent of the probationers committing a violent crime and none causing serious injury. Other intensive supervision programs have reported higher failure rates, but that appears due to the extremely close monitoring rather than heightened criminal activity.[10]

Intensive probation is one of the most underutilized alternatives to incarceration. It is often the first program to be scaled back when spending is reduced, largely because it is considered "soft" on offenders. Most probation officers around the country currently are set up to fail. With each probation officer supervising more than 100 offenders, it is impossible to provide anything but the most minimal supervision. The solution should be more supervision, not less. If one considers the $22,000 annual expense of incarcerating a prisoner, the economics of probation become compelling. A single probation officer can intensively supervise anywhere from 20 to 30 offenders with enormous effect at a fraction of the cost of prison for each offender.

Parole: The Transition from Incarceration to Freedom

Most prisoners are not released into complete freedom. They must first spend a number of years under the supervision of the department of parole. Though often misunderstood, parole serves a number of important functions. It allows the government to supervise offenders after release to help minimize the risk that they will commit new crimes. While in prison, it motivates offenders to follow the rules and take part in programs (successful completion of such programs usually impresses the parole board). People who are incarcerated with no possibility of parole have less incentive to take part in treatment programs and respect other inmates or guards.

Unfortunately, many parole officers see their jobs as limited to catching violators, rather than helping parolees deal with the problems involved in readjusting to life on the outside. When technical violations (e.g., missing a meeting) are observed, those on parole should be held accountable in some manner but not necessarily returned to prison. This is seldom done. For example, California parolees are supervised so tightly that most parolees end up right back behind bars—*even if they have not done anything criminal*. In 1991, nearly half of the people in California state prisons were there for technical violations of release, that is, violation of a condition of parole that did not itself warrant a new criminal charge.[11] Most technical parole violations could be successfully and less expensively handled without reimprisoning the offender.

An alternative approach to parole would be to provide support services to increase the likelihood that the parolee will successfully make the transition from prisoner to citizen. In Virginia, when inmates are released from prison they are given $25 and a bus ticket.[12] Unless the offender has a support network on the outside or has received training and treatment while in prison, such a release is a recipe for disaster. Virginians disappointed with supposed parolee misconduct are currently considering measures designed to eliminate parole altogether. They are not, however, considering an increase in parole supervision designed to help released inmates succeed. Such improved supervision can be a far superior means of ensuring the safety of the community at an affordable cost.

Conclusion

American courts provide for an adversarial system of justice comprised of three components: the prosecution, the defense, and the judge. The prosecution and the defense are the adversaries; the judge is the neutral arbiter and the dispenser of justice. In recent years, power in the system has shifted dramatically from the judge to the prosecutor. This shift has upset the balance of power within the justice system and threatens to crack the traditional constraints of checks and balances that keep the justice system in working order. Shifts in probation and parole mirror these imbalances. As we try to reform the criminal justice system to deal with modern problems, we must be careful not to lose sight of the importance of this balance.

NINE

PATHWAY TO A SAFER SOCIETY: 2020 VISION

The best lesson we can learn about the American criminal justice system comes from a story of two brothers who wanted to earn some extra money. In the heat of the summer they decided to open a stand to sell tomatoes. The brothers drove all night to a farm and purchased a truckload of tomatoes for 50 cents per pound. Early the next morning they opened their stand. They sold their product for 50 cents per pound. Demand proved enormous, and by the end of the day they had sold all of their supply. At first the brothers were impressed with the fullness of the cash drawer. But when they compared the earnings to the money they had spent to buy the tomatoes, they discovered they had not earned anything at all. Including the costs of the overnight haul, they had actually lost money.

The young men were undaunted and they decided to try again. To ensure a profit next time, they decided to do things differently. Next time they decided to buy more tomatoes.

For the past twenty years, criminal justice practices and policies have been much like the business practices of the brothers: so profoundly ill-conceived that they are destined to fail. As the failures have accumulated, the justice system has responded by adding more of the same policies.

Prison and jail populations in this nation have tripled since 1980 and law enforcement expenditures have quadrupled, but polls show that most Americans do not feel safe. Legislatures lengthen sentences and add more mandatory minimum penalties. More police are hired, more prisons are built. Still, we do not feel safe. In response, policymakers continue to expand the same criminal justice apparatus: more enforcement, longer sentences, more prisons.

If this "get tough" strategy worked, the results would be apparent by now. They are not. If America is ever going to be a safer society, we need a fundamentally new approach with a clear goal against which we can measure our progress. Selling ever more tomatoes at the purchase price will never yield a profit.

That goal: to change crime and social policy so that our rates of incarceration and rates of violence are normal by the standards of the industrialized world. As a nation, the United States should be outstanding in many areas. But we should not be outstanding in our rate of homicide or rate of imprisonment. The Commission believes that if our nation wanted to get serious about changing its criminal justice policy, we could reach our goal in one generation.

We use this benchmark goal because we believe it is sufficiently ambitious and attainable by the year 2020. Our rate of incarceration is 555 per 100,000 citizens; our homicide rate is about 9 per 100,000 (that means each year 9 out of every 100,000 citizens are killed by homicide). In Canada, the incarceration rate is 116 per 100,000 citizens and the homicide rate is 2.2 per 100,000. In Australia, the rate of incarceration is 91 per 100,000 citizens and the rate of homicide is 1.9. Most countries in Europe have the same general numbers, or lower.

What do these countries do differently than us? They have highly developed social safety nets that protect children from poverty. They have severe restrictions on the availability of firearms. They have much shorter prison sentences for nonviolent crimes, and their prisons have a much greater emphasis on rehabilitation. We believe the adoption of similar policies in the United States will provide us with a realistic chance of moving in the direction of greater safety and lower rates of imprisonment.

We know that some things work to make us safer. We need the political courage to do those things. For example, we know that most violent crime is committed by friends and family, not strangers on the street. Yet we refuse to commit funding to introduce an anti-violence curriculum in the schools or to provide counseling and emergency shelter to those who are battered and abused in the home. We must commit ourselves to funding anti-violence programs for schools and shelters for all those who need them.

We know that *overall* crime rates in the United States are no greater than crime rates in most industrialized countries, and that only our rate of *homicide* is unique. Yet Congress is unwilling to enact laws to significantly curtail the deadly firearms that are now available on the streets. Our Congress needs to enact meaningful gun control legislation at the federal level that applies to every state and locality.

We know that we must distinguish between violent and nonviolent crime, and design policies that securely imprison the violent offender while using less costly non-prison sanctions for nonviolent offenders. Yet we refuse to invest in such sanctions and continue to squander scarce prison space on nonviolent offenders. We need to fund the development of a host of sanctions that are tougher than probation but not as expensive as prison—things like intensive probation, house arrest, drug treatment, and boot camps with aftercare services.

We know that police enforcement of low-grade drug offenses has a disproportionate impact on the minority community, yet we continue to arrest African-Americans for drug offenses five times as often as whites even though the two races use drugs at roughly the same rates. We must address the heavy impact of police enforcement of the war on drugs in minority communities, and we must root out racial bias at those points in the criminal justice system where it occurs. We can accomplish this most effectively by calling off the "war" on drugs and replacing it with a harm-reduction approach that treats drug addiction as a public health challenge rather than a criminal justice problem.

We know that a criminal record makes a person less employable, creating an economic drain on society, yet we continue to arrest millions of people each year who spend an average of only a few days in jail for minor crimes. Our enforcement policies not only stigmatize large sections of the population as they are entering the job market, they leave our communities without adequate money to provide drug treatment, improve education, create jobs, or fight poverty—the very things that we know will prevent crime.

We know that children born into a low-income household have a greater risk of becoming violent, and that the United States tolerates the highest rate of child poverty in the industrialized world, yet we fail to provide funding for early childhood development programs that are proven to lower crime rates. We must resolve ourselves to provide funding for Head Start and other childhood development programs intended to provide all children with a fair start in life. We must support families and make sure parents have the resources to care for their children.

We know that most women in prison are primary caregivers to their children, and that children of incarcerated parents are far more likely to grow up to commit crimes, yet we fail to utilize community-based programs that allow mothers to remain with their children while they receive drug treatment, develop parenting skills, and participate in job training. And although we know that maintaining family contact is crucial, we lock up most women offenders in facilities far removed from their communities, thereby making family visitation all but impossible. There are many successful community programs that allow mothers to remain with their children while they receive drug treatment and job training. These programs must be made available to nonviolent women who are incarcerated.

We know that community policing builds trust with citizens and has enormous potential to prevent crime, yet we continue to reward police based on the traditional criteria of how many arrests an officer makes. Police departments around the country must adopt problem-oriented community policing and begin to reward officers based on how effectively they prevent crime while making the *fewest* number of arrests.

We know that most juvenile crime is nonviolent, and that small, community-based programs are far more effective in the rehabilitation of juvenile offenders than large state institutions. Yet we continue to warehouse large numbers of juvenile offenders in what are essentially prisons for young people—mixing together the majority of nonviolent offenders with the minority of violent offenders—and fail to offer meaningful training, drug treatment, or educational programs. Youthful offenders must be provided opportunities for rehabilitation and vocational training; nonviolent offenders must not be warehoused with violent offenders; and violent offenders must be placed in small, secure facilities where they can receive intensive treatment services.

And we know that most prisoners will eventually return to society. We must equip them to do so, so they will be less likely to commit new crimes. For those prisoners who need it, we must provide drug treatment and literacy and job training. We must abolish long sentences for nonviolent offenders and provide a full range of support to offenders who return to our communities.

We know many things must work together to reduce crime, yet for two decades we have continued to rely almost completely on one line of responses: more aggressive enforcement and longer prison terms.

What follows are eleven recommendations to fundamentally shift the direction of crime policy in the United States, so that all Americans will be safer, and our tax dollars will be used effectively.

Recommendation 1

Adopt a three-year moratorium on new prison construction until a systematic assessment of prison needs can be completed. Replace some prison sanctions with alternative programs that are less expensive and often more effective at reducing crime.

We believe a voluntary three-year moratorium on new prison construction will allow states to systematically examine whether all offenders currently imprisoned might be better served by a non-prison sanction. To decrease our reliance on prison as the primary response to crime, we need to develop a wide range of intermediate sanctions so there will be more options at sentencing.

Our current system is one of extremes. Sentencing judges must choose between ineffective probation or prison. It is like asking a doctor for relief from a headache and being told the only treatments are baby aspirin or a lobotomy. Moreover, we do not have a good mechanism to ensure that the harshest punishments are reserved for the most serious offenders.

Many non-prison punishments exist but are not widely available because of funding limitations.[1] These noncustodial punishments include:

- intensive probation
- day reporting centers
- work release
- halfway houses
- fines
- compensation for victims
- boot camps
- community service
- home detention
- curfews
- drug treatment
- electronic monitoring
- diversion

An emphasis on non-prison sanctions would benefit American taxpayers, since they are cheaper than prison. It costs taxpayers on average $22,000 per year to imprison one offender. Including the hidden costs of incarceration, the actual cost is much higher. Thus, the government can spend thousands of dollars per offender per year on non-prison sanctions and still come out ahead. Most non-prison sanctions cost less than half as much as prison. Taxpayers can pocket the savings or spend them on crime prevention programs.

Recommendation 2

Replace the war on drugs with a policy of harm reduction where the police work with public health and other professionals to stem substance use. Substance abuse should be treated as a public health challenge rather than a criminal justice problem.

By replacing the war on drugs with a policy of harm reduction, we will take a major step toward solving two problems caused by our crime control policies. First, we will relieve our crowded jails and prisons of the responsibility for locking up huge numbers of less serious offenders. Second, discouraging police crackdowns in minority neighborhoods will slow the growth of the racial disparities that are hurtling the nation toward a catastrophe in its race relations. The policy is called "harm reduction" because it is designed to minimize the harmful effects of drug use.

For several years, the war on drugs has been fought in earnest with few tangible results but devastating collateral consequences. While $100 billion has been spent over the last five years prosecuting the drug war, illegal drug use continues at the same levels and drugs available on the streets have not declined in their level of potency. The purpose of harm reduction is to minimize the harmful effects of drug use rather than to wage a war against drug users. It recognizes that the drug trade is driven mostly by demand created by addicts, many of whom commit crimes to support their habit. Harm reduction does not mean that police will stand on the sidelines when drugs threaten a neighborhood. It simply means that public health professionals will be afforded the opportunity to coax addicts into treatment programs, and that options after arrest will include drug treatment rather than just prison. For those who must spend time in prison, drug treatment should be made available in the prison setting.

Harm reduction includes the following elements:

1. The availability of drug treatment facilities so that all addicts who wish can overcome their habits and lead drug-free lives.

2. The use of health professionals to administer drugs to addicts as part of a treatment and detoxification program.

3. Needle exchange programs that will slow the transmission of HIV and educate drug users about how HIV is contracted and spread.

4. Special drug courts or pretrial diversion programs that compel drug treatment; the drug courts in Dade County (Miami), Florida, are an excellent model.

Harm reduction is necessary because drug abuse does not respond well to punishment. Drug cravings are irrational. When addicts want a fix, they will do almost anything to satisfy it. Most drug users do not care if the punishment is one year or five years in prison. The best way to change the addict's behavior is to eliminate the craving for the fix. Drug treatment should thus be the cornerstone of an effective drug control policy. Enforcement should focus on hard-core addicts, violent drug users, and drug distribution channels.

We recommend harm reduction because of the increasing evidence that drug treatment is effective at reducing crime and saving money. A statewide study in California found that every dollar spent on substance abuse treatment saved taxpayers seven dollars in lowered crime and health care costs.[2] The study also found that the level of criminal activity by participants decreased by 66 percent following treatment. The number of crimes involving a weapon or physical force declined by 71 percent. In the District of Columbia, where the cost of in-house drug treatment is one-tenth the cost of incarceration, inmates who are treated before release have less than half the recidivism rate of untreated inmates (see charts on page 203).

The private sector has a history of success in treating drug addiction. The nonprofit Phoenix House runs residential and outpatient programs in New York and California. In New York, the Phoenix House charges $37 per day for adults; prison in New York costs $67.40 per day.[3] Most importantly, more than 93 percent of those who take part in the Phoenix House program have not committed a new offense five years after the end of treatment.

Despite its effectiveness in reducing crime, drug treatment remains largely ignored by the criminal justice system. Three out of every four men in California prisons have a history of drug use, but

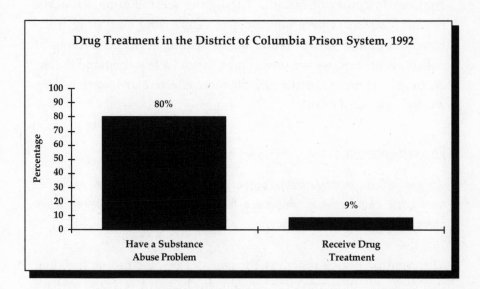

Drug Treatment in the District of Columbia Prison System, 1992

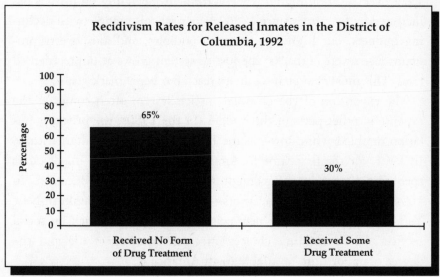

Recidivism Rates for Released Inmates in the District of Columbia, 1992

Source: Information provided by the Office of Planning Analysis, District of Columbia Department of Corrections.

only 10 percent are involved in a drug treatment program. Only 1 percent receive comprehensive full-term treatment as defined by the National Institutes of Health. The figures are the same across the nation. Most cities have long lines of people who *want* drug treatment and cannot get it. While we are willing to spend millions of dollars on prisons, we are unwilling to spend a few thousand dollars on treatment programs that are far more effective at lowering drug use and associated crime.

Recommendation 3

Criminal justice spending must be cost-effective, so it does not drain resources from other civic activities. Require a fiscal impact statement before major changes are made to crime policy.

The criminal justice system is the one area of government spending that continues to escape close scrutiny. In the past five years, we have spent over $400 billion on law enforcement. Spending on prisons has increased by five times since 1980. As our schools grapple with declining budgets, our highways fill with potholes, and antipoverty programs face severe cutbacks, the justice system grows at unprecedented rates. This must change if we are to reach our benchmark goals.

The expansion of the criminal justice system often comes at the expense of other parts of the budget. In the 1980s, the prison population doubled while low-income housing was slashed dramatically. In 1991, for the first time in American history, several major cities spent more on law enforcement than on secondary education. In 1994 and 1995, several governors—including George Pataki in New York—proposed building new prisons while cutting back on social services. These funding choices affect the quality of life and the degree of opportunity available to all Americans.

To ensure a better balance in criminal justice spending, all proposed changes in crime policy must be accompanied by a *fiscal impact statement*. This statement should be similar to a business plan. It should state how much the initiative will cost, how it will be paid for, and its expected rate of return. For example, legislators proposing a truth in sentencing law should be required to assess the cost and analyze its impact on other parts of the budget. The same should apply to those proposing "three strikes" legislation.

Criminal justice costs should be viewed as part of the larger budget. A city that expands its jail is a city that has less money to spend on youth programs that can prevent violence. We need to restore a sense of balance to criminal justice spending so we can strengthen communities, respond to victims of crime, provide opportunities to those at risk of turning to crime, and ensure adequate prison space for violent offenders. Policymakers must think of the entire system at once when allocating resources to fight crime.

Recommendation 4

Restore the internal balance of the criminal justice system so that judges can impose punishments that fit the crime and the accused.

This recommendation will give our courts the flexibility they need to lower our rates of incarceration by sentencing more nonviolent offenders to non-prison sanctions.

We have shown how strict sentencing laws shifted much of the power in the criminal justice system from the judge to the prosecutor. This shift has upset the traditional balance of power in the justice system. The enhanced power of the prosecutor threatens in some cases to crack the traditional constraints of checks and balances that keeps the justice system in working order. To restore this balance, we need to scrap laws that require judges to adhere to strict sentencing guidelines rather than use their own discretion.

This power is particularly worrisome because of intense political pressure on prosecutors to advance their careers by securing convictions in high-profile cases. We need to develop more meaningful criteria for evaluating prosecutors, relying less on conviction rates and more on the quality of the prosecutions. Few prosecutors boast of how often they dismiss trivial arrests or drop charges against innocent people, yet these are also important to the fair administration of justice. Prosecutorial decisions must not be used for personal political gain.

Another imbalance results from uneven distribution of resources. The increases in prosecutorial budgets were not matched with similar increases in funding for indigent defense. We have seen how most criminal defendants cannot afford to have their own lawyers and are typically assigned a public defender who suffers from an enormous workload. Public defenders received just 2.3 percent of the total spent on criminal justice in 1990.[4] Prosecutors received 8 percent and the police (who investigate and gather evidence for prosecutors) received 43 percent. Indigent defense must have more resources for the constitutional right to a fair trial to have meaning.

Recommendation 5

Eliminate racial and ethnic biases within the criminal justice system. Require a racial impact statement before major changes are made to crime policy.

As a nation, we need to confront the race problem squarely. We must elevate the discussion about race and crime from a polemic of racism to the impact of criminal justice policies on race relations.

We know there are huge disparities between whites and African-Americans in the criminal justice system. These disparities also affect Hispanics, Native Americans, and other minorities as well. African-Americans constitute 13 percent of the nation's monthly drug users but 75 percent of the population imprisoned for drug offenses. In Baltimore, for example, 11,107 out of 12,956 arrests for drug offenses in 1991 were of African-Americans. In that same year in Baltimore, there were 13 arrests of white youths for drug sales compared to 1,304 for African-Americans.[15]

This is a question of more than crime rates or disproportion within the system. This is a question of race relations and the American ideal. More than a century after the end of slavery and three decades after passage of the Civil Rights Act, one in three young African-American men lives under control of the criminal justice system. In some communities, *virtually everybody* is either personally under criminal justice supervision or has a close family member or friend under criminal justice supervision. The impact of law enforcement leads African-

American and other minorities to experience America very differently than whites. These differences were reflected clearly in the reaction to the verdict in the O. J. Simpson case. The differences make it increasingly difficult to seek common ground across the racial divide.

To narrow this gap, every criminal justice initiative should be required to include a *racial impact statement* assessing how the initiative will affect minority communities. If the initiative will widen racial disparities that cannot be justified by differences in crime rates or other legitimate factors, it should be discarded.

Mandatory sentences for drug offenses should be eliminated until they are enforced equally among all races. Penalties for crack cocaine should be dropped to the same level as those for powder cocaine. We should deemphasize the war on drugs as it applies to low-level nonviolent drug offenders. Cities and states should regularly review and compare arrest rates with incarceration rates, and adjust policies to correct any unwarranted racial disparities. Aggressive programs are needed to ensure that arrests, pretrial detentions, plea negotiations, and sentencing are free from racial bias. To accomplish these measures, authorities at the state level should assign at least one staff person to monitor the racial impact of policies.

Most important, policymakers and elected officials must make an honest effort to respond to complaints by minorities of bias in the system. This can best be done by increasing the number of minority decision makers who are police supervisors, prosecutorial supervisors, and judges. Racism will not diminish as long as criminal justice policy and execution remains largely in all-white hands. Our current path is one of denial—and that is not a path to a safer America.

Recommendation 6

Congress should commission an independent clearinghouse to gather and report objective criminal justice information to the public. The clearinghouse should be separate from the Department of Justice.

The establishment of an independent clearinghouse to report objective information about the criminal justice system will allow citizens and policymakers to make clear choices about policy options. We have shown how two different measures of crime rates produce different results. These results often confuse the issues in a way that makes prison a logical response to all crime, not just violent crime. We also know that the Department of Justice often publishes crime data with explanations that tend to support current policies. It will be virtually impossible for the nation to forge a new consensus on crime policy unless the data are first collected, reported, and clarified by an independent and authoritative body.

The clearinghouse should track changes in crime rates and publish the results on a state-by-state basis. It should use the scientific polling techniques of the National Crime Victimization Survey, rather than rely solely on police reports. It should think of innovative ways to communicate crime information to the media. It should consider publishing pamphlets that contain the latest information on crime and distributing them to the public in post offices. Ultimately, it should provide the public with the tools needed to hold the criminal justice system accountable. Regardless of the establishment of any clearinghouse, the media must not treat law enforcement agencies as a neutral source of crime information.

Recommendation 7

All levels of government should create crime prevention councils to develop a coordinated anti-crime strategy. These councils should be created at the city, county, state, and national levels. They should include representatives from the community, law enforcement, prosecutors, social service professionals, public health specialists, child welfare officials, crime victims, and representatives of other government agencies concerned with crime prevention.

We know that there is no national body that makes crime policy in the United States. We also know that policy choices are shaped to a large degree by police and prosecutors. We believe this process needs to be broadened to include interested citizens, victims of crime, and other government officials who can contribute to the creation of a crime prevention strategy. This recommendation will allow us to remove a major obstacle to the creation of a safe and effective policy. It also will allow us to catch up to advances made in other countries in the way crime policy is formulated. Many countries—including Canada and France—have recently created planning councils that provide a general direction to crime prevention at the national and local levels. No such councils exist at the national level in the United States, and few exist at the state and local levels.

By creating crime prevention councils, leaders can exchange ideas and craft new and effective approaches to crime prevention. Epinay, a small town outside Paris, created such a council and saw relations between police and citizens improve dramatically. The town created an office for crime victims to receive information, developed a neighborhood mediation service, computerized the police station, created auxiliary police officers, and instituted neighborhood patrols. Programs were set up to keep youth busy after school. A youth council was created to involve young people in criminal justice planning. Both crime and criminal justice system costs dropped dramatically.

How might a crime prevention council respond to a problem of firearms violence in a community in the United States? The council could meet and define the exact nature of the problem and develop a strategy. Educators might alert high school students to the dangers of firearms, social service agencies might educate parents on the risks of having handguns in the home, and police might search those who enter schools. Prosecutors might create programs that require first-time offenders to visit a morgue or an emergency room to witness the effects of firearms violence.

This kind of coordinated effort will happen only if the different parties create and implement a single strategy. Police obviously have a critical role to play to control crime and remove the violent offender from our streets. But others must become involved in order to create an anti-crime approach as comprehensive as the problem. When we cede most of the responsibility of crime prevention to law enforcement, we almost guarantee that we will continue to rely on arrests and prisons as the primary response to all crime. Crime prevention councils are the best way to engage broad sectors of the population in criminal justice planning. They are also an effective way to build the political support necessary to carry out a reform of the criminal justice system.

Recommendation 8

Reduce violence by (1) using innovative approaches developed in the field of public health, and (2) passing comprehensive gun control legislation at the federal level.

Public Health Approach

We know that the source of most fear in America is not crime but violence. We also know that there is a tremendous amount of violence in America that never makes it into the criminal justice system. The criminal justice system alone simply cannot be expected to prevent all violence, although it can be expected to control its worst forms so we feel safe.

Most violence prevention in the United States occurs informally and has nothing to do with the police: a parent tells her child not to fight, a teacher settles a dispute between students, a neighbor watches the house of a friend who is away. We should strengthen the informal mechanisms that citizens already use to prevent violence. Just as we recognize that surgical procedures are not the only pathway to physical health, we need to recognize that the formal criminal justice system is not the only pathway to a safer and less violent society.

We believe that the most promising approach to violence reduction is currently being developed in the field of public health. Doctors and public health specialists are taking a bold look at the causes of violence and what can be done to address them. The reason is that violence kills people, just like any other epidemic. David Satcher, a leading health professional and director of the federal Centers for Disease Control and Prevention, said it best: "Violence is the leading cause of lost life in this country today. If it's not a public-health problem, why are all those people dying from it?"[5]

Violence is defined by public health specialists as behavior that *intentionally threatens, attempts, or inflicts physical harm on others.*[6] When assessing how to reduce violence, a prison sentence is only one possible option. More important is to determine why people become violent and to develop strategies to reduce the risk factors that lead to violence.

The public health approach to violence prevention is not an abstract exercise but one with serious practical goals. In 1990, the U.S. Public Health Service set concrete violence reduction goals for the year 2000. These included reducing homicides from 8.5 to 7.2 per 100,000 people; reducing suicides from 11.7 to 10.5 per 100,000 people; and reducing rape from 120 to 107 per 100,000 women.[7] These measurements are far more useful than the traditional arrest rates used by police to judge the effectiveness of crime control, and they highlight a fundamental difference between the two systems. The public health approach focuses on violence and aims to reduce it, while the criminal justice approach measures the use of its apparatus and assumes that increased use will produce increased safety.[8] As a result, it bogs down in nonviolent crime. In terms of safety, what matters most is not the number of arrests and convictions but the amount of violence.

Public health strategies focus on children and youthful offenders partly because of the problem of firearms violence and partly because many older offenders start their careers as juveniles. Significant risk factors for youth violence include chronic parental unemployment, substance abuse, early onset of aggression, child abuse, victimization (i.e., being the victim of violent offenses or witnessing chronic violence in the family and community), and poor performance in school. Other risk factors for youth violence include illegal ownership of guns, drug use, involvement in gangs, and living in socially isolated neighborhoods that fail to meet the basic needs of their residents, including access to health care, educational opportunities, jobs, housing, and reasonably priced food stores.[9]

Of course, risk factors cannot predict the future of individuals. Children with more risk factors are at greater risk of becoming violent than children with fewer risk factors, but some children at great risk will grow up without becoming violent and some children at low risk will become dangerous.

The strategies to reduce risk factors are complex, but they can use-

How to Reduce Violence: The Public Health Approach

Strategy Type	Intervention Examples
Individual interventions	• Training in conflict resolution and social skills • General education • Vocational training • Public information and education campaigns • Identify and counsel victims of family violence • Psychotherapy, individual or group • Head Start • Drug treatment
Family or peer group interventions	• Pro-arrest policies for domestic assault • Battered woman's shelters • Counseling for abusive partners • Parenting training • Development of pro-social gang alternatives
Neighborhood interventions	• Better schools • Outreach to caretakers • Conflict resolution programs • After-school programs • Professional pay for teachers • Modern facilities • Coordinate neighborhood organizations • Neighborhood patrols • Parks and recreational facilities in decent condition with good lighting at night
Society-wide interventions	• Reduced violence in entertainment • Political shift from rhetoric of war to rhetoric of peace • Employment and anti-poverty policies • Nationwide effort to find solutions

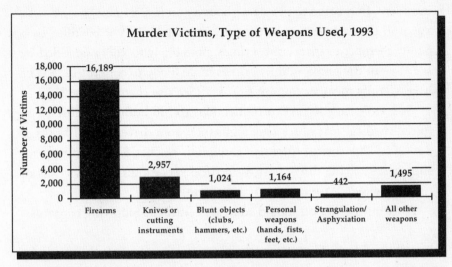

Murder Victims, Type of Weapons Used, 1993

Source: **U.S. Department of Justice, Bureau of Justice Statistics (December 1994),** *Crime in the United States—1993.* **p. 18.**

fully be divided into four levels of interventions.[10] These interventions start at the individual level and expand in ever-widening spheres to include the family, the neighborhood, and ultimately the entire social system.

Gun Control Legislation

Careful regulation of firearms and ammunition is essential if we are to reduce youth homicide and lessen violence generally. Such regulations should not affect the rights of collectors and sportsmen to own and use their weapons for legitimate purposes. Regulation of firearms should focus on those weapons—handguns and automatic firearms—that are most involved in criminal violence. Polls consistently demonstrate that most Americans support restrictions on the sale of firearms in order to reduce violence.

Contrary to popular belief, most victims of firearms violence are attacked by family members or friends rather than strangers. The availability of a lethal weapon can turn a heated argument into a homicide or a suicidal disposition into a completed suicide. Rarely are firearms used successfully in self-defense—a gun in the home is forty-three times more likely to be used to kill a family member than to kill an intruder.[11] In relation to people without a gun in the home, people with a gun in the home are eight times more likely to kill or be killed by a family member or friend, three times more likely to kill or be killed by someone in the home, and five times more likely to commit suicide or have a family member commit suicide.[12] (See also chart on page 213.)

Gun violence also takes a tremendous toll in health care costs. The initial medical cost of treating a gunshot wound averages $15,000 to $20,000. The cost of intensive care often reaches $150,000 per victim. In 1993, the direct cost of medical spending for the victims of firearms violence totaled about $3 billion.[13]

Firearms legislation should address at least the following concerns:

•Guns are mobile. Restrictions on firearms in one jurisdiction can be undermined by importation of firearms from a neighboring jurisdiction. Thus, gun control should occur at the highest jurisdictional level, the federal government.

•Guns last a long time, and more than 200 million are already in circulation. Regulation can focus on ammunition, which needs to be replaced. Gun swaps or amnesties can help to reduce the number of guns in circulation.

•Taxation on guns, ammunition, or licenses creates a deterrence to their acquisition and a new revenue source for treating victims or fighting crime.

•Waiting periods make it more likely that people will "cool down" before buying a gun for revenge. It also permits authorities to run background checks.

•Police activities that target those who carry illegal weapons can disrupt illegal gun markets.

•Technology has reached the point where "fingerprinted" weapons are made that can be fired only by the legal owner. This "safe" technology should be encouraged by law and regulation.

Recommendation 9

In order to reduce street crime, the nation must commit itself to reducing poverty by investing in children, youth, families, and communities.

Most people recognize that street crime is highest in low-income neighborhoods and lowest in wealthy neighborhoods. A program to reduce poverty levels—particularly among children—will reduce levels of crime and violence and make the country safer.

Common sense tells many Americans where it is least safe to walk alone at night, and the statistics back them up. The location of most crime in America, the victims of most crime in America, and the characteristics of most criminals in America provide solid evidence that poverty and crime are inextricably linked.[14] To reach our goal of a safer society and a lower prison population, we must commit ourselves as a nation to reducing poverty. We have the highest rates of child poverty in the industrialized world. About 46 percent of African-American children and 39 percent of Hispanic children are born into poverty in the United States, compared to 16 percent of white children and 2 percent of all children in Sweden (which has proportionately more children born out of wedlock than the United States).

Anti-poverty programs are more easily accepted when they are broadly applied. In Europe, effective anti-poverty programs have wide political support because they are designed to assist all families rather than just low-income families. The anti-poverty component of a crime prevention program for the United States might include some or all of the elements listed below:

•**A "child allowance" for families:** Many countries pay parents a standard amount per child to help with rearing costs. This could take the form of a refundable income tax credit of $800 to $1,000 per child. Some experts believe this, combined with the Earned Income Tax Credit, would lift most low-income families with children out of poverty.

•**Child support for single mothers:** A standard benefit should be paid to all single mothers for each child in their care. The benefits should be recouped from the father if he can be identified.

•**Head Start for all low-income families with children:** As the High/Scope Perry Preschool Study demonstrates (see chart below), early childhood development programs on the Head Start model are proven to lower crime and increase family stability. Currently, Head Start reaches only 35 percent of eligible children.

•**Extended unemployment benefits:** These should be connected to job training and targeted to parents with children.

•**Welfare reform:** Once these systems are in place with adequate funding, anti-poverty experts believe women receiving welfare should be ready to move to self-sufficiency by the time the youngest child is three.

•**Job training:** The federal Job Corps program helps at-risk youth overcome the barriers to employment. A study found that every dollar invested in Job Corps returned $1.46 to society through decreased income maintenance payments, reductions in costs of incarceration, and taxes paid by former Job Corps students. The pri-

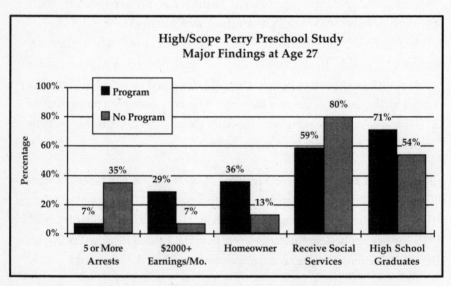

Source: Schweinhart, L. J., H. V. Barnes, and D. P. Weikart, (1993), *Significant Benefits: The High/Scope Perry Preschool Study Through Age 27*, p. xvi, Figure 1.

vate sector also has a role to play through vocational training programs, summer internships for teenagers, and a variety of programs designed to bring people into the workforce.

•**Employment:** Invest $1 billion in grassroots community development corporations in inner-city neighborhoods. These corporations are one of the most effective ways to generate jobs for the disadvantaged.

•**Urban revitalization:** Harness free-market techniques to create opportunities where currently the best hope of earning a living is to sell drugs. Community development banks can help finance small businesses to create local jobs and increase home ownership. Chicago's South Shore Bank has demonstrated that loans can be made in low-income neighborhoods at a profit. Cities and states can invest in rebuilding their infrastructure.

We currently spend $100 billion per year on the criminal justice system. The Eisenhower Foundation, which works to develop declining urban neighborhoods, has estimated that it will cost $30 billion per year over a decade to revitalize urban areas across the nation.

Recommendation 10

Enhance services provided to crime victims.

Crime victims are often left in the shadows of the criminal justice system. It is victims of crime who usually suffer the most as a result of crime. Victims are the main source of information about crimes and criminals. Over one-half of all crime known to the police comes from reports by victims, in contrast to the one-third reported by witnesses and a small proportion—mostly victimless crime—that comes from police action.

Victims of crime deserve better treatment. As things stand now, crime victims are often revictimized by the justice process. They are sometimes shuffled around by the bureaucracy, questioned insensitively by police, subpoenaed rudely by courts, mystified by procedures needed to get restitution, kept ignorant of important court dates, and denied possession of their own property being held as evidence. To the greatest degree possible, crime victims should be made to feel whole—not angry—by the criminal justice process. The system must satisfy crime victims if it is to help heal the physical and emotional trauma caused by crime. No increase in punishment alone will heal a victim as fully as sympathetic treatment by police and prosecutors, or assistance in obtaining restitution and medical care. All courts around the country should develop programs to meet the needs of victims in the criminal justice process. These needs include the right to be free from intimidation; to be told of social services and how to apply for them; to be provided a secure area during interviews and court proceedings and to be notified if their presence in court is not needed; to get property returned when it is no longer needed as evidence; to be notified in felony cases whenever the perpetrator is released from custody; and to be interviewed by a female official in the case of rape and other sexual offenses.

Recommendation 11

Shift crime policy from an agenda of "war" to an agenda of "peace."

Politicians often talk of the "war" on crime or the "war" against drugs. They speak of police and prosecutors as being on the "front lines" of these "wars." This kind of rhetoric serves only to confine our imagination in the search for solutions to the crime problem. Who is the enemy in this war? Young men who hang out on street corners because there are no parks? Teenagers who sell drugs because there is little legitimate economic opportunity in the neighborhood? The next-door neighbor who sometimes smoked marijuana and wound up serving a five-year mandatory prison sentence? The enemy in this war is *our own people.*

A war against the American people is a war that nobody can win. It brings hostility and division; it exhausts our resources and saps our moral strength. The goal is not to declare a war and win it, but to declare a peace and bring with it the terms for lasting reconciliation.

Peace can bring policies of renewal that have no place in warfare. One does not build parks or provide drug treatment for an enemy; one does not invest in job creation for people one abhors. When we shift to a rhetoric of peace, we pave the way for the reform of the criminal justice system and what we hope will be a safer America.

APPENDIX A

Report Card on Safety

The *NCJC Report Card on Safety* ranks the fifty states by how well they promote public safety. We believe the *Report Card* is the most comprehensive and innovative index of its kind. It measures the safety level in each state by examining a series of policies that are often ignored by more traditional surveys. The *Report Card* includes measures of criminal justice system performance, but also measures of poverty, education, and anti-violence initiatives that are proven to increase public safety. By ranking each state individually, the *Report Card* provides citizens with information to assess crime policy in their home state.

The *Report Card* includes the following five measures for every state:

• **Violence:** What is the level of violent crime?

• **Rational Use:** Is prison space reserved for the most dangerous offenders?

• **Poverty:** Are residents prosperous or economically distressed?

• **Violence Prevention Initiatives:** Is the government exploring new avenues to increase public safety?

•**Hope for the Future:** Do government policies plan for failure or lay the foundation for success?

On each measure, a ranking of 1 is best and a ranking of 50 is worst.

Violence

Violent crime is more frightening than any other type of crime. The threat of violent crime forces citizens to lock their doors and stay home at night. For this reason, the first item on the *Report Card* measures levels of violent crime.

States' rankings on the NCJC Violence scale are on page 223.

The precise measure is the state's homicide rate relative to its population. The *Report Card* uses homicide rates for two reasons. First, homicide is the only crime that is accurately measured on a state-by-state basis. The FBI Uniform Crime Reports is the only source for state-by-state breakdowns of crime rates, and homicide is the only crime it measures accurately enough to make cross-jurisdictional comparisons. Second, homicide is an "indicator" crime. A jurisdiction that has many homicides typically has many assaults, robberies, and other types of violent crime—and vice versa for jurisdictions with fewer homicides. Thus, homicide rates are a solid indicator of the overall level of violence.

Rational Use

This score assesses how rationally a state employs its prison resources. The scale rewards states that reserve prison resources for violent offenders and keep rates of incarceration in line with rates of violent crime. A state without a rational policy, for example, locks up large numbers of petty offenders while releasing serious offenders because it lacks prison space. Such a state would not score high on this scale.

States' rankings on the NCJC Rational Use scale are on page 224.

The score combines three different measures. The first measure is the ratio of violent to nonviolent new commitments to state prison. This indicates whether those going to prison are truly dangerous.

Violence Rankings			
State	**Rank**	**State**	**Rank**
Maine	1	Pennsylvania	26
North Dakota	2	West Virginia	27
New Hampshire	3	Indiana	28
Iowa	4	New Mexico	29
Idaho	5	Virginia	30
Montana	6	Oklahoma	31
Utah	7	Arizona	32
Minnesota	8	Florida	33
South Dakota	9	Alaska	34
Wyoming	10	Michigan	35
Vermont	11	Arkansas	36
Hawaii	12	Tennessee	37
Massachusetts	13	South Carolina	38
Nebraska	14	Nevada	39
Rhode Island	15	Missouri	40
Wisconsin	16	North Carolina	41
Oregon	17	Georgia	42
Delaware	18	Illinois	43
Washington	19	Alabama	44
New Jersey	20	Texas	45
Colorado	21	Maryland	46
Ohio	22	California	47
Connecticut	23	New York	48
Kansas	24	Mississippi	49
Kentucky	25	Louisiana	50

The second measure is the change in the rate of incarceration over the previous ten years. This long-term measure gives perspective on the growth of imprisonment over time. The final measure is the rate of incarceration of each state, which ensures that the ranking does not stray too far from the basic reliance on prisons. All three measures are weighted equally.

Poverty

Decades of research reveal a correlation between poverty or economic inequality and rates of street crime. As living conditions worsen, rates of street crime tend to increase.

States' rankings on the NCJC Poverty scale are on page 225.

The poverty score combines two different indicators of economic

Rational Use Rankings			
State	Rank	State	Rank
Oregon	1	Iowa	26
Minnesota	2	Idaho	27
Massachusetts	3	South Dakota	28
North Dakota	4	Florida	29
West Virginia	5	Connecticut	30
Montana	6	Maryland	31
Pennsylvania	7	Nevada	32
Wisconsin	8	Kentucky	33
Maine	9	Missouri	34
Vermont	10	California	35
Washington	11	Indiana	36
Nebraska	12	Colorado	37
Utah	13	Delaware	38
New Hampshire	14	Arkansas	39
Rhode Island	15	Georgia	40
Tennessee	16	North Carolina	41
Kansas	17	Ohio	42
New Mexico	18	Mississippi	43
Hawaii	19	Louisiana	44
New York	20	Alabama	45
Illinois	21	Texas	46
Alaska	22	Virginia	47
Michigan	23	Arizona	48
New Jersey	24	Oklahoma	49
Wyoming	25	South Carolina	50

well-being. The first measure is the percentage of children living in poverty. We focus on child poverty because most older offenders start their careers as juveniles. Moreover, impoverished children often lack the nutrition, attention, and access to education needed to become productive members of society. The second measure is the employment rate. Research has consistently revealed a strong correlation between rates of unemployment and underemployment and rates of crime.

Violence Prevention Initiatives

Many means of reducing violence occur outside the formal justice system. Classes in conflict resolution, educational and recreational

Poverty Rankings			
State	Rank	State	Rank
Nebraska	1	Idaho	26
New Hampshire	2	Rhode Island	27
Iowa	3	New Jersey	28
Utah	4	Massachusetts	29
Delaware	5	Pennsylvania	30
South Dakota	6	Montana	31
Wisconsin	7	Tennessee	32
North Dakota	8	Maine	33
Wyoming	9	Georgia	34
Vermont	10	Oklahoma	35
Colorado	11	Illinois	36
Connecticut	12	Arizona	37
Virginia	13	Kentucky	38
Minnesota	14	Michigan	39
Washington	15	Arkansas	40
Maryland	16	Alabama	41
Ohio	17	South Carolina	42
Kansas	18	New York	43
North Carolina	19	Texas	44
Oregon	20	Florida	45
Indiana	21	New Mexico	46
Nevada	22	California	47
Missouri	23	Mississippi	48
Alaska	24	West Virginia	49
Hawaii	25	Louisiana	50

opportunities, drug treatment, counseling, job training, improved street lighting, and many other techniques can reduce violence in a community. The development of such programs is limited only by a jurisdiction's creativity and financial commitment.

States' rankings on the NCJC Violence Prevention scale are on page 226.

This score measures how many violence prevention initiatives a state supports relative to its level of violence. We make no effort to measure the efficacy of different initiatives, preferring instead to let states experiment with a wide variety of techniques. This score rewards states that support an abundance of anti-violence initiatives.

Violence Prevention Rankings			
State	Rank	State	Rank
North Dakota	1	Kansas	26
Maine	2	Georgia	27
South Dakota	3	New Jersey	28
New Mexico	4	Arkansas	29
Idaho	5	Arizona	30
Delaware	6	Alaska	31
Hawaii	7	Missouri	32
New Hampshire	8	Illinois	33
Iowa	9	Virginia	34
Wyoming	10	Ohio	35
Minnesota	11	Mississippi	36
Massachusetts	12	Indiana	37
Nebraska	13	Oklahoma	38
West Virginia	14	Kentucky	39
Washington	15	Pennsylvania	40
Wisconsin	16	California	41
Rhode Island	17	Alabama	42
Colorado	18	Tennessee	43
Oregon	19	North Carolina	44
Utah	20	Louisiana	45
Nevada	21	Florida	46
Montana	22	New York	47
Connecticut	23	Michigan	48
Vermont	24	Texas	49
Maryland	25	South Carolina	50

Hope for the Future

Where is our nation going? Are we planning for failure by building more prisons, or are we building for the future by improving schools and giving children the skills they need to succeed? Financing is limited. Money spent on prisons is money not spent on classrooms, libraries, or parks. This score measures how spending priorities affect our hopes for the future.

States' rankings on the NCJC Hope for the Future scale are on page 227.

This score combines two different measures, weighted equally. The first measure is the percentage of teens who dropped out of high school. Most people recognize that education is necessary for people to succeed. Less than a quarter of state prison inmates have gradu-

Hope for the Future Rankings

State	Rank	State	Rank
Wisconsin	1	Missouri	26
Maine	2	Vermont	27
Connecticut	3	New Jersey	28
Iowa	4	Illinois	29
Kansas	5	Utah	30
Ohio	6	Oregon	31
Maryland	7	Wyoming	32
Minnesota	8	Arkansas	33
Virginia	9	Mississippi	34
Nebraska	10	Kentucky	35
South Carolina	11	Alaska	36
Hawaii	12	Georgia	37
Pennsylvania	13	Arizona	38
Montana	14	Colorado	39
Washington	15	Florida	40
Delaware	16	Texas	41
New Hampshire	17	West Virginia	42
Rhode Island	18	Oklahoma	43
New York	19	Louisiana	44
Indiana	20	North Carolina	45
North Dakota	21	Alabama	46
Tennessee	22	Idaho	47
Michigan	23	California	48
Massachusetts	24	Nevada	49
South Dakota	25	New Mexico	50

ated from high school. The percentage of children graduating from high school also provides a rough indication of drug use among students, teenage pregnancy, parental involvement, and many other factors that affect public well-being. The second measure is the salary ratio between public school teachers and prison guards. This indicates how the state prioritizes its resources and what kind of work it encourages talented people to seek.

The Final Grade

The final grade is the composite ranking of the states in each of the five categories. This ranking allows citizens to assess their state's overall performance on the crucial question of public safety. Following are the composite scores:

The Final Grade			
State	Rank	State	Rank
North Dakota	1	New Mexico	26
Maine	2	Maryland	27
New Hampshire	3	New Jersey	28
Iowa	4	Virginia	29
Minnesota	5	Indiana	30
Nebraska	6	Alaska	31
South Dakota	7	Tennessee	32
Wisconsin	8	Missouri	33
Oregon	9	Nevada	34
Utah	10	Illinois	35
Massachusetts	11	Kentucky	36
Hawaii	12	Georgia	37
Delaware	13	Michigan	38
Montana	14	New York	39
Vermont	15	Arkansas	40
Idaho	16	North Carolina	41
Wyoming	17	Arizona	42
Washington	18	Florida	43
Connecticut	19	Oklahoma	44
Rhode Island	20	South Carolina	45
Kansas	21	Mississippi	46
Pennsylvania	22	Alabama	47
Colorado	23	California	48
West Virginia	24	Texas	49
Ohio	25	Louisiana	50

Sources

Homicide Rates

U.S. Department of Justice, Federal Bureau of Investigation. (December 4, 1994). *Crime in the United States 1993*. Washington, D.C.: U.S. Government Printing Office.

Rates of Incarceration

U.S. Department of Justice, Bureau of Justice Statistics. (August 1995). *Prisoners in 1994*. Washington, D.C.: U.S. Government Printing Office.

U.S. Department of Justice, Bureau of Justice Statistics. (1985). *Prisoners in 1984.* Washington, D.C.: U.S. Government Printing Office.

Ratio of Violent to Nonviolent Admissions

U.S. Department of Justice, Bureau of Justice Statistics. (October 1994). *National Corrections Reporting Program, 1992.* Washington, D.C.: U.S. Government Printing Office.

In this measure, all figures are from the 1992 National Corrections Reporting Program, except for those states that did not participate. From those states, NCJC obtained data for the following years directly from the state department of corrections: Arizona, fiscal year 1995; Delaware, calendar year 1994; Indiana, fiscal year 1994; Kansas, fiscal year 1995; Montana, fiscal year 1995; New Mexico, calendar year 1994; Vermont, fiscal year 1995. Information from the following five states was unavailable: Alaska, Connecticut, Idaho, Rhode Island, and Wyoming. We attributed to each of those states the average ratio from all known states.

Unemployment

U.S. Department of Labor, Bureau of Labor Statistics. *Seasonally Adjusted Local Area Unemployment Statistics, January 1995.*

Population Counts

U.S. Department of Commerce, Bureau of the Census. (March 1994). *Population Projections for States by Age, Sex, Race and Hispanic Origin: 1993 to 2020.* Washington, D.C.: U.S. Government Printing Office, p. 17.

Children in Poverty

Annie E. Casey Foundation. (1995). *Kids Count, Data Book.* Baltimore, Maryland: Annie E. Casey Foundation.

Violence Prevention

U.S. Department of Justice, U.S. Department of Health and Human Services, U.S. Department of Education, U.S. Department of Labor, U.S. Department of Housing and Urban Development, and

U.S. Department of Agriculture. (August 1994). *Partnerships Against Violence, Promising Programs.* Washington, D.C.: U.S. Government Printing Office.

Corrections Salaries

Camp, Graham, and George Camp. (1994). *Corrections Yearbook, Adult Corrections.* South Salem, N.Y.: The Criminal Justice Institute. Additional information on New York and New Mexico was obtained directly from the states' department of corrections.

Teacher Salaries

National Education Association. (1994). *Rankings of the States, 1994.* Washington, D.C.: Research Division of the National Education Association.

Teenage Dropouts (1992)

Annie E. Casey Foundation. (1995). *Kids Count, Data Book.* Baltimore, Maryland: Annie E. Casey Foundation.

APPENDIX B

Crime Prevention Model Programs

The following is a list of model crime prevention programs identified by the National Criminal Justice Commission. The Commission conducted a nationwide survey for cost-effective programs that have been able to reduce and prevent crime to varying degrees. There are thousands of programs working to solve the problem of crime in our society. We have chosen those that we believe effectively represent an individual category or intervention approach.

Each of the following subcategories is an essential part of a comprehensive crime prevention model. The National Criminal Justice Commission believes that if one or more of these programs is implemented in a given community, the results will be positive.

Early Childhood Development/Parent Training

Early childhood development is one of the most cost-effective crime prevention options available. In the United States, Head Start provides education, social services, and medical, nutritional, and mental health services to disadvantaged preschoolers and their low-income families. Unfortunately, these programs currently reach less than half of the children living in poverty.

PROJECT HEAD START
National Office
1651 Prince Street
Alexandria, VA 22314
(703) 739-0875

Project Head Start is designed to help children of low-income families. It focuses on the development of the child's intellect, fosters emotional and social development, provides health and nutritional services, and involves parents and the community in these efforts. An evaluation of 1,500 Head Start studies found improvement in school performance; improvement in self-esteem and motivation; lowered school absenteeism; and improvement in the child's health and nutrition.

HIGH/SCOPE PERRY PRESCHOOL PROGRAM
600 North River Street
Ypsilanti, MI 48198
(313) 485-2000

The High/Scope Perry Preschool program is based on the Head Start model. Results reveal that adults born into poverty who attended a high-quality, active learning preschool program at ages three and four have half as many criminal arrests, higher earnings and property wealth, and greater commitment to marriage, according to the latest findings of the High/Scope Educational Research Foundation. Over participants' lifetimes, the public receives an estimated $7.16 return for every dollar invested.

SUCCESS FOR ALL
Center for the Education of Students Placed at Risk
3505 North Charles Street
Baltimore, MD 21218
(410) 516-8800

Success for All, which was started in Baltimore, Maryland, is a comprehensive restructuring plan designed primarily for use in elementary schools serving many disadvantaged students. The program has been evaluated in fifteen elementary schools in seven states and found to be effective in increasing reading achievement and reducing retentions and special education referrals.

THE PRENATAL/EARLY INFANCY PROJECT
School of Nursing
601 Elmwood Avenue
Rochester, NY 14642
(716) 275-3738

In this program, nurses visit pregnant women to provide information and support that encourage mothers to adopt good health habits, learn the skills needed to care for their infant children, secure access to needed community services, achieve educational or occupational goals, and prevent unwanted future pregnancies. Evaluation of this project showed that the health and social skills of participants had improved and that there was a substantial reduction in verified cases of child abuse among the children of at-risk women participants. The evaluation found that an investment in this type of program can pay for itself by the time the child is four years old.

HEALTHY START IN HAWAII
Hawaii State Department of Health
1600 Kapiolani Boulevard, Suite 600
Honolulu, HI 96814
(808) 946-4771

Healthy Start in Hawaii is designed to prevent child abuse by providing prenatal and post-birth counseling to high-risk parents. Early evaluation findings show that of ninety persons receiving weekly counseling services in the program, none committed child abuse while in the program. After leaving the program, three committed abuse.

PARENTS AS TEACHERS (PAT)
Parents as Teachers National Center, Inc.
10176 Corporate Square Drive
St. Louis, MO 63132
(314) 432-4330

In a typical PAT program, parents of an infant enroll and remain in the program until the child is three years old. Each monthly visit by a specially trained PAT professional offers the parent(s) strategies to address parental concerns and age-appropriate learning activities, and provides children with health and other social services. Three comprehensive evaluations of PAT programs have found that children who participated were significantly advanced over their peers in language, social development, problem solving, and other intellectual abilities, and also that parents knew more about child development than nonparticipants. The 1991 evaluation in the Binghamton (New York) City School District found that welfare dependence within the PAT group dropped by 10 percent while dependence nearly doubled for the control group by the child's first birthday.

MIRACLE VILLAGE
Metro Health Clement Center for Family Care
2500 East 79th Street
Cleveland, OH 44104
(216) 391-3387

A drug treatment program for inner-city mothers in Cuyahoga County links treatment for chemical dependency and such services as housing, health care, parenting and nutrition classes, remedial education, and vocational training. Miracle Village has achieved a 75 percent abstinence rate among 100 women who had been addicted to crack cocaine and failed to complete prior forms of treatment.

Vocational Training

Providing children and young adults with the necessary tools to attain and sustain a job is one of the most essential aspects of reducing crime. Employment gives juveniles responsibility and a sense of accomplishment and self-worth that cannot be found elsewhere. Job skills are essential to leading a productive, crime-free life.

JOB CORPS
U.S. Department of Labor
Office of Job Corps, Room N4510
200 Constitution Avenue, NW
Washington, DC 20210
(202) 219-8550

Managed by the U.S. Department of Labor, Job Corps is a vocational training and education program for young adults. It is primarily residential in nature, although some urban Job Corps centers offer nonresidential programs. The comprehensive services offered, including counseling, cultural and recreational activities, and medical care, has helped Job Corps return $1.46 to society for every dollar invested in the program through reductions in unemployment and incarceration.

CENTER FOR EMPLOYMENT TRAINING (CET)
701 Vine Street
San Jose, CA 95110
(800) 533-2519

CET offers innovative classroom training in more than twenty-five occupations to hard-to-serve, at-risk clients. Training incorporates basic skills remediation with occupational skills training, life skills instruction, counseling, and job placement. Since its inception, CET has trained and placed more than 60,000 persons in jobs, including welfare recipients and at-risk youths.

QUANTUM OPPORTUNITIES PROGRAM
U.S. Department of Labor
200 Constitution Avenue, NW
Washington, DC 20210
(202) 219-5472

This experimental job skills, life-mentoring program educates young teens for four years. The youths are paid a stipend of $1.33—matched in a college fund for them—for each hour they spend on extra academic study, volunteer work, or cultural and educational events, plus a $100 bonus for each 100 hours completed. Of the 100 teenagers in the program, many more improved their basic skills, had fewer babies, graduated from high school, and went on to college than a randomly selected control group of their peers.

YOUTH EDUCATION AND EMPLOYMENT PROGRAM
Juvenile and Domestic Relations Court
Chesapeake Circuit Court
300 Cedar Road
Chesapeake, VA 23320
(804) 547-6111

This program helps youth build confident, self-reliant lives through a flexible, comprehensive program of education, life/pre-employment skills training, job placement, and counseling. The program has placed 75 percent of its participants in unsubsidized employment.

LOUISIANA STATE YOUTH OPPORTUNITIES UNLIMITED
Louisiana State University
118 Hatcher Hall
College of Education
Baton Rouge, LA 70803
(504) 388-1751

Participants in this program live in dormitories on the Louisiana State University campus in Baton Rouge for eight weeks during the summer. They receive academic instruction, work minimum-wage jobs, and participate in recreational activities and career and personal counseling. Evaluations have shown significant academic gains, improved coping skills, and a 65 percent graduation success rate.

YOUTHBUILD BOSTON
173A Norfolk Avenue
Roxbury, MA 02119
(617) 445-8887

Involves unemployed, disenfranchised young people in renovating abandoned buildings as affordable housing while offering them a second chance to gain the education, skills, and personal support needed to build a better future.

YOUTH AS RESOURCES (YAR)
National Crime Prevention Council
1700 K Street, NW, 2nd Floor
Washington, DC 20006
(202) 466-6272

This may be the nation's most widespread teen community service initiative. Between 1987 and 1993, forty-five thousand youth from high-risk as well as middle-class neighborhoods participated in thirty-nine YAR programs. By completing thousands of projects through YAR, the youth participants develop a sense of self-esteem and responsibility.

Preventing Youth Violence Through Education

Violence prevention education programs have proven effective at reducing crime. Most of the model programs are comprehensive and deal with many aspects of crime prevention; some specialize in one particular violence prevention concept, such as conflict resolution, gang prevention, or mentoring. All of these programs educate youth about the consequences of crime and how to avoid involvement in crime.

AMER-I-CAN PROGRAM, INC.
292 South La Cienega Boulevard, Suite 210
Beverly Hills, CA 90211
(310) 652-7884

The Amer-I-Can Program, Inc. employs former gang members and ex-convicts to teach a two-week curriculum of life management and conflict resolution skills to current gang members and children at risk of becoming involved in gangs. There are currently 150 former gang members and ex-convicts who serve as Amer-I-Can consultants in California, Florida, Illinois, New York, Ohio, and Oregon.

STRAIGHT TALK ABOUT RISKS
Center to Prevent Handgun Violence
1225 I Street, NW, Suite 1100
Washington, DC 20005
(202) 289-7319

This comprehensive school program is designed to prevent gunshot injuries and deaths among children and teens by teaching students the protective skills needed to avoid threatening situations with firearms. In the Dade County (Florida) Public Schools program, there was a 30 percent decrease in gun injuries and deaths among school-aged youth.

DATING VIOLENCE INTERVENTION PROJECT
P.O. Box 530
Harvard Square Station
Cambridge, MA 02238
(617) 868-8328

This project trains high school students as peer leaders to educate others about dating violence. It provides a forum for teens to talk about the issues surrounding dating violence, to voice their concerns and frustrations about relationships, and to challenge each other to think differently about a particular issue.

TEEN DATING VIOLENCE PROJECT
Austin Center for Battered Women
P.O. Box 19454
Austin, TX 78760
(512) 385-5181

This project seeks to provide education about abuse, support for victims, prevention of future family violence, and empowerment of young women. The project focuses on awareness education and support groups.

PROJECT BOOTSTRAP, INC.
210 South Brooks Street, Room 101
Madison, WI 53715
(608) 257-1180

A multifaceted program designed to meet the needs of at-risk children by integrating educational support, supportive family groups, family mentoring, and alcohol and other drug abuse programs. The goal is to teach children that they can "haul themselves up from trouble by their bootstraps." Among the participants, school attendance has improved, grades have improved, behavior problems have decreased, and violence among Bootstrap families has decreased.

YALE UNIVERSITY CHILD STUDY CENTER
230 South Frontage Road
New Haven, CT 06520
(203) 785-6862

This innovative project brings together New Haven police officers and mental health professionals to address the psychological burdens on children and families imposed by their chronic exposure to urban violence.

PEACEBUILDERS
Heartsprings, Inc.
P.O. Box 12158
Tucson, AZ 85732
(602) 322-9977

This is a program designed to create an environment that reduces violence. The program involves schools, parents, and entire communities so that peaceful behavior becomes an integral part of a child's life. It is currently working effectively in twenty-nine schools in California, and has been implemented in schools in Texas and Tucson and Sierra Vista, Arizona.

TEENS ON TARGET
3012 Summit Avenue, Suite 3670
Oakland, CA 94609
(510) 444-6191

Selected high school students are trained in an intensive summer program to be violence prevention advocates, particularly in the areas of guns, drugs, and family violence. These students become peer educators to other high school students and mentors to younger students in the middle and elementary schools.

THE OMEGA BOYS CLUB
P.O. Box 884463
San Francisco, CA 94188
(415) 826-8664

This is an innovative and highly successful youth development and delinquency prevention program that serves African-American youths at risk for violence and other problems through academic counseling, cultural awareness, and family meetings.

Conflict Resolution

Conflict resolution is designed to provide students with the opportunity to learn to control impulses, develop problem-solving skills, and manage their anger. Usually this curriculum is delivered in the classroom setting, although other settings, such as churches, multi-service centers, boys' and girls' clubs, recreation centers, housing developments, juvenile detention centers, and neighborhood health centers are also appropriate. Courses in conflict resolution have been developed for students in both elementary and high schools.

THE BOSTON CONFLICT RESOLUTION PROGRAM
Boston Area Educators for Social Responsibility
19 Garden Street, Suite 70
Cambridge, MA 02138
(617) 492-8820

This violence prevention program helps elementary school teachers and students understand and deal with conflicts frequently encountered in schools. The program also provides teacher training, implements peer mediation programs, and develops curricula and instructional resources.

CHILDREN'S CREATIVE RESPONSE TO CONFLICT
P.O. Box 271
523 North Broadway
Nyack, NY 10960
(914) 353-1796

The goal of this program is to teach educators and children the skills of conflict resolution, including themes of cooperation, communication, affirmation, problem-solving, mediation, and bias awareness.

STUDENT CONFLICT RESOLUTION EXPERTS (SCORE)
Office of the Attorney General
1 Ashburton Place
Boston, MA 02108
(617) 727-2200

SCORE trains students to intervene in tense situations to help their peers resolve conflicts peacefully. A second level of the program—Conflict Intervention Teams—provides trained teams of adult and student mediators to intervene in schoolwide outbreaks of violence. Since its inception, it has mediated more than 1,300 disputes, with about 98 percent resulting in "agreements."

PEER MEDIATION PROGRAM
Community Mediation Center
134 Grand Avenue
New Haven, CT 06513
(203) 782-3500

This program also teaches students and teachers how to mediate disputes. The police and school officials in New Haven say the program has helped reduce violence both inside and outside the schools.

RESOLVING CONFLICT CREATIVELY PROGRAM
163 Third Avenue, Suite 103
New York, NY 10003
(212) 387-0225

This conflict resolution program is being offered in more than 14 school districts and 120 schools. The program trains teachers and students in mediation. Evaluations have shown overall positive results in solving conflicts peacefully.

"OUCH!" VIOLENCE PREVENTION PROGRAM
Amherst H. Wilder Foundation
919 Lafond Avenue
St. Paul, MN 55104
(612) 642-4000

The program is aimed at teaching children and school staff alternatives to violence: to recognize and label violence in day-to-day life; to label both hurtful acts and works as violence; to teach the difference between anger and violence; to teach about the cycle of violence; to identify consequences and alternatives to violence; and to recognize that help is available when someone is a victim of violence.

Gang Prevention

The goal of gang prevention programs is to prevent teenagers from joining gangs by working with the youths and their families to increase awareness of constructive alternatives. These programs seek to provide alternatives to youths at risk of gang activity and to reduce gang recruitment and violence through crisis intervention.

COMMUNITY YOUTH GANG SERVICES (CYGS)
144 South Fetterly Avenue
Los Angeles, CA 90022
(213) 266-4264

CYGS is a comprehensive project of gang prevention activities, including crisis intervention teams to negotiate gang disputes, educational programs, and job development skills. Volunteers work with program staff and local agencies and community groups to develop cultural, recreational, and other activities that are alternatives to gang involvement.

ALTERNATIVES TO GANG MEMBERSHIP
16400 Colorado Avenue
Paramount, CA 90723
(213) 220-2140

Through an elementary school anti-gang curriculum, an intermediate school follow-up program, and neighborhood meetings, the program teaches children the harmful consequences of gang activity and positive alternatives to gangs. The program has undergone four separate studies showing that after completion of the program, 90 percent of the participants responded negatively to gang activity.

YOUTH GANG UNIT SCHOOL SAFETY PROGRAM
Ron Wheeler
Cleveland Board of Education
Youth Gang Unit
1380 East 6th Street, Room 106A
Cleveland, OH 44114
(216) 574-8552

Through education, awareness, mediation, and police involvement, the program attempts to help youth steer away from gang activity and other violent activities. According to police reports, the program's proactive efforts contributed to a 39 percent reduction in school gang-related incidents in the 1992–93 school year.

GANG PREVENTION/INTERVENTION COALITION
Yakima County Substance Abuse Coalition
1211 South 7th Street
Yakima, WA 98901
(509) 575-6114

The mission of the Coalition is to reduce the rate of youth violence by providing positive opportunities for youth in several community centers. Through education and information, prevention and intervention activities, and mentors, youth violence has decreased by 80 percent over three years in the six neighborhoods where the Coalition operates.

Mentoring

Mentors are positive, caring role models for young people in need. Adult role models may be teachers, counselors, friends, or simply members of the community. Mentors provide youngsters with much-needed attention and interest. With this added confidence and regular support, youngsters are more apt to choose positive paths.

RECLAIM OUR YOUTH MENTORSHIP PROJECT
Superior Court of the District of Columbia
500 Indiana Avenue, NW
Washington, DC 20001
(202) 879-4883

The Project has the goal of preventing crime by providing a positive role model and a positive action plan to rehabilitate youth facing delinquency proceedings.

PROJECT RAISE
605 North Utah Street
Baltimore, MD 21201
(410) 685-8316

Mentors contact the students at least weekly and meet with them face to face at least every other week. The mentors serve as role models, provide academic support, and strive to boost the youths' self-confidence.

MENTORING AND RITES OF PASSAGE
Northwestern Illinois University
Department of Psychology
5300 North St. Louis Avenue
Chicago, IL 60615
(312) 794-2568

The project is designed to reduce violent behaviors and injuries among residents 8 to 18 years of age in the Robert Taylor Public Housing Development. Youths are provided with adult mentors and a series of activities designed to assist adolescents in their transition into adulthood.

Beyond Expectations

5500 North St. Louis Avenue
Department of Psychology
Northeastern Illinois University
Chicago, IL 60625
(312) 794-2568

This program seeks to reduce violent behavior through community mentors who encourage the development of positive relationships.

African American Male Education Network (AMEN)

9824 Southwestern Avenue, Suite 175
Evergreen Park, IL 60643
(708) 720-0235

The program centers its activities on Rites of Passage programs, which foster self-esteem and pride in one's cultural heritage and provide guidance for youth as they move from one stage of life to another.

Youth Sanctuaries/Recreational Programs

Youth sanctuaries provide children with a safe haven offering comprehensive services such as health care, mental health therapy, family counseling, employment training, substance abuse counseling, tutorial assistance, and recreational programs. These sanctuaries provide idle children with youthful activities and life-preparing skills.

Boys and Girls Clubs of America

1230 West Peachtree Street, NW
Atlanta, GA 30309
(404) 815-5749

A Columbia University study found that public housing projects containing Boys and Girls Clubs have crime rates 13 percent lower than projects without them. Prevalence of drug activity is 22 percent lower in projects with a Club, while crack cocaine presence is 25 percent lower.

PREVENTION CLUBS

Dorchester Youth Collaborative
1514 A Dorchester Avenue
Boston, MA 02122
(617) 288-1748

Aimed at high-risk youth, the Prevention Club acts as a physical sanctuary from the streets, acting as an extended family providing positive role models on a daily basis. Researchers from Rutgers University tracked youths in the program and found a reduced rate of school dropout and a decreased number of arrests. When the police were brought in to serve as mentors to the youth, crime declined in the target area by over 20 percent.

NEUTRAL ZONE

P.O. BOX 195
Mountlake Terrace, WA 98043
(206) 670-2875

The Neutral Zone is a program designed to provide an alternative for youths to being out on the streets of the city between the hours of 10 P.M. and 2 A.M. It offers a variety of recreational activities and social services for high-risk youth, many of whom may be involved in gangs. A comprehensive evaluation found that crime was reduced in the area after the program was implemented, the view of police officers as positive role models by youth was enhanced, and almost all participants recommended the program to their friends.

MIDNIGHT BASKETBALL LEAGUE

P.O. Box 2982
Hyattsville, MD 20784
(301) 772-1711

These leagues are being established throughout the country to provide youth with recreational activities as an alternative to violent behavior. They provide educational activities, job skills, conflict resolution skills, and social service referrals. Once the first league started in Maryland, there was a reported 60 percent drop in drug-related crime.

WINTON HILLS

Winton Hills Community Center
5170 Winnetka Avenue
Cincinnati, OH 45232
(513) 641-0422

Public housing residents responded to a crime epidemic by launching late-night and weekend basketball along with other supervised recreation activities. In the program's first thirteen weeks, reported crime dropped by 24 percent.

Community-Wide Prevention/Urban Projects

Some of the most successful crime reduction efforts occur when the entire community takes part in crime prevention. These efforts cover all aspects of crime prevention, from measures aimed at reducing criminal opportunities to programs that promote social development and strengthen our communities.

SAFE STREETS NOW!

408 13th Street, Suite 452
Oakland, CA 94612
(510) 836-4622

This nonprofit organization uses educational workshops to address the problem of drug retailing in neighborhoods through community mobilization. It motivates individuals to create a community that reflects the standards of the residents.

TASK FORCE ON VIOLENT CRIME

614 Superior Avenue West, Suite 300
Cleveland, OH 44113
(216) 523-1128

The Cleveland community has started a number of crime prevention campaigns such as the anti–armed robbery campaign, which reduced armed robbery by 30 percent, and the second-offender campaign, which educates offenders on mandatory sentences. The task force also coordinates other crime prevention efforts such as dropout prevention, substance abuse programs, and police mini-stations.

THE SEATTLE COMMUNITY CRIME PREVENTION PROGRAM
1904 Third Avenue, Suite 614
Seattle, WA 98101
(206) 625-0577

The program substantially reinforced the relationship between police and the community, which provided for a useful partnership in dealing with the joint task of controlling crime and public security. The city created a community advisory committee that promoted a more proactive police response to citizen concerns, resulting in less crime.

OPERATION PEACE
Department of Public Health
1600 Arch Street, 7th Floor
Philadelphia, PA 19103
(215) 686-5047

The Centers for Disease Control and Prevention helped establish a community-wide, comprehensive violence prevention initiative. This neighborhood-based effort deals with all aspects of crime prevention.

CHILDREN AT RISK PROGRAM
Center on Addiction and Substance Abuse
Columbia University
152 West 57th Street
New York, NY 10019
(212) 841-5230

This is an intensive two-year intervention for high-risk youth in high-risk neighborhoods. Communities develop these programs by building on the strengths, cultural background, and history of the target neighborhood. Each program includes family and education services, mentoring and intervention, and community policing.

SAFE STREETS CAMPAIGN
934 Broadway
Tacoma, WA 98402
(206) 272-6824

Through its community-wide crime prevention efforts, Tacoma was the only city in the United States with a population over 100,000 to register a crime reduction of nearly 12 percent in 1990.

All gang-related graffiti was removed and 250 drug dealing locations have been closed since June 1990.

TRUST FOR PUBLIC LANDS
666 Pennsylvania Avenue, SE, Suite 401
Washington, DC 20003
(202) 543-7552

This is a conservation group that has launched a major effort to make twelve American cities safer through the construction of urban parks and recreation areas. In Philadelphia, where police helped neighborhood volunteers clean up vacant lots and plant gardens, reported burglaries and thefts in the precinct dropped from about forty per month to about four.

SAN FRANCISCO LEAGUE OF URBAN GARDENERS (SLUG)
2088 Oakdale Avenue
San Francisco, CA 94124
(415) 285-7584

SLUG is an organization that works with residents of housing projects and other low-income communities to maintain housing, local parks, and abandoned lots. Through this process, SLUG provides jobs, teaches skills, and offers residents a platform on which to organize and address neighborhood problems. Of the more than sixty gardens that SLUG has put in place, not one has been vandalized.

PHILADELPHIA ANTI-GRAFFITI NETWORK (PAGN)
1220 Sansom Street, 3rd Floor
Philadelphia, PA 19107
(215) 686-1550

Young people learn to paint murals in this project organized to develop their talent and stop the onslaught of graffiti on the city's buildings. PAGN has recruited hundreds of community organizations and more than 8,000 volunteers to clean up some 40,000 properties.

Preventing Future Criminal Activity

The following is a brief directory of criminal justice intervention programs. They include programs for victim restitution, job placement, substance abuse treatment, rehabilitation, and sentencing alternatives.

NOVA ANCORA
Innovations Program
John F. Kennedy School of Government
79 JFK Street
Cambridge, MA 02138
(617) 495-0558

Nova Ancora, a nonprofit agency sponsored by the New York City Department of Probation, tries to reduce recidivism by placing probationers in small businesses and manufacturing firms so they learn marketable job skills. Nova Ancora has placed probationers in auto parts, taxi service, housing construction, upholstery, cable TV, and other growth businesses. The recidivism rate for the probationers was less than 3 percent, compared with a 30 percent rate for those not participating in the program.

FIRST TIME/LAST TIME YOUTH PROGRAM
360 Delaware Avenue, Suite 106
Buffalo, NY 14202
(716) 853-9598

This program assists youthful offenders between the ages of 16 and 21 who have been charged with various criminal offenses. Youths are made aware of positive alternatives to crime, guided through their incarceration experience, and given drug and alcohol counseling, family dispute resolution counseling, employment readiness training, and referrals to educational programs.

EARN-IT
City Hall
3 Washington Street
Keene, NH 03431
(603) 357-9811

Earn-It is a victim restitution program that serves as a sentencing alternative for Juvenile Court. Since its inception in 1988, over $40,000 worth of community service work (calculated at minimum wage) has been completed by Earn-It youth; over $32,000 has been collected from Earn-It youth ordered to pay fines or restitution; and more than 75 percent of Earn-It youth have successfully repayed both their victims and the community.

SHERIFF'S WORK ALTERNATIVE PROGRAM (SWAP)
Cook County Jail
2600 South California Avenue
Chicago, IL 60608
(312) 890-6061

Created as a response to overcrowded jails, the SWAP program allows offenders to "work off" their sentence through various jobs, ranging from shoveling snow to washing county vehicles. Participating DUI offenders have a 3 percent recidivism rate, while other participating offenders have a 20 percent recidivism rate, compared to a 70 to 75 percent recidivism rate for offenders who serve jail sentences.

PROJECT TRADE
Home Builders Institute
1090 Vermont Avenue, NW, Suite 600
Washington, DC 20005
(202) 371-0600

This project represents Training, Restitution, Apprenticeship, Development, and Education. Minimum-security inmates are given training in a job skill such as carpentry, and upon release enter an apprenticeship program to pay restitution to the community by building low-income housing.

THE ARGUS COMMUNITY LEARNING FOR LIVING CENTER
760 East 160th Street
Bronx, New York 10456
(718) 993-5300

This program provides vocational training, substance abuse treatment, housing, family planning, health care, and early education. An evaluation by the Eisenhower Foundation found that youth participating in this program received higher-paying jobs with greater benefits than those that did not. Another evaluation discovered no criminal involvement of the youth in the vocational training program, and 87 percent were successfully placed in training-related jobs.

LEGIT
The Osborne Association
383 Pearl Street, 5th Floor
Brooklyn, NY 11230
(718) 624-8423

Legit is a youth entrepreneurial program. Many inner-city young-sters who sell drugs have considerable business acumen and entrepre-neurial spirit that can be harnessed in legitimate businesses of their own.

THE PHOENIX HOUSE
164 West 74th Street
New York, NY 10023
(212) 595-5810

The Phoenix House is the largest private nonprofit drug abuse services agency in the country and provides treatment for approxi-mately 1,800 adults and adolescents nationwide. Phoenix House was among the first to adopt self-help methods that make the individual the focus of treatment and address the underlying causes of drug abuse.

DELANCEY STREET
Delancey Street Foundation
600 Embarcadero
San Francisco, CA 94107
(415) 957-9800

Delancey Street is considered a leading self-help residential educa-tion center for former substance abusers and ex-convicts. Residents learn academic and vocational skills, interpersonal and social survival skills, values, and the sense of responsibility and self-reliance neces-sary to live a drug-free existence. In the twenty-two years of opera-tion, there has never been an incident of physical violence in Delancey Street, nor have there been any arrests.

TRANSITION AFTERCARE GROUP PROGRAM
Morehouse School of Medicine
720 Westview Drive, S.W.
Atlanta, GA 30310
(404) 752-1754

This aftercare program is designed to reduce recidivism among juvenile offenders. The program provides case management, treatment services, and career, educational, and vocational training activities.

CASE MANAGEMENT FOR AT-RISK CHILDREN IN DETENTION
Department of Juvenile Justice
City of New York
365 Broadway, 2nd Floor
New York, NY 10013
(212) 925-7779

This program was designed to remedy the problem of "dead time" spent by children in custody awaiting court appearances. The program helps the 4,000 children in detention each year to break the cycle of delinquency through a holistic approach that provides educational, medical, and social services and helps clients adjust to the community after their release.

COURT EMPLOYMENT PROJECT (CEP)
Center for Alternative Sentencing and Employment Services
346 Broadway
New York, NY 10013
(212) 553-6636

This program for youthful felony offenders provides counseling, educational training, job training and placement, drug counseling, parenting skills, and anger control counseling. Rearrest rates for felony offenders sentenced to standard sentencing options were 96 to 150 percent higher than for offenders sentenced to six months in CEP followed by five years on probation.

FAMILY TIES
365 Broadway
New York, NY 10013
(212) 925-7779, ext. 218

Family Ties identifies the needs of each delinquent child and works to strengthen family functions through intensive home-based services, therapy, counseling, and decisionmaking and anger management skills. Approximately eight in ten of all juveniles who participated in Family Ties during 1991 and 1992 remained uninvolved with the juvenile justice system six months later. Over a period of a year or more, the success rate was 82 percent. For every $1 spent on the program, almost $7 in savings to the public were generated by averting juvenile placements in youth detention facilities.

FLORIDA AUGUSTUS SECURE CARE UNIT (FASCU)

4501 Lannie Road
Jacksonville, FL 32218
(904) 765-2266

FASCU is a unique program for the habitual and serious juvenile offender. The secure facility provides diagnostic evaluations, mental health services, educational services, vocational services, job training and placement, and aftercare and reentry services.

APPENDIX C

The National Criminal Justice Commission Members

MICHAEL ARMSTRONG
Kirkpatrick & Lockhart
New York, New York
A former Air Force pilot, Mr. Armstrong has had a renowned career as a federal prosecutor and public servant. Mr. Armstrong served for five years as a prosecutor in the U.S. Attorney's Office in the Southern District of New York, where he rose to become chief of the Securities Fraud Division. He later became Chief Counsel to the Commission to Investigate Alleged Police Corruption in New York City in the early 1970s. Known as the Knapp Commission, the investigation untangled one of the most extensive webs of police corruption in American history. Mr. Armstrong later served as district attorney of Queens County, New York. He is now counsel to the New York Urban League, a director of the New York Legal Aid Society, and a partner in the firm of Kirkpatrick & Lockhart.

PROFESSOR DERRICK BELL
New York University School of Law
New York, New York
A native of Pittsburgh, Professor Bell is considered one of the most creative teachers and legal scholars in the country. His *Race, Racism,*

and American Law was first published in 1971 and, now in its third (1982) edition, is still used in civil rights courses at both the law school and undergraduate levels across the country. His two most recent books, *Faces at the Bottom of the Well: The Permanence of Racism* and *And We Are Not Saved: The Elusive Quest for Racial Justice*, utilize fiction to illustrate contemporary racial dilemmas in America. After an early career as a Justice Department lawyer and a staff attorney for the NAACP Legal Defense Fund, Professor Bell joined the Harvard Law School faculty in 1969 and became its first tenured African-American professor in 1971. In 1980, Professor Bell became dean of the University of Oregon Law School and in 1985 was selected as Teacher of the Year by the Society of American Law Schools. He returned to Harvard in 1986, and the university terminated his position there in 1992 when he refused to end an unpaid leave taken to protest the lack of diversity on the law school faculty. Professor Bell currently teaches at the New York University Law School and lectures around the country.

JAMES BERNARD
New York, New York

In 1989, James Bernard co-founded *The Source* with three business partners. Under his editorial direction, the magazine became "the Bible" of the hip-hop community and its circulation soared to 150,000 with virtually no money spent on promotion or publicity. Last year, he co-authored the second edition of *The Book of Rock Lists* with ex–*Rolling Stone* writer Dave Marsh and has written about music and pop culture for the *New York Times,* the *Village Voice, Entertainment Weekly,* and *Reconstruction.* A former union organizer, Mr. Bernard has appointments pending to the boards of Housing Works, a Manhattan-based agency servicing homeless people with AIDS, and the Eisenhower Foundation, a Washington D.C.–based urban policy think tank with a focus on youth and violence prevention. He recently served as the assistant to the Executive Producer of the Million Man March. Mr. Bernard, who now lives in Brooklyn, graduated from Hillsboro High School in Nashville, Tennessee, Brown University, and Harvard Law School.

REED BRODY
Attorney
New York, New York

Mr. Brody, who has worked on justice issues in over forty countries, is currently assisting the government of Haiti in bringing criminal prosecutions against human rights violators. As director of the Human Rights Division of the United Nations Observer Mission in El Salvador (ONUSAL), he coordinated programs to support that country's judiciary, human rights institutions, and civilian police. His previous positions include executive director of the International Human Rights Law Group and executive secretary of the Geneva-based International Commission of Jurists. At the 1993 U.N. World Conference on Human Rights, Mr. Brody coordinated the lobbying efforts of over 3,000 human rights activists. As a U.N. expert, he assisted the government of Mongolia in preparing its 1991 constitution. He is a principal architect of U.N. standards on detention, "disappearances," and the independence of the judiciary. A graduate of Columbia Law School, Mr. Brody is a former New York Assistant Attorney General and the author of a book documenting human rights violations by the contras in Nicaragua.

SARAH BUEL, ESQUIRE
Assistant District Attorney
Norfolk County District Attorney's Office
Dedham, Massachusetts

Ms. Buel has spent the past seventeen years working with battered women and abused children as an advocate, public policy analyst, and prosecutor. She currently prosecutes domestic violence cases as an assistant district attorney in Norfolk County, Massachusetts. Ms. Buel is the former director of the Domestic Violence Unit at the Suffolk County District Attorney's Office in Boston. She is a former Evelyn Green Davis Fellow in Law at the Bunting Institute at Radcliffe College, the nation's oldest and largest center of advanced study for women scholars and artists. Ms. Buel lectures extensively at law and medical schools and recently traveled to thirty-eight states gathering research for a book on family and domestic violence. For her work in the field of family and domestic violence, Ms.Buel was recently named one of the top twenty young lawyers in the country by the American Bar Association.

CONSTANCE R. CAPLAN
The Time Group, Caplan Family Trust
Baltimore, Maryland

As president of the Time Group, Ms. Caplan manages an extensive portfolio of multifamily housing in the Baltimore metropolitan market and is the current executive director of the Caswell J. Caplan Charitable Income Trusts. From 1976 to 1986, she served as the Criminal Justice Coordinator in Baltimore County and also worked for the Governor's Commission on Law Enforcement and Administration of Justice for four years. In 1991, she was named by Mayor Kurt Schmoke to be co-chairperson of the Downtown Security Task Force. Ms. Caplan has participated in many civic activities and has sat on a number of boards, including the American Federation of Arts, the Baltimore Mentoring Institute, and the Mt. Vernon Community Policing Committee.

PROFESSOR NILS CHRISTIE
The Faculty of Law, University of Oslo
Oslo, Norway

One of the most respected criminologists in Europe, Professor Christie is a senior lecturer on the faculty of law at the University of Oslo and is a past president of the Scandinavian Council for Criminology. He is considered an international expert on rates of incarceration and has consulted with corrections officials in numerous countries around the world. Mr. Christie is the author of ten books and several academic articles covering topics as diverse as crime control, education, drugs, and the autonomy of the mentally retarded. His *Limits to Pain* has been translated into twelve languages. His most recent book, *Crime Control as Industry: Towards Gulags, Western Style?*, argues that criminal justice policy in the United States is driven partly by financial pressures from private companies that benefit from the expansion of the corrections system.

LYNN A. CURTIS, EXECUTIVE DIRECTOR
The Eisenhower Foundation
Washington, D.C.

As President of the Milton S. Eisenhower Foundation, Dr. Curtis has devoted much of the last decade to implementing in American inner cities the recommendations of the presidential crime, riot, and violence commissions of the 1960s. Dr. Curtis was co-director of the Crimes of Violence Task Force of the National Violence Commission (known as the Eisenhower Commission) and executive director of President Carter's interagency urban policy group. He has written or edited seven books on urban issues, including *American Violence and Public Policy*, published by Yale University Press in 1985, and the Eisenhower Foundation's twenty-five-year update of the Kerner Commission, released in 1993. He is a member of the executive committee of the American Academy of Political and Social Science, a trustee of the Parliamentary Human Rights Foundation, and Vice-Chair of Partners for Democratic Change, the international organization that trains officials in Eastern Europe and Russia in democratic methods of decisionmaking. Under the leadership of Dr. Curtis, the Eisenhower Foundation continues to take delegations of American police chiefs and inner-city community organizations to Japan to study community policing practices and has launched the Corporation for Investment in What Works.

Kathleen DiChiara, Executive Director
Community FoodBank of New Jersey
Hillside, New Jersey

Kathleen DiChiara founded the Community FoodBank of New Jersey from the back of her station wagon in 1975 as a personal response to neighborhood hunger. Under her stewardship, the organization has grown over the past two decades into the largest source of donated food in New Jersey. The FoodBank operates out of a 280,000-square-foot warehouse in Hillside and gives away 10 to 12 million pounds of food annually. It employs 52 people, half of whom are ex-offenders, and counts on the work of 5,000 volunteers. Ms. DiChiara has been honored by the Pope, two Presidents, the Governor of New Jersey, and many civic and community organizations. She was most recently named by *N.J. Woman* magazine as one of the fifteen most accomplished women in the state.

Eddie Ellis, Education Coordinator
Neighborhood Defender Services of Harlem
New York, New York

Mr. Ellis recently was released after serving twenty-three years in the New York State prison system. While incarcerated, Mr. Ellis won praise as a member of a prisoner-organized think tank that produced a study that demonstrated that 75 percent of those incarcerated in New York State prisons come from seven neighborhoods in New York City. Working with fellow prisoner alumni, Mr. Ellis has formed the Community Justice Institute to lobby for nontraditional approaches to rehabilitation, including a prisoner-run model penitentiary. Mr. Ellis is currently coordinator of community education for the Neighborhood Defender Service in Harlem and a fellow at the Ralph Bunche Institute for Public Policy at the City University of New York. While in prison, he obtained a B.S., magna cum laude, in business administration from Marist College and an M.A. from the New York Theological Seminary. A former Black Panther, Mr. Ellis was targeted for arrest and conviction by the COINTELPRO program of the FBI and maintains his innocence. The story of Mr. Ellis was featured in 1992 on the front page of the *New York Times*.

ELAINE JONES, DIRECTOR-COUNSEL
NAACP Legal Defense Fund
New York, New York
Elaine R. Jones is the first woman to head the NAACP Legal Defense and Educational Fund, the nation's oldest and largest non-profit civil rights law firm. It was founded in 1940 by the late Thurgood Marshall and is considered the legal arm of the movement for racial justice. A native of Norfolk, Virginia, Ms. Jones was a Peace Corps volunteer in Turkey before becoming the first African-American woman to graduate from the law school at the University of Virginia. Ms. Jones joined LDF as an attorney in 1970 and served as a counsel of record in *Furman v. Georgia*, a landmark U.S. Supreme Court case that at the time abolished the death penalty in thirty-seven states. In recognition of her success as a litigator and civil rights activist, Ms. Jones has received numerous honors, including the Career Achievement Award of the Women's Bar Association. She was also the first African-American to serve on the Board of Governors of the American Bar Association. Ms. Jones has lectured at several American and international law schools, including Tel Aviv University School of Law and the University of Khartoum in the Sudan.

BONG HWAN KIM, EXECUTIVE DIRECTOR
Korean Youth & Community Center
Los Angeles, California

As executive director of the Korean Youth & Community Center, Mr. Kim emerged from the riots in Los Angeles as a key mediator between the African-American and Korean-American communities. He serves on several boards of community and national organizations, including the National Immigration Forum, California Tomorrow, the Black-Korean Alliance, and the California Attorney General Violence Prevention Public Policy Council. Since taking over the Korean Youth & Community Center in 1987, Mr. Kim has significantly expanded its revenue base and dramatically expanded its community-based development activities. Mr. Kim also lectures at universities and other institutions on inner-city revitalization and race relations. Mr. Kim is the recipient of numerous awards, including the NAACP Equality Award and the California Wellness Foundation Violence Prevention Leadership Award.

PROFESSOR CORAMAE RICHEY MANN
Indiana University
Bloomington, Indiana

Professor Mann teaches in the Department of Criminal Justice at Indiana University and is a specialist on female crime, juvenile delinquency, and the impact of criminal justice policies on racial minorities. She is the author of *When Women Kill (1996), Unequal Justice: A Question of Color* (1993), *Female Crime and Delinquency* (1984), and academic articles on topics ranging from female homicide to white-collar crime in the oil industry of Nigeria. Before teaching, Professor Mann was a practicing clinical psychologist in the Cook County Municipal Court. She worked in the Office of Economic Opportunity during the War on Poverty and as the director of the Chicago office of the Planned Parenthood Association. While teaching at Florida State University in the late 1970s, she was appointed by the governor to serve on the state's Juvenile Justice and Delinquency Prevention Task Force. Dr. Mann has done extensive research on the ecology of crime and is co-editing a book with Commission member Marjorie Zatz called *Images of Color, Images of Crime.* She received the 1995 Bruce Smith Award from the Academy of Criminal Justice Sciences and the 1966 Distinguished Scholar

Award from the Women and Crime division of the American Society of Criminology.

PROFESSOR KIMBERLY L. MARTUS
Justice Center, University of Alaska
Anchorage, Alaska

Ms. Martus is a professor in the Justice Center at the University of Alaska, Anchorage. Her teaching, research, and service work involves federal Indian law, development of tribal justice systems, and revitalization of Native dispute resolution forums. Her Jures Doctorate was conferred in 1993 by the University of New Mexico School of Law, where she practiced in Pueblo tribal courts, founded a lay advocate training program for tribal courts, and assisted in revising the New Mexico children's code to strengthen Indian Child Welfare Act provisions. Upon returning to Alaska she served as the first director for the Alaska Native Justice Center, providing advocacy, research, and development of criminal justice policy for Alaska Natives. She was appointed by the governor to the Public Safety Transition Team, and by the State Supreme Court Chief Justice to the advisory committee for Foster Care/Court Improvement Project. She is an enrolled member of the Cahuilla Band of Mission Indians.

JEROME G. MILLER
President, National Center on Institutions and Alternatives
Alexandria, Virginia

Co-founder of the National Center on Institutions and Alternatives and Clinical Director of the Augustus Institute in Alexandria, Virginia, Dr. Miller has a doctorate in psychiatric social work and is recognized as one of the nation's leading authorities on corrections, alternative programs, and clinical work with violent juvenile and adult offenders. Prominently known for closing all the state reform schools in Massachusetts and replacing them with community-based programs while serving as Commissioner of the Massachusetts Department of Youth Services, Dr. Miller was later appointed Director of the Illinois Department of Children and Family Services and Commissioner of Children and Youth for the Commonwealth of Pennsylvania. While serving as Special Assistant to the Governor in Pennsylvania, Dr. Miller devised strategies and programs that removed 1,000 youthful offenders from the state's adult prisons.

From 1989 to 1994 Dr. Miller was jail and prison monitor for the United States Court in the Middle District of Florida. He was appointed by the Federal Court in August 1995 as Receiver for the District of Columbia's child welfare system. Dr. Miller served as a Psychiatric Social Work Officer in the United States Air Force and was an Associate Professor in the School of Social Work at Ohio State University.

PROFESSOR NORVAL MORRIS
The University of Chicago, The Law School
Chicago, Illinois

A former dean of the University of Chicago Law School and the recipient of several research awards, Professor Morris is one of the leading criminologists in the country. He has authored or co-authored several critically acclaimed books, including the recent *Between Prison and Probation: Intermediate Punishments in a Rational Sentencing System* and *The Honest Politician's Guide to Crime Control*. He is a specialist in police tactics and policy and is currently co-editing a series of books with Michael Tonry called *Studies in Crime & Public Policy*, to be published by Oxford University Press. Professor Morris was a member of the Task Force on Prisoner Rehabilitation under President Nixon, has served on several advisory commissions to the Governor of Illinois, and is a former special assistant to the Attorney General of the United States under President Carter. He is currently the Julius Kreeger Professor of Law and Criminology, Emeritus, at the University of Chicago.

EDWIN C. MOSES
Olympic Champion
Atlanta, Georgia

A physics graduate of Morehouse College, Edwin C. Moses is one of the most accomplished track stars ever and a leader of the Olympic movement. He shocked the nation in 1976 by winning the Olympic gold medal in the 400-meter hurdles after quietly training at public high schools in Atlanta (Morehouse did not have a track). He then used his background in science to design a unique training regimen that resulted in 122 straight victories over 10 years—possibly the longest string of unbroken success by an individual athlete in history. His world record in the event, set in 1983, still stands. Mr. Moses is a director of the United States Olympic Committee and is a member of the Athletes Commission of the International Olympic Committee. In 1992, he was selected by the IOC to travel to South Africa to determine if that country should be readmitted to the Olympics. Mr. Moses is a founding partner of the Platinum Group, which represents world-class athletes in their business endeavors, and is a member of the President's Commission on White House Fellowships. He received his MBA from Pepperdine University in 1994.

PROFESSOR CHARLES OGLETREE JR.
Harvard Law School
Cambridge, Massachusetts
Professor Ogletree is considered one of the leading experts on criminal law in the country and is now serving as a special consultant to Attorney General Janet Reno on juvenile justice issues. Before joining the faculty at Harvard Law School, he was a trial attorney and deputy director of the District of Columbia Public Defender Service. At Harvard, he is director of the popular Trial Advocacy Workshop and the founder of the Criminal Justice Institute. Professor Ogletree has been the moderator for many public television programs, including *Hard Drugs, Hard Choices* (1990) and *Kids, Color and Crime* (1993). He recently received the Albert M. Sacks–Paul A. Freund Award at Harvard Law School for Excellence in Teaching. He is also the author of the 1993 *Harvard Law Review* article "Beyond Justifications: Seeking Motivations to Sustain Public Defenders."

DR. CHUKWUDI ONWUACHI-SAUNDERS
Centers for Disease Control and Prevention
Philadelphia, Pennsylvania
Dr. Chukwudi Onwuachi-Saunders is a medical epidemiologist with the Centers for Disease Control and Prevention. Currently on assignment to the city of Philadelphia, Dr. Onwuachi-Saunders has developed a nationally renowned violence prevention program called Operation Peace in Philadelphia (OPP). She is an expert in injury control and is a leading authority on interpersonal violence. She received her doctorate in medicine from the University of Lagos in Lagos, Nigeria, and her masters in Public Health from Johns Hopkins University School of Hygiene and Public Health.

JoAnne Page, Director
The Fortune Society
New York, New York

Ms. Page is director of The Fortune Society, the oldest and most established ex-offender advocacy and service organization in the country. Under the leadership of Ms. Page, The Fortune Society has helped thousands of ex-offenders find jobs and develop the resources they need to lead productive lives. The majority of her sixty-five-person staff are ex-offenders who have graduated from programs offered by Fortune. Ms. Page makes frequent television appearances to speak on criminal justice issues, and has been a guest in such diverse settings as *Donahue*, CNN, and Court TV. A graduate of Yale Law School, Ms. Page for six years developed and managed programs that provided alternatives to incarceration for the Court Employment Project in New York. She is a trustee of the Milton S. Eisenhower Foundation, serves on the board of directors of the New York State Defenders Association, and is a leading advocate for changes in the criminal justice system, including reform of mandatory sentencing laws and helping prisoners exercise their right to vote.

Chief Nicholas Pastore
New Haven Police Department
New Haven, Connecticut

Chief Pastore has had a long and distinguished police career and recently was featured on *60 Minutes* for his innovative approach to implementing community policing in New Haven. During his career with the New Haven Department of Police Service, Mr. Pastore has held the ranks of detective in the Gambling and Narcotics Division, commander of the Criminal Intelligence Division, Deputy Chief Inspector of Internal Affairs, and Chief Inspector of Investigative Services. For his dedication, Chief Pastore has received many community service and outstanding achievement awards and commendations. He also has addressed various conferences and published two reports on community policing in New Haven.

Captain William Pinkney
Motivational Speaker
Chicago, Illinois

Captain Pinkney is the only African-American to circumnavigate the earth alone in a sailboat via the five great capes and one of only four people in the country ever to accomplish the feat. A native of Chicago and a veteran of the U.S. Navy, Captain Pinkney now travels widely delivering motivational speeches to groups ranging from children in elementary schools to corporate executives. His voyage was featured in a National Geographic special and was the subject of an award-winning documentary narrated by Bill Cosby. Over 30,000 students plotted his daily progress on the 47-foot cutter "Commitment" through the use of a satellite transponder and computer downlinks. A former marketing executive with Revlon, Captain Pinkney is a serious student of the maritime history of African-Americans and is currently writing a book on sailing for first graders that will be published by Open Court. Captain Pinkney is a U.S. Coast Guard licensed captain and Past Commodore of the Belmont Yacht Club in Chicago.

PROFESSOR DAVID ROTHMAN
Center for the Study of Society & Medicine, Columbia University
New York, New York

David J. Rothman is Bernard Schoenberg Professor of Social Medicine and Director of the Center for the Study of Society and Medicine at the Columbia College of Physicians and Surgeons, and Professor of History at Columbia University. Trained in social history at Harvard University, Professor Rothman has explored American practices toward the deviant and dependent. His study of the origins of mental hospitals, prisons, reformatories, and almshouses, *The Discovery of the Asylum* (1971), was co-winner of the Albert J. Beveridge Prize. Together with Sheila M. Rothman, Professor Rothman analyzed the process of deinstitutionalization in *The Willowbrook Wars* (1984), and in 1987 he received an honorary Doctor of Law Degree from the John Jay School of Criminal Justice. In his recent publications, Professor Rothman has addressed issues in the history of human experimentation, the history of drug regulation and clinical trials with a particular focus on AIDS, and the barriers to national health insurance. Currently, Professor Rothman is exploring the links between human rights and medicine, using Romania and Zimbabwe as test cases, and is completing a book for the 20th Century Fund on the American experience with rationing scarce medical resources.

PROFESSOR ANDREW RUTHERFORD
The University–Southampton
Southampton, England

Professor Rutherford is one of the premier authorities in England on penal reform and is a specialist on therapeutic options for offenders in the United States and Europe. Presently, he is a professor on the faculty of law at the University of Southampton. A former Guggenheim Fellow, Professor Rutherford directed a national survey on prisons and jails in the United States in 1978. Mr. Rutherford has been involved in comparative studies of penal policy in the United States, Japan, the Netherlands, France, and the Federal Republic of Germany. He is a consultant to the British Broadcasting Corporation and has published several articles and books on criminal justice, including *Criminal Justice and the Pursuit of Decency* (1993). He is currently chairman of the Howard League of Penal Reform.

RICHARD SANDLER, ESQUIRE
Victor & Sandler
Los Angeles, California

A graduate of the UCLA School of Law, Mr. Sandler has been a member of the bar of the state of California and the American Bar Association for almost two decades. He is a founding partner of Victor & Sandler, where he conducts a general practice and specializes in securities law and white-collar RICO investigations. Mr. Sandler is a member of the Board of Directors of The Foundations of the Milken Families and is active in community affairs. He is a member of the executive board of Heal L.A., a director of the Western Council of the Boy Scouts of America, and a board member of the Jewish Community Foundation and Valley Beth Shalom Synagogue.

DONALD SANTARELLI, ESQUIRE
Bell, Boyd & Lloyd
Washington, D.C.

A former prosecuting attorney in the District of Columbia, Mr. Santarelli is currently chairman of the National Committee on Community Corrections and is a founding partner in the law firm of Santarelli, Smith & Carrocio, a firm specializing in a federal practice. Santarelli, Smith & Carrocio was recently merged into the national firm of Bell, Boyd & Lloyd. From 1973 to 1974, Mr. Santarelli was the administrator of the Law Enforcement Assistance Administration, a $1 billion yearly program in the Department of Justice that assisted state and local governments to reduce crime and improve the justice system. He also served as associate deputy attorney general responsible for all criminal justice matters under President Nixon from 1969 to 1972. Mr. Santarelli has served on several boards by presidential appointment, including those of the Corporation for Public Broadcasting, the Legal Services Corporation, and the Overseas Private Investment Corporation. He is presently the vice-chairman for governmental affairs of the American Bar Association Criminal Justice Section.

VINCENT SCHIRALDI, EXECUTIVE DIRECTOR
Center on Juvenile and Criminal Justice
San Francisco, California
Vincent Schiraldi is the founder and executive director of the Center on Juvenile and Criminal Justice in San Francisco. Mr. Schiraldi is a leading authority in California on the development of model programs in the areas of alternative sentencing, depopulation of juvenile detention facilities, pretrial release for homeless defendants, and independent living settings for parolees. He served on the California Blue Ribbon Commission on Inmate Population Management, was founding chair of San Francisco's Juvenile Probation Commission, and served on the Criminal Justice Subcommittees of the California Commission on the Status of African-American Men and the Little Hoover Commission. Mr. Schiraldi holds a masters degree in social work from New York University.

KENNETH SCHOEN, DIRECTOR FOR JUSTICE PROGRAMS
The Edna McConnell Clark Foundation
New York, New York
For the past fourteen years Mr. Schoen has served as the director of the Justice Program for the Edna McConnell Clark Foundation, one of the nation's leading private foundations on criminal justice. As program director, Mr. Schoen has been on the cutting edge in funding criminal justice reforms around the country. He also serves as special master for the federal court overseeing a consent decree affecting the New York City corrections system. From 1973 to 1979, Mr. Schoen served as Commissioner of the Minnesota Department of Corrections. He was

the architect of a community corrections law in Minnesota that has served as a model for several states around the country. Mr. Schoen also played a leading role in designing a secure prison that many experts believe is the most humane in the country. He has served as the superintendent of the Minnesota Home School, a juvenile correctional facility in Sauk Centre, Minnesota, and as an adjunct professor at the John Jay School of Criminal Justice in New York City.

MARY ANN TALLY, ESQUIRE
North Carolina Academy of Trial Lawyers
Raleigh, North Carolina

A native of Knoxville and a Phi Beta Kappa graduate of the University of Tennessee, Ms. Tally is a leader or member of several commissions in North Carolina devoted to the improvement of the criminal justice system. She is the general counsel to the North Carolina Academy of Trial Lawyers and chairperson of the Board of Directors of the Farmworkers Legal Services of North Carolina. Ms. Tally served as the Public Defender for the Twelfth Judicial Circuit in North Carolina from 1976 to 1993. During her tenure as Public Defender, she was vice-chairperson of the North Carolina Commission on Alternatives to Incarceration, president of the North Carolina Association of Public Defenders, and a member of the North Carolina Criminal Code Commission. Ms. Tally is also the recipient of the North Carolina Jaycees Award as one of the five outstanding young women in North Carolina.

PROFESSOR JAMES VORENBERG
Harvard Law School
Cambridge, Massachusetts

The former dean of Harvard Law School, Professor Vorenberg has devoted much of his career to the study and improvement of the criminal justice system. In 1964, Professor Vorenberg became the first director of the Office of Criminal Justice in the Department of Justice under Attorney General Robert F. Kennedy. A year later, he was appointed by President Johnson to be executive director of the national criminal justice commission (called the President's Commission on Law Enforcement and Administration of Justice) that produced the noted study *The Challenge of Crime in a Free Society*. Professor Vorenberg was an assistant to Special Investigator Archibald

Cox during the Watergate investigations. As dean of Harvard Law School from 1981 to 1989, Professor Vorenberg developed new academic programs in human rights, law and economics, international criminal justice, and the legal profession. He also established the first loan repayment plan to encourage law graduates to take jobs in the public sector. Professor Vorenberg is a longtime director of the NAACP Legal Defense Fund and was the first chairman of the Massachusetts State Ethics Commission.

PROFESSOR IRVIN WALLER
International Centre for Prevention of Crime
Montreal, Canada
Irvin Waller is director general of the International Centre for Prevention of Crime, which is an international nongovernmental organization established to harness the world's crime prevention know-how to reduce delinquency and violent crime. Its board represents its principal partners, which are federations of cities, national crime prevention agencies, and organizations concerned with criminal justice from Europe, Latin America, Africa, and Asia. Its work program is reviewed by a governmental advisory committee, which includes Quebec and Canada, England and Wales, and France. Dr. Waller has been consulted for more than two decades by local and national governments around the world on crime-reduction strategies. He has been an adviser to the United Nations, the Council of Europe, and the Organization for Economic Cooperation and Development. He was a principal contributor to, and advocate for, the Declaration on the Basic Principles of Justice for Victims of Crime and Abuse of Power approved in 1985 by the U.N. General Assembly. Dr. Waller is currently on leave from his post as professor of criminology at the University of Ottawa. He is president of the World Society of Victimology and has authored extensive scientific publications on crime prevention, policing, victim assistance, and correctional policy.

HUBERT WILLIAMS, PRESIDENT
The Police Foundation
Washington, D.C.
Hubert Williams is president of The Police Foundation, a private, nonprofit research and technical assistance organization in Washington,

D.C. As a leading advocate for higher professional standards and uniform practices in policing, Mr. Williams has presided over the design and implementation of scientific field experiments that are at the forefront of modern police policy and procedure. A thirty-year veteran of policing, Mr. Williams served for eleven years as director of police in Newark, New Jersey. He earned a bachelor of science degree from the John Jay College of Criminal Justice and a J.D. from Rutgers University School of Law, and was a research fellow at Harvard Law School's Center for Criminal Justice. Mr. Williams was the founding president of the National Organization of Black Law Enforcement Executives and serves as a member of numerous boards and committees, including the Rand Corporation's Drug Policy Research Center, Innovations in State and Local Government, and John Jay College. He served as Deputy Special Adviser to the Los Angeles Board of Police Commissioners in the investigation of the police response to the Los Angeles riots.

LUIS WILMOT, REGIONAL COUNSEL
Mexican American Legal Defense Fund
San Antonio, Texas

Mr. Wilmot is regional counsel of the Southwest office of the Mexican American Legal Defense and Educational Fund in San Antonio. A former staff attorney with the United States Commission on Civil Rights, Mr. Wilmot has a long history of fighting to protect the civil rights of recent immigrants. He filed the lawsuit that ultimately prompted the Supreme Court, in *Plyler v. Doc* (1982), to recognize that undocumented students had a constitutional right to a public education. Mr. Wilmot is the founder and former director of Centro Para Immigrantes, the first office in Houston representing indigent immigrants before the Immigration and Naturalization Service. Mr. Wilmot later served as director of litigation in the Office of People's Counsel in the District of Columbia, where he represented D.C. utility ratepayers in ratemaking proceedings. Most recently, he was appointed by Texas Governor Ann Richards to direct the Office of Public Utility Counsel in Austin, Texas. He served in that post for two years before joining MALDEF.

PROFESSOR MARJORIE S. ZATZ

Arizona State University
Tempe, Arizona

Marjorie S. Zatz is a professor of Justice Studies and Women's Studies at Arizona State University. She has written extensively on criminal justice issues in the United States and Latin America. She is the author of *Producing Legality: Law and Socialism in Cuba* (1994) and coeditor with William Chambliss of *Making Law: The State, the Law, and Structural Contradictions* (1993). Professor Zatz has published numerous academic articles on racial and ethnic discrimination in court processing and sanctioning, the impact of criminal justice policies on Chicano youths and American Indians, gender and the legal profession, and social and legal change in Cuba and Nicaragua. With Coramae Richey Mann, she is currently coediting a book entitled *Images of Color: Images of Crime.* Professor Zatz is a member of the executive board of the American Society of Criminology and chair of the Crime and Delinquency Division of the Society for the Study of Social Problems.

NOTES

CHAPTER ONE: CRIME AND POLICY

1. Boggess, Scott, and John Bounds. July 1993. *Did Criminal Activity Increase During the 1980s? Comparisons Across Data Sources.* Working Paper Series, #4431. Cambridge, Mass.: National Bureau of Economic Research.

2. See generally Miller, Jerome G. Spring 1996. *Search and Destroy.* Cambridge, Mass.: Cambridge University Press; Reiss, Albert J., Jr., and Jeffrey A. Roth, eds. 1993. *Understanding and Preventing Violence.* Washington, D.C.: National Academy Press; Currie, Elliott. 1985. *Confronting Crime: An American Challenge.* New York: Pantheon Books.

3. Reiss, Albert J., Jr., and Jeffrey A. Roth, eds. 1993. *Understanding and Preventing Violence.* Washington, D.C.: National Academy Press: 414.

4. U.S. Department of Justice, Federal Bureau of Investigation. December 4, 1994. *Crime in the United States—1993*; 1974. *Crime in the United States—1973.* Washington, D.C.: U.S. Government Printing Office.

5. Centers for Disease Control and Prevention. October 14, 1994. *Morbidity and Mortality Weekly Report*: 726.

6. U.S. Department of Justice, Bureau of Justice Statistics. July 1994. *Murder in Families.* Washington, D.C.: U.S. Government Printing Office.

7. U.S. Department of Justice, Bureau of Justice Statistics. March

1994. *Criminal Victimization in the United States—1992*. Washington, D.C.: U.S. Government Printing Office: 23, Table 4.

8. Ibid., p. 28, Table 10.

9. These statistics are from 1988 or 1991, dependent on the country. Van Dijk, Jan J. M., and Pat Mayhew. November 1992. *Criminal Victimisation in the Industrialised World*. The Hague, Netherlands: Ministry of Justice/University of Leyden: 33, 23, 10.

10. Ibid.

11. U.S. Department of Justice, Bureau of Justice Statistics. March 1994. *Criminal Victimization in the Unites States—1992*. Washington, D.C.: U.S. Government Printing Office: 91, Table 86.

12. Ibid., p. 91, Table 88.

13. U.S. Department of Justice, Bureau of Justice Statistics. June 1994. *Prisoners in 1993*. Washington, D.C.: U.S. Government Printing Office: 13, Table 18.

14. U.S. Department of Justice, Bureau of Justice Statistics. August 1995. *Prisoners in 1994*. Washington, D.C.: U.S. Government Printing Office: 10, Appendix Table 2.

15. Zimring, Franklin, and Gordon Hawkins. 1994. The Growth of Imprisonment in California. *British Journal of Criminology*. Vol. 34, special issue: 88.

16. U.S. Advisory Commission on Intergovernmental Relations. May 1993. *The Role of General Government Elected Officials in Criminal Justice*. Washington, D.C.: U.S. Advisory Commission on Intergovernmental Relations.

17. Fabelo, Tony. January 1993. *Sentencing Dynamics Study*. Austin, Tex.: Criminal Justice Policy Council: 26.

18. U.S. Department of Justice. February 4, 1994. *An Analysis of Nonviolent Drug Offenders with Minimal Criminal Histories*. Washington, D.C.: U.S. Government Printing Office.

19. Valentine, Paul. May 24, 1993. "You Can't Build Your Way Out," Maryland Official Says. *Washington Post*.

20. Ibid.

21. Data compiled by Franklin E. Zimring and Gordon Hawkins in Stoff, D. M., J. Breiling, and J. Maser, eds. 1996. *Handbook of Anti-Social Behavior*. New York: John Wiley and Sons.

22. U.S. Department of Justice, Bureau of Justice Statistics Bulletins. *Prisoners* series, 1980–93. Washington, D.C.: U.S. Government Printing Office.

23. Data compiled by Franklin E. Zimring and Gordon Hawkins in Stoff, D. M., J. Breiling, and J. Maser, eds. 1996. *Handbook of Anti-Social Behavior*. New York: John Wiley and Sons.

24. Egan, Timothy. February 15, 1994. A Three Strikes Penal Law Shows It's Not as Simple as It Seems. *New York Times*.

25. Schiraldi, Vincent, Peter Y. Sussman, and Lanric Hyland. October 1994. *Three Strikes: The Unintended Victims*. San Francisco: Center on Juvenile and Criminal Justice: 15–17.

26. Ibid., p. 17.

27. California Legislative Analyst's Office. January 6, 1995. *The "Three Strikes and You're Out" Law—A Preliminary Assessment*. Sacramento, Calif.: California Legislative Analyst's Office: 8.

28. Zimbardo, Philip. November 1994. *Transforming California's Prisons into Expensive Old Age Homes for Felons: Enormous Hidden Costs and Consequences for California's Taxpayers*. San Francisco: Center on Juvenile and Criminal Justice.

29. Greenwood, Peter, et al. 1994. *Three Strikes and You're Out— Estimated Benefits and Costs of California's New Mandatory Sentencing Law*. Santa Monica, Calif.: Rand Corporation.

30. California Legislative Analyst's Office. January 6, 1995. *The "Three Strikes and You're Out" Law—A Preliminary Assessment*. Sacramento, Calif.: California Legislative Analyst's Office.

31. The data presented by the Los Angeles Public Defender's Office were based on the first six months of actual experience with Assembly Bill 971—the "three strikes" law. Schiraldi, Vincent, and Michael Godfrey. October 1994. *Racial Disparities in the Charging of Los Angeles County's "Third Strike" Cases*. San Francisco: Center on Juvenile and Criminal Justice.

32. U.S. Department of Justice, Bureau of Justice Statistics. August 1995. *Probation and Parole Violators in State Prison, 1991*. Washington, D.C.: U.S. Government Printing Office: 10; U.S. Department of Justice, Federal Bureau of Investigation. August 30, 1992. *Crime in the United States—1991*. Washington, D.C.: U.S. Government Printing Office: 10.

33. Virginia House Appropriations Committee. Staff report. September 19, 1994. *Analysis of Potential Costs Under the Governor's Sentencing Reform Plan*. Richmond, Va.: Office of the Governor.

34. Baker, Donald P., and Peter Baker. December 21, 1994. Allen's Tax Break Would Force Trade-Offs in N. VA. *Washington Post*.

35. See generally Governor's Commission on Parole Abolition and Sentencing Reform. August 1994. *Final Report*. Richmond, Va.: Office of the Governor.

36. Baker, Peter. September 19, 1994. Many Ex-Offenders Succeed After Release. *Washington Post*.

37. Sileo, Chi Chi. December 6, 1993. Sentencing Rules That Shackle Justice. *Insight:* 11.

38. Ibid.

39. Associated Press. March 10, 1994. Justice Kennedy Assails Mandatory Sentences. *Washington Post*; Sileo, Chi Chi. December 6, 1993. Sentencing Rules That Shackle Justice. *Insight*.

40. Families Against Mandatory Minimums. January/February 1993. *FAMM-gram-action kit*. Issue no. 10; Sileo, Chi Chi. December 6, 1993. Sentencing Rules That Shackle Justice. *Insight:* 11.

41. Wilkins, William W. September/October 1993. Testimony of Judge William W. Wilkins Jr., chairman, United States Sentencing Commission: July 28, 1993. *Federal Sentencing Reporter.* Vol. 6, no. 2., p. 68; Campaign for an Effective Crime Policy. October 1993. *Evaluating Mandatory Minimum Sentences.* Washington, D.C.: Campaign for an Effective Crime Policy; United States Sentencing Commission. 1991. *Mandatory Minimum Penalties in the Federal Criminal Justice System: A Special Report to Congress.* Washington, D.C.: The Commission; Schulhofer, Stephen. Summer 1993. Rethinking Mandatory Minimums. *Wake Forest Law Review* 28:199; Miller, Marc, and Daniel J. Freed. September/October 1993. The Chasm Between the Judiciary and Congress over Mandatory Minimum Sentences. *Federal Sentencing Reporter.* Vol. 6, no. 2.

42. See generally Currie, Elliott. 1985. *Confronting Crime: An American Challenge.* New York: Pantheon Books.

43. See generally Schweinhart, L. J., H. V. Barnes, and D. P. Weikart. 1993. *Significant Benefits: The High/Scope Perry Preschool Study Through Age 27.* Ypsilanti, Mich.: High/Scope Press.

44. U.S. Department of Commerce, Bureau of the Census. March 1994. *Current Population Reports.* Washington, D.C.: U.S. Government Printing Office; Carnegie Task Force on Meeting the Needs of Young Children. April 1994. *Starting Points: Meeting the Needs of Our Youngest Children.* New York: Carnegie Corporation.

45. Reiss, Albert J., Jr., and Jeffrey A. Roth, eds. 1993. *Understanding and Preventing Violence.* Washington, D.C.: National Academy Press; Currie, Elliott. 1985. *Confronting Crime: An American Challenge.* New York: Pantheon Books.

46. See generally Carnegie Task Force on Meeting the Needs of Young Children. April 1994. *Starting Points: Meeting the Needs of Our Youngest Children.* New York: Carnegie Corporation.

47. Ibid., p. 17.

48. Rainwater, Lee, and Timothy M. Smeeding. August 1995. *Luxembourg Income Study: Working Paper No. 127: Doing Poorly: The Real Income of American Children in a Comparative Perspective.* Syracuse, N.Y.: Maxwell School of Citizenship and Public Affairs, Syracuse University.

49. Currie, Elliott. 1985. *Confronting Crime: An American Challenge.* New York: Pantheon Books: 167–169.

50. U.S. Department of Commerce, Bureau of the Census. March 1994. *Current Population Reports.* Washington, D.C.: U.S. Government Printing Office.

51. Ibid.

52. These child poverty rates take into account government benefits as a source of income. Rainwater, Lee, and Timothy M. Smeeding. August 1995. *Luxembourg Income Study: Working Paper No. 127: Doing Poorly: The Real Income of American Children in a Comparative Perspective.* Syracuse, N.Y.: Maxwell School of Citizenship and Public Affairs, Syracuse University: Table A–2.

53. For a complete discussion of social trends and their relationship to criminal justice issues, see National Criminal Justice Commission. June 1994. Breakdown of Caregiving Institutions. Unpublished paper. Alexandria, Va.: National Criminal Justice Commission.

Chapter Two: Prisons

1. Zachary, G. Pascal. September 29, 1995. Economists Say Prison Boom Will Take Toll. *Wall Street Journal:* B1.

2. U.S. Department of Justice, Bureau of Justice Statistics. April 1995. *Jails and Jail Inmates 1993–1994.* Washington, D.C.: U.S. Government Printing Office; *Prisoners in 1994.* August 1995. Washington, D.C.: U.S. Government Printing Office.

3. U.S. Department of Justice, Bureau of Justice Statistics. August 27, 1995. *The Nation's Correctional Population Tops 5 Million.* Press release.

4. U.S. Bureau of the Census. November 1993. *Population Projections of the United States, by Age, Sex, Race, and Hispanic Origin: 1993 to 2050.* Washington, D.C.: U.S. Government Printing Office: 14, Table 2.

5. The total number of admissions, including transfers and readmissions, is 13,245,000. U.S. Department of Justice, Bureau of Justice Statistics. April 1995. *Jails and Jail Inmates 1993–1994.* Washington, D.C.: U.S. Government Printing Office.

6. Miller, Jerome G. March 1994. *African-American Males in the Criminal Justice System.* Unpublished paper presented at the National Criminal Justice Commission Conference, Alexandria, Virginia.

7. Miller, Jerome G. June 1, 1993. *The Duval County Jail Report.* Alexandria, Va.: National Center on Institutions and Alternatives.

8. The number of criminal records as of December 31, 1993, was 47,833,600, and in 1993 alone the FBI received almost 4.2 million fingerprint records. U.S. Department of Justice, Bureau of Justice Statistics.

January 1995. *Survey of Criminal History Information Systems, 1993.* Washington, D.C.: U.S. Government Printing Office: 19.

9. Austin, James, and John Irwin. 1994. *It's About Time: America's Imprisonment Binge.* Belmont, Calif.: Wadsworth: 160.

10. Office of the Comptroller of the Department of Defense. March 1994. *National Defense Budget Estimates for FY 1995.* Washington, D.C.: Department of Defense.

11. Camp, Camille G., and George M. Camp. Various years. *The Corrections Yearbook; Adult Corrections 1981* through *1994.* South Salem, N.Y.: Criminal Justice Institute.

12. *Violent Crime Control and Law Enforcement Act of 1994.* Public Law 103-322. September 13, 1994.

13. The Sentencing Project reports the incarceration rate in Russia to be 558 per 100,000. Mauer, Marc. September 1994. *Americans Behind Bars: The International Use of Incarceration, 1992–93.* Washington, D.C.: The Sentencing Project: 4. However, data from Russia suffers from serious problems of reliability. Austin, James. March 1994. *An Overview of Incarceration Trends in the United States and Their Impact on Crime.* Unpublished paper presented at the National Criminal Justice Commission Conference, Alexandria, Virginia.

14. Mauer, Marc. September 1994. *Americans Behind Bars: The International Use of Incarceration, 1992–93.* Washington, D.C.: The Sentencing Project.

15. Ibid.

16. U.S. Department of Justice, Bureau of Justice Statistics. August 1995. *Prisoners in 1994.* Washington, D.C.: U.S. Government Printing Office.

17. U.S. Department of Justice, Bureau of Justice Statistics. August 1995. *Prisoners in 1994.* Washington, D.C.: U.S. Government Printing Office.

18. See for example July 1995. Breaking the Silence on Prison Rape and AIDS. *Corrections Compendium.* Vol. XX, no. 7, p. 14.

19. Terry, Don. September 13, 1992. More Familiar, Life in a Cell Seems Less Terrible. *New York Times:* 1; also see generally Miller, Jerome G. 1996. *Search and Destroy.* Cambridge, Mass.: Cambridge University Press.

20. Terry, Don. September 13, 1992. More Familiar, Life in a Cell Seems Less Terrible. *New York Times:* 1.

21. See, e.g., Nossiter, Adam. September 17, 1994. Making Hard Times Harder: States Cut Jail TV and Sports. *New York Times.*

22. Clark, Charles S. February 4, 1994. Prison Overcrowding. *The Congressional Quarterly Researcher.* Vol. 4, no. 5, p. 100; U.S. Department of Justice, Bureau of Justice Statistics. April 1992. Bulletin. *Prisons and Prisoners*

in the United States. Washington, D.C.: U.S. Government Printing Office: 8.

23. *LeMaire v. Maass,* 745 F. Supp. 623 (D. Or. 1990).

24. Donaldson, Stephen. 1995. *Rape of Incarcerated Prisoners: A Preliminary Statistical Look.* New York: Stop Prisoner Rape, Inc.

25. Editorial. September 21, 1994. Blunt talk from U.S. attorney. *Washington Post.*

26. ACLU National Prison Project. January 1, 1995. *Status Report: State Prisons and the Courts.* Washington, D.C.: American Civil Liberties Union.

27. Nossiter, Adam. September 17, 1994. Making Hard Times Harder: States Cut Jail TV and Sports. *New York Times.*

28. Bass, Paul. May 26, 1994. Hit and Run. *New Haven Advocate.*

29. U.S. Department of Justice, Bureau of Justice Statistics. October 1994. *National Corrections Reporting Program, 1992.* Washington, D.C.: U.S. Government Printing Office: 39; Camp, Camille G., and George M. Camp. 1994. *The Corrections Yearbook 1994: Adult Corrections.* South Salem, N.Y.: Criminal Justice Institute, Inc.: 18; U.S. Department of Justice, Bureau of Justice Statistics. October 27, 1994. Press release. *State and Federal Prison Population Tops One Million.*

30. Andersen, Eric. Winter 1985. Denmark's Radical Approach to Super-Max Yields Success. *The National Prison Project: A Project of the American Civil Liberties Union Foundation.* No. 6: 8-9.

31. U.S. Department of Justice, Bureau of Justice Statistics. March 1994. Special Report. *Women in Prison.* Washington, D.C.: U.S. Government Printing Office: 6-7.

32. Miller, Jerome G. 1992. *Search and Destroy: The Plight of African-American Males in the Criminal Justice System.* Unpublished paper. Alexandria, Va.: National Center on Institutions and Alternatives.

33. Camp, Camille G., and George M. Camp. 1994. *The Corrections Yearbook 1994: Adult Corrections.* South Salem, N.Y.: Criminal Justice Institute: 48-49.

34. Ibid., pp. 37, 48-49.

35. Proband, Stan. October 1995. Corrections Leads State Appropriations Increases for '96. *Overcrowded Times.*

36. Gold, Steve. 1990. *Trends in State Spending.* Albany, N.Y.: Center for the Study of the States, Nelson A. Rockefeller Institute of Government.

37. Proband, Stan. October 1995. Corrections Leads State Appropriations Increases for '96. *Overcrowded Times.*

38. U.S. Department of Justice, Bureau of Justice Statistics. September 1992. Bulletin. *Justice Expenditure and Employment, 1990.* Washington, D.C.: U.S. Government Printing Office: 2.

39. Moore, John W. July 30, 1994. Locked In. *National Journal:* 1785.

40. The Edna McConnell Clark Foundation. April 1993. *Americans Behind Bars*. New York: The Edna McConnell Clark Foundation: 4.

41. Moore, John W. July 30, 1994. Locked In. *National Journal:* 1785.

42. This is arrived at by dividing the FY94 total operating and capital costs of $20.1 billion by the number of inmates in the state systems on June 30, 1994, 919, 143. See Camp, Camille G., and George M. Camp. 1994. *The Corrections Yearbook 1994: Adult Corrections*. South Salem, N.Y.: Criminal Justice Institute: 1, 48–49; U.S. Department of Justice, Bureau of Justice Statistics. October 27, 1994. Press release. *State and Federal Prison Population Tops One Million*. Washington, D.C.: U.S. Government Printing Office. 1993 median household after-tax income is $26,112. U.S. Bureau of the Census. 1993. Unpublished data. Current Population Survey.

43. The average family will pay $6,498 in federal taxes per year in 1992 (provided by the Congressional Budget Office. January 1994. *An Economic Analysis of the Revenue Provisions of OBRA-93:32*). The most recent published figure on the annual cost of an inmate in the federal system is $20,885. See Federal Bureau of Prisons. 1995. *State of the Bureau, 1993*. Sandstone, Minn.: Federal Prisons Industry: 63.

44. Branham, Lynn S. April 1992. *The Use of Incarceration in the United States: A Look at the Present and the Future*. Chicago, Ill.: American Bar Association: 21.

45. See Cory, Bruce, and Stephen Gettinger. 1984. *Time to Build? The Realities of Prison Construction*. New York: The Edna McConnell Clark Foundation.

46. The Edna McConnell Clark Foundation. April 1993. *Americans Behind Bars*. New York: The Edna McConnell Clark Foundation: 5. Also see Loeb, Carl M., Jr. October 1978. The Cost of Jailing in New York City. *Crime and Delinquency*: 446-52.

47. Irwin, John, and James Austin. 1994. *It's About Time: America's Imprisonment Binge*. Belmont, Calif.: Wadsworth: 144; see also McDonald, D. 1980. *The Price of Punishment*. Boulder, Colo.: Westview Press; and Loeb, Carl. October 1978. The Cost of Jailing in New York City. *Crime and Delinquency*: 446-52.

48. See Cory, Bruce, and Stephen Gettinger. 1984. *Time to Build? The Realities of Prison Construction*. New York: The Edna McConnell Clark Foundation.

49. U.S. Department of Justice, Bureau of Justice Statistics. *Tuberculosis in Correctional Facilities, 1993*. Washington, D.C.: U.S. Government Printing Office.

50. Sennott, Charles M. May 2, 1994. AIDS Adds a Fatal Factor to Prison Assault: Rape Behind Bars (second of three parts). *Boston Globe;*

January 1994. Prison and AIDS. *Stanford Law Review* 44:1541.

51. Hanlon, Sean M. December 24, 1993. State Prisons Taking a Hit from AIDS. *Washington Times.*

52. U.S. Department of Justice, Bureau of Justice Statistics. 1993. *Sourcebook of Criminal Justice Statistics 1992.* Washington, D.C.: U.S. Government Printing Office: 609, Table 6.69.

53. See, e.g., Cromwell, Paul. June 1994. The Greying of America's Prisons. *Overcrowded Times.*

54. Wikberg, Ron. May/June 1988. The Longtermers. *The Angolite.* Vol. 13, no. 3, p. 40.

55. Mandel, Michael J., Paul Magnusson, James E. Ellis, Gail DeGeorge, and Keith L. Alexander. December 13, 1993. The Economics of Crime. *Business Week:* 74.

56. Ibid., p. 78.

57. Ibid., p. 73.

58. U.S. Department of Justice, Bureau of Justice Statistics. November 1993. *Federal Criminal Case Processing, 1982-1991; With Preliminary Data for 1992.* Washington, D.C.: U.S. Government Printing Office: 18, Table 18.

59. U.S. Department of Justice. February 4, 1994. *An Analysis of Nonviolent Drug Offenders with Minimal Criminal Histories.* Washington, D.C.: U.S. Government Printing Office.

60. See generally Killias, Martin, Andre Kuhn, and Simone Ronez. June 1995. Sentencing in Switzerland. *Overcrowded Times.* Vol. 6, no. 3.

61. Simon, Paul. December 21, 1994. *In New Survey, Wardens Call for Smarter Sentencing, Alternatives to Incarceration, and Prevention Programs.* Washington, D.C.: Office of Senator Paul Simon, U.S. Senate.

62. See generally MacKenzie, Doris Layton. August 1994. Boot Camps: A National Assessment. *Overcrowded Times;* Campaign for an Effective Crime Policy. March 1994. *Evaluating Boot Camp Prisons.* Washington, D.C.: Campaign for an Effective Crime Policy; U.S. Department of Justice, National Institute of Justice. November 1994. *Multisite Evaluation of Shock Incarceration.* Washington, D.C.: U.S. Government Printing Office.

63. Roberts, Julian V. April 1992. American Attitudes About Punishment: Myth and Reality. *Overcrowded Times.* Vol. 3, no. 2, p. 1.

64. Ibid.

65. Doble, John, and Josh Klein. 1989. *Punishing Criminals. The Public's View—An Alabama Survey.* New York: The Edna McConnell Clark Foundation; Doble, John, Stephen Immerwahr, and Amy Richardson. 1991. *Punishing Criminals: The People of Delaware Consider the Options.* New York: The Edna McConnell Clark Foundation.

CHAPTER THREE: FEAR, POLITICS AND THE PRISON-INDUSTRIAL COMPLEX

1. For a similar story, see Steffens, Lincoln. 1931. "I Make a Crime Wave," chapter XIV in *The Autobiography of Lincoln Steffens*. New York: Harcourt Brace: 285-291.

2. *New York Times*/CBS News poll conducted January 15-17, 1994.

3. Browne, Jeff. October 23, 1994. Survey Reveals Four Broad Misperceptions (Four-part Series on Crime Myths). *Milwaukee Journal*; Zucchino, David. October 30, 1994. Today's Violent Crime Is Old Story with a Twist. *The Philadelphia Inquirer;* Kappeler, Victor E., Mark Blumberg, Gary W. Potter. 1993. *The Mythology of Crime and Criminal Justice*. Prospect Heights, Ill.: Waveland Press, Inc.: 53.

4. See, e.g., Adler, Stephen, and Wade Lambert. March 12, 1993. Just About Everyone Violates Some Laws, Even Model Citizens. *Wall Street Journal*.

5. Dunn, Katherine. April 10, 1994. Crime and Embellishment. *Los Angeles Times Magazine*: 24.

6. Ibid., p. 26.

7. Kappeler, Victor E., Mark Blumberg, and Gary W. Potter. 1993. *The Mythology of Crime and Criminal Justice*. Prospect Heights, Ill.: Waveland Press, Inc.: 53.

8. Ibid.

9. Lichter, S. Robert, and Linda S. Lichter, eds. January/February 1994. *Media Monitor: 1993—The Year in Review*. Vol. VIII, no. 1. Washington, D.C.: Center for Media and Public Affairs; see also Davis, F. 1951. Crime News in Colorado Newspapers. *American Journal of Sociology* 57:325-330; and Durham, Alexis M., H. Preston Elrod, and Patrick T. Kinkade. 1995. Images of Crime and Justice: Murder and the "True Crime" Genre. Unpublished manuscript. Tampa, Fla.: University of Tampa: 8.

10. Lichter, Robert S., and D. Edmundson. June 1992. *A Day in the Life of Television Violence*. Washington, D.C.: Center for Media and Public Affairs.

11. Gerbner, George. July 1994. Television Violence: The Art of Asking the Wrong Question. *Currents in Modern Thought*: 385-97.

12. Seagal, Debra. November 1993. Tales from the Cutting Room Floor: The Reality of "Reality-Based" Television. *Harper's Magazine:* 51.

13. A study of television news from 1974 to 1986 for the three major networks found that violent crime was disproportionately featured relative to property crime. A study in New Orleans found that 80 percent of television newscast crime stories dealt with murder or robbery when those crimes accounted for only 12 percent of all crimes. Durham, Alexis M., H. Preston Elrod, and Patrick T. Kinkade. 1994. Images of Crime

and Justice: Murder and the "True Crime" Genre. Unpublished manuscript. Tampa, Fla.: University of Tampa: 9.

14. Brillon, Y., C. Louis-Guerin, and M. Lamarche. 1984. *Attitudes of the Canadian Public Toward Crime Policies.* Montreal: International Center for Comparative Criminology.

15. Surette, Ray. 1992. *Media, Crime, and Criminal Justice: Images and Realities.* Pacific Grove: Brooks Cole: 35.

16. For an excellent study of this phenomenon in the context of the true crime genre of novels, see Durham, Alexis M., H. Preston Elrod, and Patrick T. Kinkade. 1994. Images of Crime and Justice: Murder and the "True Crime" Genre. Unpublished manuscript.

17. Gerbner, George. July 1994. Television Violence: The Art of Asking the Wrong Question. *Currents in Modern Thought*: 396; see also Gerbner, George, Michael Morgan, and Nancy Signorielli. *Television Violence Profile No. 16: The Turning Point.* Philadelphia: University of Pennsylvania, The Annenberg School for Communication.

18. Carlson, J. 1985. *Prime Time Enforcement.* New York: Praeger: 190.

19. Davis, F. 1951. Crime News in Colorado Newspapers. *American Journal of Sociology* 57:325-330.

20. Sheley, J., and C. Askins. 1981. Crime, Crime News, and Crime Views. *Public Opinion Quarterly* 45:492-506.

21. Hoover, Ken. February 3, 1994. S.F. Erred in Data on Teenage Killings. *San Francisco Chronicle.*

22. Gest, Ted, Gordon Witkin, Katia Hetter, and Andrea Wright. January 17, 1994. Violence in America. *U.S. News & World Report.* Vol. 116, no. 2. For an excellent analysis of this story, see Jackson, Janine, and Jim Naureckas. May/June 1994. Crime Contradictions. *Extra:* 10.

23. U.S. Department of Justice, Bureau of Justice Statistics. July 1994. *Criminal Victimization in the United States: 1973–92, Trends.* Washington, D.C.: U.S. Government Printing Office: 103–04, 110.

24. U.S. Department of Justice, Bureau of Justice Statistics. *Survey of State Prison Inmates, 1991.* Washington, D.C.: U.S. Government Printing Office.

25. See, e.g., DiIulio, John J. January 20, 1995. *Crime in America: Three Ways to Prevent It.* Congressional Testimony. Washington, D.C.: Brookings Institution.

26. U.S. Department of Justice, Bureau of Justice Statistics. August 1995. *Probation and Parole Violators in State Prison, 1991.* Washington, D.C.: U.S. Government Printing Office: 10; U.S. Department of Justice, Federal Bureau of Investigation. August 30, 1992. *Crime in the United States—1991.* Washington, D.C.: U.S. Government Printing Office: 10.

27. U.S. Department of Justice, Bureau of Justice Statistics. July

1987. Bulletin. *Recidivism of Felons on Probation, 1986–89.* Washington, D.C.: U.S. Government Printing Office: 6.

28. Tonry, Michael. February 1993. General Barr's Last Stand. *Overcrowded Times.* Vol. 4, no. 1, pp. 2–3.

29. U.S. Department of Justice, Bureau of Justice Statistics. July 1987. Bulletin. *Making Confinement Decisions.* Washington, D.C.: U.S. Government Printing Office.

30. Greenwood, Peter, and Susan Turner. March 1987. *Selective Incapacitation Revisited.* Santa Monica, Calif.: Rand Corporation.

31. Zimring, Franklin, and Gordon Hawkins. October 1988. The New Mathematics of Imprisonment. *Crime and Delinquency.* Vol. 34, no. 4, pp. 425-436.

32. Fischer, Craig, ed. April 1, 1992. Washington Report: Justice Department Raises Eyebrows with Focus on Need for Prisons. *Criminal Justice Newsletter.* Vol. 23, no. 7. Washington, D.C.: Pace Publications.

33. Ibid.

34. Ibid.

35. U.S. Department of Justice, Federal Bureau of Investigation. December 4, 1994. *Crime in the United States—1993.* Washington, D.C.: U.S. Government Printing Office: Section V.

36. Davis, Robert, and Sam Vincent Meddis. December 5, 1994. Random Killings Hit a High. *USA Today:* 1A.

37. U.S. Department of Justice, Bureau of Justice Statistics. October 27, 1994. Press release. *State and Federal Prison Population Tops One Million.* Washington, D.C.: U.S. Government Printing Office.

38. U.S. Department of Justice, Bureau of Justice Statistics. December 1986. *Historical Corrections Statistics in the United States, 1850–1984.* Rockville, Md.: Westat, Inc.: 65; U.S. Department of Justice, Bureau of Justice Statistics. October 27, 1994. Press Release. *State and Federal Prison Population Tops One Million.* Washington, D.C.: U.S. Government Printing Office.

39. But see Bovard, James. January 30, 1994. Kids, Cops and Caseworkers: America's Newest Parent Traps; DARE Scare: Turning Children into Informants? *Washington Post:* C3.

40. Sowell, Thomas. October 14, 1994. Feds Who DARE Not Tell the Results. *Washington Times:* A18; Monroe, Sylvester. October 17, 1994. D.A.R.E. Bedeviled. *Time:* 49; Elliott, Jeff. March 1995. Drug Prevention Placebo: How DARE Wastes Time, Money, and Police. *Reason:* 14–21.

41. Ennett, Susan T., et al. September 1994. How Effective Is Drug Abuse Resistance Education? A Meta-Analysis of Project DARE Outcome Evaluations. *The American Journal of Public Health.* Vol. 84, no. 9, pp. 1394–1401.

42. U.S. Department of Justice. February 1994. *An Analysis of Nonviolent Drug Offenders with Minimal Criminal Histories.* Washington, D.C.: U.S. Government Printing Office.

43. Kurtz, Howard. November 2, 1994. Ads Use Crimes' Pain for Candidates' Gain. *Washington Post:* A1; September 9, 1994. In 1994 Political Ads, Crime Is the Weapon of Choice. *Washington Post:* A1.

44. Meddis, Sam Vincent. December 13, 1994. Success of Expansion of Matter of Debate. *USA Today:* 10A.

45. See, e.g., Associated Press. October 27, 1994. TV Ads in Governor's Race Focus on Crime. *New York Times.*

46. Montgomery, David. August 22, 1994. Md. Governor's Race Offers High-Cost Crime Plans. *Washington Post:* D1.

47. Butterfield, Fox. June 26, 1995. Aggressive Strategy by N.R.A. Has Left Its Finances Reeling. *New York Times:* 1.

48. See Mauer, Marc. *Did the Growth of Imprisonment During the 1980s Work?: The NRA and the Misuse of Criminal Justice Data.* Washington, D.C.: The Sentencing Project.

49. U.S. Department of Justice, Bureau of Justice Statistics. September 1992. Bulletin. *Justice Expenditure and Employment, 1990.* Washington, D.C.: U.S. Government Printing Office: 4, Table 4; U.S. Department of Defense. March 1994. *National Defense Budget Estimates for FY 1995.* Washington, D.C.: Office of the Comptroller of the Department of Defense: 147, Table 7-1.

50. Law Enforcement Technology for the 21st Century. May 15-17, 1995. Conference sponsored by the National Institute of Justice and American Defense Preparedness Association. Washington, D.C.

51. Thomas, Paulette. May 12, 1994. Making Crime Pay: Triangle of Interests Creates Infrastructure to Fight Lawlessness. *Wall Street Journal:* A1.

52. Ramirez, Anthony. August 14, 1994. Privatizing America's Prisons, Slowly. *New York Times:* sec. 3, p. 1.

53. Thomas, Charles W. March 1, 1995. *Private Adult Correctional Facility Census,* 8th ed. Gainesville, Fla.: Private Corrections Project, University of Florida: vii.

54. Ibid.

55. See, e.g., Robbins, Ira P. April–May 1986. Privatization of Corrections: Defining the Issues. *Judicature.* Vol. 69, no. 6, pp. 325–31.

56. Ramirez, Anthony. August 14, 1994. Privatizing America's Prisons, Slowly. *New York Times:* sec. 3, p. 1.

57. Thomas, Paulette. May 12, 1994. Making Crime Pay: Triangle of Interests Creates Infrastructure to Fight Lawlessness. *Wall Street Journal:* A1.

58. Ramirez, Anthony. August 14, 1994. Privatizing America's Prisons, Slowly. *New York Times:* sec. 3, p. 1.

59. Thomas, Paulette. May 12, 1994. Making Crime Pay: Triangle of Interests Creates Infrastructure to Fight Lawlessness. *Wall Street Journal:* A6.

60. Securities and Exchange Commission (SEC). *Annual Report of Form 10-K Under the Securities Exchange Act of 1934 for the Fiscal Year Ended December 31, 1993: Corrections Corporation of America.* Washington, D.C.: SEC: 11.

61. Goins, Ted. 1994. *Institutional Research.* Richmond, Va.: Branch Cabell.

62. Lilly, J. Robert, and Paul Knepper. April 1993. The Corrections-Commercial Complex. *Crime and Delinquency.* Vol. 39, no. 2, p. 154; Robbins, Ira P. April–May 1986. Privatization of Corrections: Defining the Issues. *Judicature.* Vol. 69, no. 6, p. 326.

63. Lilly, J. Robert, and Paul Knepper. April 1993. The Corrections-Commercial Complex. *Crime and Delinquency.* Vol. 39, no. 2, p. 155.

64. Meddis, Sam Vincent, and Deborah Sharp. December 13, 1994. Prison Business Is a Blockbuster. *USA Today:* 10A.

65. Ibid.

66. Ibid.

67. Beale, Calvin L. June 1993. Prisons, Population and Jobs in NonMetro America. *Rural Development Perspectives.* Vol. 8, no. 3, pp. 16–19.

68. Ibid., p. 17.

69. See, e.g., Welch, Randy. March 1991. Praying for Prisons. *State Legislatures:* 28–30; Lane, Laura. February 20, 1994. Prisons a Growing Industry. *Sunday Herald-Times* (Bloomington/Bedford, Ind.): A1, A10; Beale, Calvin L. June 1993. Prisons, Population and Jobs in NonMetro America. *Rural Development Perspectives.* Vol. 8, no. 3, pp. 16–19; LaGanga, Maria, L. October 18, 1994. New Prisons No Panacea for Ills of Rural California. *Los Angeles Times.*

70. Welch, Randy. March 1991. Praying for Prisons. *State Legislatures:* 29.

71. LaGanga, Maria L. October 18, 1994. New Prisons No Panacea for Ills of Rural California. *Los Angeles Times:* A6.

72. Welch, Randy. March 1991. Praying for Prisons. *State Legislatures:* 28.

73. *New York Times* News Service. February 4, 1993. With Private Prison, Town Hopes Crime Will Pay. *Chicago Tribune:* 6.

74. LaGanga, Maria L. October 18, 1994. New Prisons No Panacea for Ills of Rural California. *Los Angeles Times:* A6.

75. Ibid.

76. Carlson, Katherine A. (January 1992). Doing Good and Looking Bad: A Case Study of Prison/Community Relations. *Crime and Delinquency,* Vol. 38, No. 1: 56-69.

77. Morain, Dan. Firm Reaps Profit from Desolate Prison Site. *Los Angeles Times.*

78. See, e.g., December 1991. The Growing Clout of Prison Guards. *Governing:* 37; Schiraldi, Vincent. October 1994. *The Undue Influence of California's Prison Guards' Union: California's Correctional-Industrial Complex.* San Francisco: Center on Juvenile and Criminal Justice; Domanick, Joe. September 2–8, 1994. Who's Guarding the Guards? *LA Weekly:* 20–26; Hurst, John. February 6, 1994. The Big House That Don Novey Built: Working the PR, Spreading Big Bucks, A Canny Union Boss Demands More Prisons and Top Pay for His Guards. *Los Angeles Times Magazine:* 16.

79. December 1991. The Growing Clout of Prison Guards. *Governing:* 37.

80. Ibid.

81. Ibid.

82. Foote, Caleb. June 1993. *The Prison Population Explosion: California's Rogue Elephant.* San Francisco: Center on Juvenile and Criminal Justice: 12.

83. Alexander, Kim. July 1993. *Deep Pockets: 1991–92 Top Ten Contributors to California Legislative Campaigns.* Sacramento, Calif.: California Common Cause; Foote, Caleb. June 1993. *The Prison Population Explosion: California's Rogue Elephant.* San Francisco, Calif.: Center on Juvenile and Criminal Justice: 12.

CHAPTER FOUR: RACE AND CRIMINAL JUSTICE

1. Stout, David. May 9, 1995. Black Businessman Ponders Ordeal as a Suspect. *New York Times:* B1.

2. Williams, Hubert, and Patrick Murphy. December 1989. *The Evolving Strategy of Police: A Minority View.* National Institute of Justice, Perspectives on Policing. Washington, D.C.: U.S. Government Printing Office.

3. Mann, Coramae Richey. 1993. *Unequal Justice.* Bloomington, Ind.: Indiana University Press: vii.

4. Mauer, Marc. September 1994. *Americans Behind Bars: The International Use of Incarceration, 1992–93.* Washington, D.C.: The Sentencing Project.

5. Miller, Jerome G. September 1992. *Hobbling a Generation: Young African-American Males in the Criminal Justice System of America's Cities: Baltimore, Maryland.* Alexandria, Va.: National Center on Institutions and Alternatives.

6. Miller, Jerome G. April 17, 1992. *Hobbling a Generation: Young*

African-American Males in Washington, D.C.'s Criminal Justice System. Alexandria, Va.: National Center on Institutions and Alternatives.

7. Mauer, Marc. October 1995. *Young Black Americans and the Criminal Justice System: Five Years Later.* Washington, D.C.: The Sentencing Project.

8. Blumstein, Alfred, and Elizabeth Graddy. 1983. Prevalence and Recidivism in Index Arrests: A Feedback Model. *Law and Society Review.* Vol. 16, no. 2, pp. 279–80.

9. Tillman, Robert. August 1987. The Size of the "Criminal Population": The Prevalence and Incidence of Adult Arrest. *Criminology.* Vol. 25, no. 3, pp. 561–79.

10. Miller, Jerome G. June 1, 1993. *The Duval County Jail Report.* Alexandria, Va.: National Center on Institutions and Alternatives: 133.

11. Sherman, Arloc. 1994. *Wasting America's Future.* Children's Defense Fund. Boston, Mass.: Beacon Press.

12. Currie, Elliott. 1985. *Confronting Crime: An American Challenge.* New York: Pantheon Books: 144.

13. Ibid., p. 146

14. From 1980 to 1993 the total populations in state and federal prisons and local jails increased an average of 8 percent per year. Given this rate of increase, the NCJC projected the total incarcerated population forward to the year 2020 (it should be noted that the most recent BJS bulletin, *Prisoners in 1994*, revealed a 9 percent increase in state and federal prisoners from 1993 to 1994). To determine the racial makeup of the incarcerated population we relied on the rate at which each racial/ethnic group accounted for the increase of inmates from 1986 to 1991 in state prisons. We used state prisons due to the availability of complete information and because the majority of inmates are held in state prisons. 46 percent of the increase in prison inmates was accounted for by African-Americans, 28 percent by whites, and 26 percent by Hispanics/Other. Starting with the actual racial/ethnic makeup of prison and jail inmates in 1992 and using the trends noted above, we projected forward to the year 2020. Given the population projections of the U.S. Bureau of the Census in the year 2020, we calculated that 63.3 percent of African-Americans and 25.6 percent of Hispanics between the ages of 18 and 34 will be incarcerated.

15. U.S. Department of Justice, Federal Bureau of Investigation. December 4, 1994. *Crime in the United States—1993.* Washington, D.C.: U.S. Government Printing Office: 235; U.S. Bureau of the Census. March 1994. *U.S. Population Estimates, by Age, Sex, Race, and Hispanic Origin: 1990 to 1993.* Washington, D.C.: U.S. Government Printing Office: 13.

16. U.S. Department of Justice, Bureau of Justice Statistics. August

1995. *Prisoners in 1994*: 1. The incarceration rate for blacks is 1,471 and for whites is 207. U.S. Department of Justice, Federal Bureau of Investigation. December 4, 1994. *Crime in the United States—1993*. Washington, D.C.: U.S. Government Printing Office: 235; U.S. Bureau of the Census. March 1994. *U.S Population Estimates, by Age, Sex, Race, and Hispanic Origin: 1990 to 1993*. Washington, D.C.: U.S. Government Printing Office: 13.

17. See, e.g., Kempf, Kimberly L. August 1992. *The Role of Race in Juvenile Justice Processing in Pennsylvania*. Grant #89-90/J/01/3615. Pennsylvania Commission on Crime and Delinquency; Morris, Norval. August–September 1988. Race and Crime: What Evidence Is There That Race Influences Results in the Criminal Justice System? *Judicature*. Vol. 72, no. 2, pp. 111–113.

18. May 1988. Developments in the Law—Race and the Criminal Process. *Harvard Law Review*. Vol. 101, no. 7, p. 1525.

19. See generally Zatz, Marjorie. 1987. The Changing Forms of Racial/Ethnic Biases in Sentencing. *Journal of Research in Crime and Delinquency*. Vol. 24, no. 1; Zatz, Marjorie. 1984. Race, Ethnicity, and Determinate Sentencing: A New Dimension to an Old Controversy. *Criminology*. Vol. 22.

20. Schmitt, Christopher, H. December 9, 1991. Ethnic Disparities Start with Arrests. *San Jose Mercury News:* 8A; and Ewing, Jack, and Brant Houston. June 17, 1991. Some Judges Punish People Without Benefit of Trial. *The Hartford Courant:* A1.

21. May 1988. Developments in the Law—Race and the Criminal Process. *Harvard Law Review*. Vol. 101, no. 7., p. 1496.

22. Schmitt, Christopher, H. December 9, 1991. Ethnic Disparities Start with Arrests. *San Jose Mercury News*: 8A.

23. Valentine, Paul. January 5, 1995. Maryland Settles Lawsuit Over Racial Profiles. *Washington Post:* B1.

24. Lopez, Christopher. List Brands 2 of 3 Young Black Men. *The Denver Post*.

25. May 1988. Developments in the Law—Race and the Criminal Process. *Harvard Law Review*. Vol. 101, no. 7, p. 1525.

26. May 1988. Developments in the Law—Race and the Criminal Process. *Harvard Law Review*. Vol. 101, no. 7, p. 1526.

27. Ewing, Jack, and Brant Houston. June 17, 1991. Some Judges Punish People Without Benefit of Trial. *The Hartford Courant:* A1.

28. Schmitt, Christopher, H. December 8, 1991. Plea Bargaining Favors Whites as Blacks, Hispanics Pay Price. *San Jose Mercury News:* 1.

29. Ibid.

30. Ibid.

31. Ibid.

32. Florida House of Representatives Criminal Justice Committee, Chairman Elvin Martinez. September 1992. *Report on Habitual Offender Law.* Tallahassee, Florida.

33. Baldus, David C., Charles A. Pulaski Jr., and George Woodworth. Fall 1983. Comparative Review of Death Sentences: An Empirical Study of the Georgia Experience. *Journal of Criminal Law & Criminology* 74:661. For a judicial description of the study, see *McCleskey v. Kemp*, 107 S. Ct. 1756 (1987).

34. May 1988. Developments in the Law—Race and the Criminal Process. *Harvard Law Review.* Vol. 101, no. 7, pp. 1473–1641.

35. Crutchfield, Robert D., George S. Bridges, and Susan R. Pitchford. May 1994. Analytical and Aggregation Biases in Analyses of Imprisonment: Reconciling Discrepancies in Studies of Racial Disparity. *Journal of Research in Crime and Delinquency.* Vol. 31, no. 2, pp. 166–82.

36. Blumstein, Alfred. 1983. On the Racial Disproportionality of the United States' Prison Populations. *Journal of Criminal Law & Criminology.* Vol. 73, p. 1259.

37. Morris, Norval. August–September 1988. Race and Crime: What Evidence Is There That Race Influences Results in the Criminal Justice System? *Judicature.* Vol. 72, no. 2, p. 113.

38. Walker, William O., ed. 1992. *Drug Control Policy: Essays in Historical and Comparative Perspective.* University Park, Pa.: The Pennsylvania State University Press: 26.

39. U.S. Department of Health and Human Services. 1994. *National Household Survey on Drug Abuse—1992.* Washington, D.C.: U.S. Government Printing Office: 20–21.

40. Butterfield, Fox. October 5, 1995. More Blacks in Their 20's Have Trouble with the Law. *New York Times:* A18.

41. Tonry, Michael. 1995. *Malign Neglect—Race, Crime, and Punishment in America.* New York: Oxford University Press: 105.

42. Ibid., pp. 107–10.

43. U.S. Department of Justice, Federal Bureau of Investigation. 1986 and 1990. *Crime in the United States—1985 and 1986.* Washington, D.C.: U.S. Government Printing Office.

44. Tonry, Michael. 1995. *Malign Neglect: Race, Crime, and Punishment in America.* New York: Oxford University Press: 81.

45. U.S. Department of Justice, Bureau of Justice Statistics. 1994. *Sourcebook of Criminal Justice Statistics—1993.* Washington, D.C.: U.S. Government Printing Office: 340. The data are from the U.S. Department of Health and Human Services' "National Household Survey on Drug Abuse." This is also substantiated by the *National Survey Results on*

Drug Use from Monitoring the Future Study, 1975–1993 by the U.S. Department of Health and Human Services. Washington, D.C.: U.S. Government Printing Office.

46. Meddis, Sam Vincent. July 26, 1993. In Twin Cities, a Tale of Two Standards. *USA Today:* 6A.

47. Ibid.

48. U.S. Department of Justice, Bureau of Justice Statistics. September 1994. *Comparing Federal and State Prison Inmates, 1991.* Special report, pp. 3–4; January 1988. *Profile of State Prison Inmates, 1986,* p. 3; December 1986. *Historical Corrections Statistics in the United States, 1850–1984,* p. 158.

49. U.S. Department of Justice, Bureau of Justice Statistics. December 1993. *Sentencing in the Federal Courts: Does Race Matter? The Transition to Sentencing Guidelines, 1986-90.* Washington, D.C.: U.S. Government Printing Office: 97, 109.

50. Reinarman, Craig, and Harry G. Levine. Winter 1989. Crack in Context: Politics and Media in the Making of a Drug Scare. *Contemporary Drug Problems.*

51. Benjamin, Daniel K. and Roger Leroy Miller. 1991. *Undoing Drugs: Beyond Legalization.* New York: Basic Books: 75–76.

52. Tidwell, Mike. 1992. *In the Shadow of the White House: Drugs, Death, and Redemption on the Streets of the Nation's Capital.* Rocklin, Calif.: Prima Publishing: 189.

53. Several judges, including Judge Jack B. Weinstein of Brooklyn and Judge Whitman Knapp of Manhattan, have refused to handle any more drug cases; U.S. District Judge Stanley S. Harris and Circuit Court Judge Audrey Melbourne of Maryland have noted the devastating impact of the mandatory minimums in their sentencing hearings; and Judge Alan Nevas, appointed by President Reagan, remarked that the mandatory minimum sentences for crack cocaine are the "unfairest sentences I have ever had to impose." May 26, 1993. Powder Cocaine vs. Crack Cocaine: Balanced Justice? *USA Today.*

54. *United States v. Majied.* No. 8: CR91-00038 (02) 1993 U.S. Dist. Lexis 15156 (D. Neb. July 29, 1993).

55. *State v. Russell,* 477 N.W. 2d 886 (Minn. 1991).

56. Commission to Study the Impact of Substance Use on the Criminal Justice System in Monroe County, Jim Gocker, chairman. May 1992. Report to Monroe County Bar Association Board of Trustees. *Justice in Jeopardy.* Rochester, N.Y.: Monroe County Bar Association.

57. Tonry, Michael. 1995. *Malign Neglect: Race, Crime, and Punishment in America.* New York: Oxford University Press: 32.

58. Snyder, Howard. 1992. *Arrests of Youth 1990.* Washington, D.C.:

U.S. Government Printing Office; Criminal Justice Policy Council. 1992. *Sentencing Dynamics Study*. Texas Punishment Standards Commission.

59. Miller, Jerome G. September 1992. *Hobbling a Generation: Young African-American Males in the Criminal Justice System of America's Cities: Baltimore, Maryland*. Alexandria, Va.: National Center on Institutions and Alternatives.

60. Wilson, John J., and James C. Howell. July 1, 1993. *A Comprehensive Strategy for Serious, Violent, and Chronic Juvenile Offenders*. Washington, D.C.: Office of Juvenile Justice and Delinquency Prevention: 3.

61. Dannefer, Dale, and Russell Schutt. 1987. Race and Juvenile Justice Processing in Court and Police Agencies. *American Journal of Sociology*. Vol. 87, no. 5, pp. 1113–32.

62. Kempf, Kimberly L. August 1992. *The Role of Race in Juvenile Justice Processing in Pennsylvania*. Grant #89-90/J/01/3615. Pennsylvania Commission on Crime and Delinquency.

63. McGarrell, Edmund F. January 1993. Trends in Racial Disproportionality in Juvenile Court Processing: 1985–1989. *Crime and Delinquency*. Vol. 39, no. 1, pp. 29–48.

64. Miller, Jerome. March 1994. *African-American Males in the Criminal Justice System*. Unpublished paper presented at the National Criminal Justice Commission Conference, Alexandria, Virginia.

65. Gellman, B., and S. Horowitz. March 29, 1990. Letter Stirs Debate After Acquittal: Writer Says Jurors Bowed to Racial Issue in D.C. Murder Case. *Washington Post:* A1.

66. Miller, Jerome G. March 1994. *African-American Males in the Criminal Justice System*. Unpublished paper presented at the National Criminal Justice Commission Conference, Alexandria, Virginia.

67. Chambliss, William. Moral Panics and Racial Oppression. In Hawkins, Darney. 1993. *Ethnicity, Race and Crime*. New York: SUNY Press; Lopez, Christopher. List Brands 2 of 3 Young Black Men. *The Denver Post;* Criminal Justice Institute, Harvard Law School, and The William Monroe Trotter Institute, University of Massachusetts at Boston. March 1993. *Beyond the Rodney King Story: An NAACP Report on Police Conduct and Community Relations*. The National Association for the Advancement of Colored People.

68. Chambliss, William. Moral Panics and Racial Oppression. In Hawkins, Darney. 1993. *Ethnicity, Race and Crime*. New York: SUNY Press.

69. Hagan, John. 1992. The Poverty of a Classless Criminology. *Journal of Criminology*. Vol. 30, no. 1.; Hagan, John. 1993. The Social Embeddedness of Crime and Unemployment. *Criminology*. Vol. 31, no. 4, p. 465.

70. Wilson, William J. 1987. *The Truly Disadvantaged*. Chicago: University of Chicago Press.

71. Milloy, Courtney. June 7, 1995. Jails or Jobs? Employment Is Cheaper. *Washington Post:* B1.

72. Ibid.

73. Miller, Jerome G. 1996. *Search and Destroy*. Cambridge University Press.

74. Shapiro, Andrew. November 1993. Challenging Criminal Disenfranchisement Under the Voting Rights Act: A New Strategy. *The Yale Law Journal* 103:537.

75. Ibid.

76. *United States v. Louisiana,* 225 F. Supp. 353 (Eastern Dist. of Louisiana, 1963).

77. Shapiro, Andrew. December 20, 1993. Giving Ex-cons the Vote. *The Nation.*

CHAPTER FIVE: YOUTH VIOLENCE AND JUVENILE JUSTICE

1. Office of Juvenile Justice and Delinquency Prevention. 1994. *Conditions of Confinement*. Washington, D.C.: U.S. Department of Justice, Office of Justice Programs, Office of Juvenile Justice and Delinquency Prevention.

2. Jones, Michael A., and Barry Krisberg. June 1994. *Images and Reality*. San Francisco: National Council on Crime and Delinquency: 15–16.

3. National Center for Health Statistics. August 23, 1994. *Death for Selected Causes, By 5 Year Age Groups, Color and Sex: United States, 1979–92*; U.S. Bureau of the Census. March 1994. *U.S. Population Estimates, by Age, Sex, Race, and Hispanic Origin: 1990 to 1993*. Washington, D.C.: U.S. Government Printing Office.

4. Ibid.

5. Young homicide victims are more likely to be killed by their parents or legal guardians than they are by other children. Abuse by parents and guardians kills about 5,000 children and harms about 165,000 children each year. National Center for Health Statistics. 1990. *Health in the United States, 1989*. Hyattsville, Md.: Public Health Service, U.S. Department of Health and Human Services.

6. U.S. Department of Justice, Federal Bureau of Investigation. 1993. *Crime in the United States, 1992.* Washington, D.C.: U.S. Government Printing Office: 227.

7. Ibid.

8. Grace, Julie. September 12, 1994. There Are No Children Here. *Time*. Vol. 144, no. 11, p. 43.

9. Jones, Charisse. August 1, 1995. Bullet Claims a Role Model, Leaving Pain in Coney Island. *New York Times:* A1.

10. U.S. Department of Justice, Office of Juvenile Justice and Delinquency Prevention. August 1994. *Conditions of Confinement: Juvenile Detention and Corrections Facilities.* Washington, D.C.: U.S. Government Printing Office: 22, 42.

11. DeComo, R., S. Tunis, B. Krisberg, and N. Herrera. 1993. *Juveniles Taken into Custody Research Program: FY 1992 Annual Report.* Washington, D.C.: Office of Juvenile Justice and Delinquency Prevention.

12. Jones, Michael A., and Barry Krisberg. June 1994. *Images and Reality.* San Francisco: National Council on Crime and Delinquency: 30.

13. 16.6 percent involved violent crime charges and 83.3 percent involved property crime charges. Snyder, Howard, and Melissa Sickmund. May 1995. Juvenile Offenders and Victims: A Focus on Violence. OJJDP Report. Pittsburg: National Center on Juvenile Justice: 27; see also Feld, Barry C. 1987. The Juvenile Court Meets the Principle of the Offense: Legislative Changes in Juvenile Waiver Statutes. *Journal of Criminal Law and Criminology* 78:501.

14. Office of Juvenile Justice and Delinquency Prevention. 1992. *Juvenile Court Statistics, 1991.* Washington, D.C.: U.S. Government Printing Office.

15. Harris, Ron. August 22, 1993. A Nation's Children in Lockup. First of a four-part series. *Los Angeles Times:* A1.

16. Davis, Robert. February 3, 1994. For Kids, Life on a Hair-Trigger. *USA Today:* 3A.

17. U.S. Department of Justice, National Institute of Justice 1993. *Street Gang Crime in Chicago.* Research in Brief. Washington, D.C.: U.S. Government Printing Office.

18. Anderson, Elijah. May 1994. The Code of the Streets. *Atlantic Monthly:* 81–94.

19. Office of Juvenile Justice and Delinquency Prevention. 1993. *Juvenile Court Statistics 1992.* Washington, D.C.: U.S. Government Printing Office.

20. Office of Juvenile Justice and Delinquency Prevention. 1994. *Conditions of Confinement.* Washington, D.C.: U.S. Department of Justice, Office of Justice Programs, Office of Juvenile Justice and Delinquency Prevention.

21. Harris, Ron. August 22, 1993. A Nation's Children in Lockup. First of four-part series. *Los Angeles Times:* A1.

22. Center for the Study of Youth Policy. November 1989. *Programs for Serious and Violent Juvenile Offenders.* Ann Arbor, Mich.: Center for the Study of Youth Policy: 19.

23. Ibid.

24. Ibid.

25. For a first-person account of how the Massachusetts system became transformed, see Miller, Jerome G. 1991. *Last One Over the Wall*. Columbus: Ohio State University Press.

26. See, e.g., Miller, Jerome G. 1991. *Last One Over the Wall*. Columbus: Ohio State University Press; and generally, Jones, Michael A., and Barry Krisberg. June 1994. *Images and Reality*. San Francisco: National Council on Crime and Delinquency.

27. Jones, Michael A., and Barry Krisberg. June 1994. *Images and Reality*. San Francisco: National Council on Crime and Delinquency: 40.

28. Office of Juvenile Justice and Delinquency Prevention. December 1993. *Comprehensive Strategy for Serious, Violent, and Chronic Juvenile Offenders*. Washington, D.C.: U.S. Government Printing Office.

CHAPTER SIX: WOMEN AND THE CRIMINAL JUSTICE SYSTEM

1. Rafter, Nicole Hahn. 1990. *Partial Justice: Women, Prisons, and Social Control*. New Brunswick, N.J.: Transaction Books.

2. American Correctional Association. 1990. *The Female Offender: What Does the Future Hold?* Washington, D.C.: St. Mary's Press.

3. Stark, E., and A. Flitcraft. 1985. Woman-Battering, Child Abuse and Social Heredity: What Is the Relationship? *Marital Violence*, Sociological Review Monograph #31; Stark, E., and A. Flitcraft. October 1985. Spouse Abuse. *Surgeon General's Workshop on Violence and Public Health Source Book*, presented at the Surgeon General's Workshop on Violence and Public Health, Leesburg, Virginia; see also "In the United States, a woman is more likely to be assaulted, injured, raped, or killed by a male partner than by any other type of assailant." In Browne, A., and K. Williams. November 1987. Resource Availability for Women at Risk: Its Relationship to Rates of Female-Perpetrated Homicide. Paper presented at the American Society of Criminology, Montreal, Quebec.

4. U.S. Department of Justice, Bureau of Justice Statistics. 1994. *Sourcebook of Criminal Justice Statistics—1993*. Washington, D.C.: U.S. Government Printing Office: 600.

5. U.S. Department of Justice, Bureau of Justice Statistics. August 27, 1995. The Nation's Prison Population Grew Almost 9 Percent Last Year. Press release. Washington, D.C.: U.S. Government Printing Office: 4.

6. U.S. Department of Justice, Bureau of Justice Statistics. August 27, 1995. The Nation's Correctional Population Tops 5 Million. Press release. Washington, D.C.: U.S. Government Printing Office: 8.

7. Mauer, Marc. February 1990. *Young Black Men and the Criminal Justice System: A Growing National Problem*. Washington, D.C.: The Sentencing Project: 3.

8. According to the UCR, arrests of women for aggravated assault rose 94.8 percent from 1984 to 1993 (compared to a 64 percent increase for men). U.S. Department of Justice, Federal Bureau of Investigation. 1992. *Uniform Crime Reports 1990*. Washington, D.C.: U.S. Government Printing Office: 222, Table 33.

9. U.S. Department of Justice, Federal Bureau of Investigation. 1994. *Crime in the United States—1993*. Washington, D.C.: U.S. Government Printing Office: 222, Table 33; U.S. Department of Justice, Bureau of Justice Statistics. 1994. *Sourcebook of Criminal Justice Statistics—1993*. Washington, D.C.: U.S. Government Printing Office: 600; June 1994. *Prisoners in 1993*. Washington, D.C.: U.S. Government Printing Office: 4, Table 5.

10. U.S. Department of Justice, Federal Bureau of Investigation. 1991. *Crime in the United States—1990*. Washington, D.C.: U.S. Government Printing Office; 1992. *Crime in the United States—1991;* 1993. *Crime in the United States—1992;* 1994. *Crime in the United States—1993*.

11. U.S. Department of Justice, Bureau of Justice Statistics. 1988. *Profile of State Prison Inmates 1986*. Washington, D.C.: U.S. Government Printing Office: 3, Table 3; U.S. Department of Justice, Bureau of Justice Statistics. 1994. *Women in Prison*. Bulletin. Washington, D.C.: U.S. Government Printing Office: 3, Table 2.

12. Chesney-Lind, Meda. 1995. Rethinking Women's Imprisonment: A Critical Examination of Trends in Female Incarceration. *The Criminal Justice System and Women*, 2nd ed. New York: McGraw-Hill: 105–117.

13. Bloom, Barbara, Meda Chesney-Lind and Barbara Owen. May 1994. *Women in California Prisons: Hidden Victims of the War on Drugs*. San Francisco: Center on Juvenile and Criminal Justice: 3.

14. Wagner, Dennis. 1986. *Women in Prison: How Much Community Risk?* Madison, Wis.: Wisconsin Department of Health and Social Services.

15. Immarigeon, Russ, and Meda Chesney-Lind. 1992. *Women's Prisons: Overcrowded and Overused*. San Francisco: National Council on Crime and Delinquency.

16. American Correctional Association. 1990. *The Female Offender: What Does the Future Hold?* Washington, D.C.: St. Mary's Press; see also U.S. Department of Justice, Bureau of Justice Statistics. 1994. *Women in Prison*. Bulletin. Washington, D.C.: U.S. Government Printing Office.

17. Browne, Angela. 1987. *When Battered Women Kill*. New York: The Free Press; Ewing, C. 1987. *Battered Women Who Kill*. Lexington, Mass.: Lexington Books.

18. Huling, Tracy. 1991. *Breaking the Silence*. New York: Correctional Association of New York, Inc.

19. Chesney-Lind, Meda. 1995. Rethinking Women's Imprisonment:

A Critical Examination of Trends in Female Incarceration. *The Criminal Justice System and Women*, 2nd ed. New York: McGraw-Hill: 105–117, 110.

20. U.S. Department of Justice, Bureau of Justice Statistics. 1994. *Women in Prison*. Bulletin. Washington, D.C.: U.S. Government Printing Office.

21. LeClair, Daniel. October 1990. *The Incarcerated Female Offender: Victim or Villain?* Boston: Massachusetts Division of Correction, Research Division.

22. Austin, James. June 1991. *The Consequences of Escalating the Use of Imprisonment: The Case Study of Florida. Focus Report.* San Francisco: National Council on Crime and Delinquency.

23. U.S. Department of Justice, Bureau of Justice Statistics. 1988. *Profile of State Prison Inmates 1986*. Washington, D.C.: U.S. Government Printing Office: 3, Table 3; U.S. Department of Justice, Bureau of Justice Statistics. 1994. *Women in Prison*. Bulletin. Washington, D.C.: U.S. Government Printing Office: 3, Table 3.

24. Steffensmeier, D., et. al. August 1993. Gender and Imprisonment Decisions. *Criminology*. Vol. 31, no. 3; Daly, Kathleen. 1994. *Gender, Crime and Punishment*. New Haven, Conn.: Yale University Press.

25. U.S. Department of Justice, Bureau of Justice Statistics. 1994. *Women in Prison*. Washington, D.C.: U.S. Government Printing Office: 4.

26. Raeder, Myrna. 1993. Gender and Sentencing: Single Moms, Battered Women and Other Sex-Based Anomalies in the Gender-Free World of the Federal Sentencing Guidelines. *Pepperdine Law Review.* Vol. 20, no. 3., pp. 905-90.

27. U.S. Department of Justice, Bureau of Justice Statistics. 1989. *Prisoners in 1988*. Bulletin. Washington, D.C.: U.S. Government Printing Office; U.S. Department of Justice, Bureau of Justice Statistics. 1993. *Prisoners in 1992*. Bulletin. Washington, D.C.: U.S. Government Printing Office.

28. In 1991, state prison inmates alone had 826,964 children under the age of eighteen. U.S. Department of Justice, Bureau of Justice Statistics. 1994. *Women in Prison*. Washington, D.C.: U.S. Government Printing Office: 6, Table 9. Other sources estimate that as many as two million children have a parent imprisoned. Breen, Peter. 1994. *Advocacy Efforts on Behalf of Children of Incarcerated Parents*. San Francisco: Center Force.

29. Bloom, Barbara, and David Steinhart. 1993. *Why Punish the Children? A Reappraisal of the Children of Incarcerated Mothers in America*. San Francisco: National Council on Crime and Delinquency.

30. Johnston, Denise. 1993. *Report No. 13: Effects of Parental*

Incarceration. Pasadena, Calif.: The Center for Children of Incarcerated Parents.

31. U.S. Department of Justice, Bureau of Justice Statistics. 1994. *Women in Prison.* Washington, D.C.: U.S. Government Printing Office: 7.

32. Ibid., p. 6.

33. Ibid.

34. Bloom, Barbara, and David Steinhart. 1993. *Why Punish the Children? A Reappraisal of the Children of Incarcerated Mothers in America.* San Francisco: National Council on Crime and Delinquency; Breen, Peter. 1994. *Advocacy Efforts on Behalf of Children of Incarcerated Parents.* San Francisco: Center Force; Genty, Philip. 1991–92. Procedural Due Process Rights of Incarcerated Parents in Termination of Parental Rights Proceedings: A Fifty State Analysis. *Journal of Family Law.* Vol. 30, no. 4; Johnston, Denise. 1993. *Report No. 12: Incarcerated Mothers.* Pasadena, Calif.: The Center for Children of Incarcerated Parents; Laszlo, Anna T., Barbara Smith, and Sharon Goretsky Elstein. April 1994. Children on Hold: What Happens When Their Primary Caretaker Is Arrested? Paper presented at the American Bar Association Annual Conference on Children and the Law. Washington, D.C.

35. The states with such statutes are: Alabama, Arizona, California, Colorado, Georgia, Idaho, Iowa, Kansas, Louisiana, Mississippi, Missouri, Montana, Nevada, New Hampshire, New Mexico, New York, Oklahoma, Oregon, Rhode Island, Wisconsin, and Wyoming. Genty, Philip. 1991–92. Procedural Due Process Rights of Incarcerated Parents in Termination of Parental Rights Proceedings: A Fifty State Analysis. *Journal of Family Law.* Vol. 30, no. 4, pp. 757–846.

36. Genty, Philip. 1991–92. Procedural Due Process Rights of Incarcerated Parents in Termination of Parental Rights Proceedings: A Fifty State Analysis. *Journal of Family Law.* Vol. 30, no. 4, pp. 757–846.

37. Ibid.

38. Hayes, Lindsay M., et al. 1989. *The Female Offender in Delaware: Population Analysis and Assessment.* Alexandria, Va.: National Center on Institutions and Alternatives; Roche, Timothy J. 1989. *Addendum to NCIA's Report on the Female Offender in Delaware.* Alexandria, Va.: National Center on Institutions and Alternatives.

39. Brott, Armin. July 31, 1994. Battered-Truth Syndrome. *Washington Post:* C1. Citing Rita Smith, coordinator of National Coalition Against Domestic Violence.

40. Ingrassia, Michelle, and Melinda Beck. July 4, 1994. Patterns of Abuse. *Newsweek:* 26–28.

41. U.S. Department of Justice, Federal Bureau of Investigation. 1993.

Uniform Crime Reports 1993. Washington, D.C.: U.S. Government Printing Office: 17, Table 2.8. In 1993, 5,278 females were murdered, and the sex of the offender was known in 58 percent of the cases.

42. U.S. Department of Justice, Bureau of Justice Statistics. August 1995. *Violence Against Women: Estimates from the Redesigned Survey.* Special Report. Washington, D.C.: U.S. Government Printing Office: 1.

43. Women and Violence. Hearings Before the U.S. Senate Judiciary Committee, August 29 and December 11, 1990, Senate Hearing 101-939, pt. 2: 128; Eagen. January 29, 1988. Abused by the System. *Boston Sunday Herald Magazine:* 7, 14.

44. Buel, Sarah M. 1994. *Family Violence: Recommendations for Courts and Communities*: 6. Taken from the keynote address given by the author at the Courts and Communities: Confronting Violence in the Family Conference on March 25, 1993, San Francisco. 15.

45. Browne, Angela. 1987. *When Battered Women Kill.* New York: The Free Press.

46. 1985. *Delinquent Youth and Family Violence: A Study of Abuse and Neglect in the Homes of Serious Juvenile Offenders.* Commonwealth of Massachusetts. Boston: Department of Youth Services: 18.

47. Ibid., p. 95.

48. Stark, E., and A. Flitcraft. 1985. Woman-Battering, Child Abuse and Social Heredity: What Is the Relationship? *Marital Violence,* Sociological Review Monograph #31, ed. N. Johnson. London: Routledge and Kegan Paul.

49. U.S. Department of Justice, Bureau of Justice Statistics. October 1992. *The Cycle of Violence.* Washington, D.C.: U.S. Government Printing Office: 1.

50. Ibid.

51. Rhoades, P., and S. Parker. 1981. *The Connections Between Youth Problems and Violence in the Home.* Portland: Oregon Coalition Against Domestic and Family Violence: 18.

52. Sendi, I., and P. Blomgren. 1975. A Comparative Study of Predictive Criteria in the Predisposition of Homicidal Adolescents. *American Journal of Psychiatry* 132:404–07, as cited in Laird, A. May 22, 1989. *Children Who Witness Their Mothers Being Beaten: The Need for Child Protective Services, Policies and Intervention.* Master's Thesis, Urban Studies and Planning, Massachusetts Institute of Technology: 23.

53. Chesney-Lind, Meda. 1995. Rethinking Women's Imprisonment: A Critical Examination of Trends in Female Incarceration. *The Criminal Justice System and Women,* 2d ed. New York: McGraw-Hill.

54. Ibid.

CHAPTER SEVEN: TOWARD A NEW MODEL OF POLICING

1. Ryan, Michael. January 9, 1994. It's All About Dignity and Respect. *Connecticut Post, Parade:* 12–14.

2. Ibid.

3. U.S. Department of Justice, Bureau of Justice Statistics. August 1995. *Prisoners in 1994.* Washington, D.C.: U.S. Government Printing Office; U.S. Department of Justice, Bureau of Justice Statistics. 1995. *Jails and Jail Inmates 1993–1994.* Washington, D.C.: U.S. Government Printing Office; U.S. Department of Justice, Federal Bureau of Investigation. 1994. *Crime in the United States—1993.* Washington, D.C.: U.S. Government Printing Office.

4. U.S. Department of Justice, Federal Bureau of Investigation. 1994. *Crime in the United States—1993.* Washington, D.C.: U.S. Government Printing Office: 293.

5. Ibid.

6. U.S. Department of Justice, Bureau of Justice Statistics. September 1992. Bulletin. *Justice Expenditures and Employment, 1990.* Washington, D.C.: U.S. Government Printing Office: 2.

7. Public Law 103-322. H.R. 3355. September 13, 1994. *Violent Crime Control and Law Enforcement Act of 1994.*

8. Bayley, David. 1994. *Police for the Future.* New York: Oxford University Press: 15–35.

9. Ibid.

10. Ibid.

11. Kelling, George, Tony Pate, Duange Dieckman, and Charles Brown. 1974. *The Kansas City Preventive Patrol Experiment: A Summary Report.* Washington, D.C.: Police Foundation.

12. U.S. Department of Justice, Federal Bureau of Investigation. December 4, 1994. *Crime in the United States—1993.* Washington, D.C.: U.S. Government Printing Office: 105–159, 296–354.

13. Moran, Richard. February 23, 1994. Why More Police Won't Reduce Crime. Testimony Before the Subcommittee on Crime and Criminal Justice, Committee on the Judiciary, United States House of Representatives, Washington, D.C.

14. Ryan, Michael. January 9, 1994. It's All About Dignity and Respect. *Connecticut Post, Parade:* 12–14.

15. Pooley, Eric. July 11, 1994. *New York's Untouchables.* New York: NYPD Special Report: 17.

16. The City of New York: Commission to Investigate Allegations of Police Corruption and the Anti-Corruption Procedures of the Police Department. Milton Mollen, chair. July 7, 1994. *Commission Report:* 1–2.

17. Ibid.

18. Ibid., p. 36.

19. Krauss, Clifford, and Adam Nossiter. May 2, 1995. Bronx Abuse Complaints Stir Crackdown on Police; May 3, 1995. Sixteen Police Officers Are Indicted in Bronx Precinct Graft Inquiry. *New York Times.*

20. Pierre-Pierre, Garry. April 2, 1995. Settling Suits for Brutality Rises in Cost. *New York Times:* sec. 1, p. 39.

21. Harriston, Keith, and Mary Pat Flaherty. August 28, 1994. D.C. Police Force Still Paying for Forced Hiring Binge. First of a four-part series: Law and Disorder: The District's Troubled Police. *Washington Post:* A1.

22. Ibid.

23. Ibid.

24. Cornwell, Tim. June 25, 1995. Crooked Cops Make a Killing in the Big Easy. *The Observer:* 21.

25. Walker, Sam. June 6, 1995. New Orleans Tries to Police Its Thin Blue Line. *Christian Science Monitor:* 1.

26. Ibid.

27. See generally, Amnesty International. June 1992. *Police Brutality in Los Angeles, California, United States of America.* New York: Network Printing of New York; The Criminal Justice Institute, Harvard Law School, and The William Monroe Trotter Institute, University of Massachusetts at Boston. March 1993. *Beyond the Rodney King Story: An NAACP Report on Police Conduct and Community Relations.* Washington, D.C.: The National Association for the Advancement of Colored People; Mann, Coramae Richey. 1993. *Unequal Justice.* Bloomington, Ind.: Indiana University Press: 134; Independent Commission on the Los Angeles Police Department. Warren Christopher, chair. 1991. *Report of the Independent Commission on the Los Angeles Police Department.*

28. Independent Commission on the Los Angeles Police Department. Warren Christopher, chair. 1991. *Report of the Independent Commission on the Los Angeles Police Department: Summary Report:* 3.

29. Ibid., p. 4.

30. Ibid., p. i.

31. Ibid.

32. The Criminal Justice Institute, Harvard Law School, and The William Monroe Trotter Institute, University of Massachusetts at Boston. March 1993. *Beyond the Rodney King Story: An NAACP Report on Police Conduct and Community Relations.* Washington, D.C.: The National Association for the Advancement of Colored People.

33. Independent Commission on the Los Angeles Police Department. Warren Christopher, chair. 1991. *Report of the Independent Commission on the Los Angeles Police Department: Summary Report:* 6.

34. Ibid., p. 7.

35. The Criminal Justice Institute, Harvard Law School, and The William Monroe Trotter Institute, University of Massachusetts at Boston. March 1993. *Beyond the Rodney King Story: An NAACP Report on Police Conduct and Community Relations*. Washington, D.C.: The National Association for the Advancement of Colored People.

36. Ibid., p. vi.

37. Feldman, Paul, and Edward Boyer. April 20, 1995. Street Gang Crackdown Producing Mixed Results. *Los Angeles Times:* sec. A, p. 1.

38. Ibid.

39. Adams, Lorraine. July 30, 1995. 180 Degrees Separate Black, White Views of O. J. Simpson Case. *Washington Post*.

40. Horowitz, Craig. August 14, 1995. The Suddenly Safer City. *New York Times:* 20.

41. Violante, Thomas R. December 3, 1993. New Haven Toll: 10 Gangs Demolished, 200 Jailed. *Connecticut Post:* A1.

42. Polk, Nancy. June 28, 1992. Police Officers "Must Play by the Rules." *New York Times*.

43. Rosenbaum, Dennis, ed. 1994. *Challenge of Community Policing: Testing the Promise*. Thousand Oaks, Calif.: Sage Publications: 293.

44. Olesky, Walter. August 1992. Police Don't Live Here. They Don't Really Care. *Law and Order:* 45.

45. Wilson, James Q., and George L. Kelling. March 1982. Broken Windows. *Atlantic Monthly:* 29–38; Wilson, James Q., and George L. Kelling. February 1989. Making Neighborhoods Safe. *Atlantic Monthly:* 46–52.

46. Wilson, James Q., and George L. Kelling. February 1989. Making Neighborhoods Safe. *Atlantic Monthly:* 48.

47. Spelman, William, and John Eck. January 1987. *Problem-Oriented Policing*. National Institute of Justice, Research in Brief. Washington, D.C.: U.S. Government Printing Office.

48. Ibid.

49. Ibid.

50. Ryan, Michael. January 9, 1994. It's All About Dignity and Respect. *Connecticut Post, Parade:* 12–14.

51. Hampton, Ronald. 1994. From Just Us to Justice for All: A Perspective on Community Policing. Unpublished manuscript.

52. Rosenbaum, Dennis, ed. 1994. *Challenge of Community Policing: Testing the Promise*. Thousand Oaks, Calif.: Sage Publications: 250. See also U.S. Department of Justice, National Institute of Justice, Perspectives on Policing. November 1988. *Implementing Community Policing*. Washington, D.C.: U.S. Government Printing Office; and U.S. Department of Justice,

National Institute of Justice, Perspectives on Policing. July 1993. *Implementing Community Policing: The Administrative Problem.* Washington, D.C.: U.S. Government Printing Office.

53. Ryan, Michael. January 9, 1994. It's All About Dignity and Respect. *Connecticut Post, Parade:* 12–14.

54. The Criminal Justice Institute, Harvard Law School, and The William Monroe Trotter Institute, University of Massachusetts at Boston. March 1993. *Beyond the Rodney King Story: An NAACP Report on Police Conduct and Community Relations.* Washington, D.C.: The National Association for the Advancement of Colored People: 195.

55. Whetstone, Thomas. September 1993. Training Police Officers. *Law and Order:* 150.

56. Kilborn, Peter T. October 10, 1994. Police Profile Stays Much the Same. *New York Times:* B1.

57. Goldberg, Jeffrey. July 11, 1994. Through Blue Eyes. New York, NYPD Special Report: 30. Also note: In 1992 the police force was 11.4 percent black. Sack, Kevin. September 4, 1995. Racism of Rogue Police: Officer Casts Suspicion on Police Nationwide. *New York Times.*

CHAPTER EIGHT: THE APPARATUS OF JUSTICE—COURTS, PROSECUTION, DEFENSE, PROBATION, AND PAROLE

1. U.S. Department of Justice, Bureau of Justice Statistics. September 1992. Justice Expenditure and Employment, 1990. Washington, D.C.: U.S. Govenment Printing Office: 4.

2. *Gideon v. Wainwright,* 372 U.S. 335 (1962).

3. Tuohy, Lynn. January 8, 1995. CCLU Suit Lays Bare a Public Defense System in Crisis. *Hartford Courant.*

4. U.S. Department of Justice, Bureau of Justice Statistics. September 1992. *Justice Expenditure and Employment, 1990.* Bulletin. Washington, D.C.: U.S. Government Printing Office: 3.

5. Tuohy, Lynn. January 8, 1995. CCLU Suit Lays Bare a Public Defense System in Crisis. *Hartford Courant.*

6. Camp, Camille Graham, and George M. Camp. 1994. *Corrections Yearbook 1994: Probation and Parole.* South Salem, N.Y.: Criminal Justice Institute.

7. Costell, Anthony, Rick Garnett, and Vincent Schiraldi. September 1991. *Parole Violators in California: A Waste of Money, a Waste of Time.* San Francisco: Center on Juvenile and Criminal Justice: 8.

8. Camp, Camille Graham, and George M. Camp. 1994. *Corrections Yearbook 1994: Probation and Parole.* South Salem, N.Y.: Criminal Justice Institute: 15.

9. U.S. Department of Justice, National Institute of Justice. January

1987. *New Dimensions in Probation: Georgia's Experience with Intensive Probation Supervision.* Washington, D.C.: U.S. Government Printing Office.

10. See generally Petersilia, Joan, and Susan Turner. October 1993. Evaluating Intensive Supervision Probation and Parole. *Overcrowded Times*; and Petersilia, Joan, and Susan Turner. May 1993. *Evaluating Intensive Probation/Parole: Results of a Nationwide Experiment.* Washington, D.C.: National Institute of Justice.

11. Wooten, Harold. March 1994. *Prison and Parole Systems: A Partial Solution to Crime and Punishment, or Out of Touch and Perhaps Out of Time?* Prepared for the National Criminal Justice Commission. See also Costell, Anthony, Rick Garnett, and Vincent Schiraldi. September 1991. *Parole Violators in California: A Waste of Money, a Waste of Time.* San Francisco: Center on Juvenile and Criminal Justice.

12. Baker, Peter. September 1994. Many Ex-Offenders Succeed After Release. *Washington Post.*

CHAPTER NINE: PATHWAY TO A SAFER SOCIETY—2020 VISION

1. Model legislation for community corrections is available from the Criminal Justice Section of the American Bar Association. See Branham, Lynn. April 1992. *The Use of Incarceration in the United States: A Look at the Present and the Future.* Washington, D.C.: American Bar Association.

2. State of California, Pete Wilson, governor. April 1994. *Evaluating Recovery Services: The California Drug and Alcohol Treatment Assessment.* Sacramento, Calif.: California Department of Alcohol and Drug Programs.

3. Graham, Camille, and George M. Camp. 1994. *The Corrections Yearbook 1994: Adult Corrections.* South Salem, N.Y.: Criminal Justice Institute: 50.

4. U.S. Department of Justice, Bureau of Justice Statistics. September 1992. Justice Expenditure and Employment, 1990. Bulletin. Washington, D.C.: U.S. Government Printing Office: 3.

5. Stevens, Jane Ellen. August/September 1994. Treating Violence as an Epidemic. *Technology Review.* Vol. 97, no. 6, p. 23.

6. Reiss, Albert J., Jr., and Jeffrey A. Roth, eds. 1993. *Understanding and Preventing Violence.* Washington, D.C.: National Academy Press: 2.

7. Stevens, Jane Ellen. August/September 1994. Treating Violence as an Epidemic. *Technology Review.* Vol. 97, no. 6, p. 25.

8. U.S. Department of Justice, Bureau of Justice Statistics. 1993. *Performance Measures for the Criminal Justice System.* Washington, D.C.: U.S. Government Printing Office.

9. McCart, Linda. 1994. *Kids and Violence.* Washington, D.C.: National Governors' Association.

10. See, for example, Elliot, Delbert S. March 1994. *Youth Violence: An*

Overview. Boulder, Colo.: Center for the Study and Prevention of Violence; Tolan, Patrick, and Nancy Guerra. July 1994. *What Works in Reducing Adolescent Violence: An Empirical Review of the Field*. Boulder, Colo.: Center for the Study and Prevention of Violence; Eron, Leonard D., Jacquelyn H. Gentry, and Peggy Schlegel, eds. 1994. *Reason to Hope—A Psychological Perspective on Violence and Youth*. Washington, D.C.: American Psychological Association; Mercy, James A., Mark L. Rosenberg, Kenneth E. Powell, et al. Winter 1993. Public Health Policy for Preventing Violence. *Health Affairs*. Vol. 12, no. 4, pp. 7–29; Currie, Elliott. 1985. *Confronting Crime: An American Challenge*. New York: Pantheon Books; U.S. Department of Justice, Office of Juvenile Justice and Delinquency Prevention. 1993. *Comprehensive Strategy for Serious, Violent, and Chronic Juvenile Offenders*. Washington, D.C.: U.S. Government Printing Office.

11. Kellerman, Arthur T., and Donald T. Reay. June 12, 1986. Protection or Peril? An Analysis of Firearms-Related Deaths in the Home. *New England Journal of Medicine* 314:1557.

12. Coalition to Stop Handgun Violence. 1994. *Costs of Guns to Society: Who Pays?* Materials distributed at conference sponsored by Coalition to Stop Handgun Violence, Washington, D.C.: 5.

13. The Carter Center. 1994. *Not Even One: A Report on the Crisis of Children and Firearms*. Atlanta, GA: The Carter Center: 9.

14. Currie, Elliott. 1985. *Confronting Crime: An American Challenge*. New York: Pantheon Books: 148.

15. Miller, Jerome G. September 1992. *Hobbling a Generation: Young African-American Males in the Criminal Justice System of America's Cities: Baltimore, Maryland*. Alexandria, Va.: National Center on Institutions and Alternatives.

INDEX

DATE DUE

GAYLORD			PRINTED IN U.S.A.